Teaching Sport and Physical Activity

Insights on the Road to Excellence

Paul G. Schempp, EdD
University of Georgia

Human Kinetics

Library of Congress Cataloging-in-Publication Data

Schempp, Paul G.
  Teaching sport and physical activity : insights on the road to
excellence / Paul G. Schempp.
        p. cm.
Includes bibliographical references and index.
  ISBN 0-7360-3387-4 (softcover)
  1. Physical education and training--Study and teaching (Secondary) 2.
Physical education teachers--Training of. I. Title.
  GV361 .S25 2003
  613.7'071'2--dc21   2002152966

ISBN: 0-7360-3387-4

The Web addresses cited in this text were current as of January 2003, unless otherwise noted.

Acquisitions Editor: Scott Wikgren; **Developmental Editor:** Myles Schrag; **Assistant Editors:** Jennifer L. Davis, Sandra Merz Bott, Derek Campbell; **Copyeditor:** Patricia L. MacDonald; **Proofreader:** Pamela Johnson; **Indexer:** Bobbi Swanson; **Permission Manager:** Dalene Reeder; **Graphic Designer:** Nancy Rasmus; **Graphic Artist:** Yvonne Griffith; **Photo Manager:** Leslie A. Woodrum; **Cover Designer:** Jack W. Davis; **Photographer (cover):** ©Mug Shots/Corbis; **Art Manager:** Kelly Hendren; **Printer:** Versa Press

Printed in the United States of America   10 9 8 7 6 5 4 3 2 1

Human Kinetics
Web site: www.HumanKinetics.com

United States: Human Kinetics, P.O. Box 5076, Champaign, IL 61825-5076
800-747-4457
e-mail: humank@hkusa.com

Canada: Human Kinetics, 475 Devonshire Road Unit 100, Windsor, ON N8Y 2L5
800-465-7301 (in Canada only)
e-mail: orders@hkcanada.com

Europe: Human Kinetics, 107 Bradford Road, Stanningley, Leeds LS28 6AT, United Kingdom
+44 (0) 113 255 5665
e-mail: hk@hkeurope.com

Australia: Human Kinetics, 57A Price Avenue, Lower Mitcham, South Australia 5062
08 8277 1555
e-mail: liahka@senet.com.au

New Zealand: Human Kinetics, P.O. Box 105-231, Auckland Central
09-523-3462
e-mail: hkp@ihug.co.nz

Dedicated . . .

   . . . to my teachers.

   They taught me how.

   . . . to my students.

   They taught me why.

Contents

**part V   Development: Becoming a Better
Teacher and Coach**

Foreword

Like most college students, I took courses to earn a degree that would lead to getting a job. College classes, for the most part, are rites of passage. During my junior year at the University of Oregon, I took my seat in a course called Teaching Human Movement. I didn't expect to learn much at the time, but I tried to remain open-minded. My passion was, and still is, basketball. I wanted to be a coach. Becoming a physical education teacher was important, but ultimately coaching was what I saw in my future. As the course progressed, Dr. Schempp piqued my attention with the points he made, the examples he gave, and the stories he told. He made the theory come alive in practice. What caught my attention even more—and I told him so—was that he often used coaches as examples for teaching. Many of those people were basketball coaches that I was already familiar with: John Thompson, Bobby Knight, Dean Smith, Mike Krzyzewski, Rick Pitino, and Jim Boeheim were all used as examples for various teaching strategies, skills, and perspectives. I had always thought that much of coaching was about teaching, and much of teaching was a lot like coaching, but this was the first time I heard it in a college class. It was the first time I had heard someone link excellence in coaching with excellence in teaching. To this day, I see much of my success as a coach linked to my ability and skill as a teacher.

Most coaches realize that a critical part of coaching is teaching. In fact, coaching is teaching and all of the skills that teaching requires: knowing the sport or activity; planning; developing people skills such as communication, motivation, mentoring, and being a role model; understanding your players or students; and, of course, knowing how to teach.

Although subject knowledge and management skills are vital, coaches and teachers also need to enjoy what they are doing. Infusing that enthusiasm into your students will help them reach their goals. If you have a unique talent for teaching or coaching, what better reward is there than seeing your students or athletes learn and succeed? Dr. Schempp is this type of teacher: caring, compassionate, competent, and able to bring fun to learning. I was fortunate to have him as a teacher when I was a student who dreamed of coaching basketball but didn't yet know what all that dream entailed. Many of the lessons from Dr. Schempp's class are included in this book and presented in his friendly, approachable style. The lessons have proven invaluable in my teaching and coaching career.

I am not the only person in the Gonzaga men's basketball program that has worked with Dr. Schempp. My director of basketball operations, Jerry Krause, is a Hall of Fame coach and author of 13 books on coaching basketball. Dr. Krause met Dr. Schempp at West Point when they planned the graduate program for military officers to complete before being appointed as physical education faculty members at the military academy. At the time, Dr. Krause was the director of instruction for the physical education department. Dr. Schempp served as the advisor and mentor for officers completing their degrees at the University of Georgia. The vast experience these two men have as teachers has been integral to my continual professional development.

Dr. Schempp knows prominent physical education teachers and coaches from all over the world in a variety of sports. He has worked alongside them and studied them, and he is one of them. The result of all this globetrotting and extensive fieldwork is a man who knows the inner workings of teaching sport and physical activity from many different perspectives. He understands the fundamentals of the profession because his experience is vast enough to include many voices, and he has studied enough to know the traits that make for solid teaching no matter what the sport or activity.

I highly recommend this book for people who aspire to be great teachers and coaches. As Dr. Schempp writes in these pages, the road to excellence is long and there is no substitute for experi-

ence. But with insights from mentors such as Paul Schempp and teaching aids such as this book, that road is a little bit shorter and smoother.

Mark Few
Men's basketball coach
Gonzaga University, Spokane, Washington

Preface

Learning to teach begins early in life. Our parents are usually our first real teachers, and the lessons they leave us with have a profound and potent impact on our lives. In addition to teaching writing, math, science, or music, our school teachers also give us a firsthand look at the duties and responsibilities of teachers. Physical education teachers are particularly powerful sources of career education for those aspiring to become physical educators. Coaches provide another important source of information when it comes to understanding what teachers do and why. The very fact that you are holding this book means someone taught you to read—and taught you something about teaching, as well.

This book won't try to tell you all there is to know about teaching. It can't. No book can. You'll learn more about teaching from your experiences with teachers and the experiences you had or will have as a teacher or coach than from any book. What this book can do, however, is introduce you to some of the ideas good teachers think about, provide you with information to help you sharpen your teaching skills and understand your students and their learning a bit better, and offer some guidelines to help you become a better teacher. In short, this book can get you moving along the road to excellence in your profession.

It has been a longtime goal of mine to become a good teacher. I've observed many great teachers, read what others have written about good teaching, and conducted a number of research studies on teachers and teaching. The information in this book represents knowledge gained in my experiences as both a teacher and a researcher of teachers. Having spent the better portion of the last 25 years attempting to understand what it takes to teach well, I figured it was time to sit down and try to organize that knowledge into something someone else might find useful. In those 25 years, I've been fortunate to have lived in the United States, Germany, and Singapore and to have visited 21 other countries on four continents. In these travels, I met teachers and coaches of all sorts, ranging from school physical education teachers who teach the most novice learners to elite amateur and professional coaches in a variety of sports who help the very best get better.

This book is really about them. What these caring, committed, and accomplished people taught me about teaching sport and physical activity has, in large part, influenced both the contents and style of this book. In this book, you'll find personal accounts from just a few of these excellent teachers and coaches.

Interestingly, almost every teacher and coach I met wanted to become better. It is my hope, therefore, that this book offers some insights and assistance to those who share my quest to become a better teacher. But there is no substitute for experience when it comes to understanding the knowledge, skills, and perspectives needed to teach. Although I hope you'll find this book helpful, without trying out the ideas and suggestions with your students or athletes and without attempting to find yourself as a teacher or coach, the words on these pages will remain only inert ideas. Time with students and other teachers is essential to the education of a teacher. I began to learn that lesson in my student teaching, and I am reminded of it every time I step before a group of students. The greatest lessons will come when you are teaching, and this book can help you make the most of those lessons when they arise.

Teaching Sport and Physical Activity is designed as a comprehensive guide for new teachers, but it also offers experienced teachers and coaches some new ideas that might serve their instructional practices. Although every practicing teacher, coach, or activity leader knows something, and perhaps even a great deal, about teaching, it's uncommon to find teachers who believe they "know it all." Therefore, this book was also written for experienced teachers who are searching for some fresh ideas to invigorate their teaching as well as looking to test and validate the practices they currently use. Being the best teacher possible requires new knowledge to go along with accumulated experience—and that is why this book may help you. Whether you are a sports coach, a physical education teacher, a private instructor, or a physical activity leader, if teaching is a fundamental part of what you do, or want to do, this book was written for you.

Within the pages of this book, topics vital to good teaching will be presented and discussed to get you thinking about what you need to do and what you need to learn to be the teacher or coach you strive to be. You won't find all the answers in this book, or any book, for that matter. You will, however, find answers to some of the questions you might have and perhaps to questions you have yet to discover. But most important, this book should guide you along your own unique path toward excellence as you pose your own questions and discover the answers that will most help you to teach and your students to learn.

The opening chapters address the issues surrounding the decision to become a teacher. It's important for teachers and coaches to examine these issues because their occupational satisfaction and their effectiveness as teachers are largely shaped by their reasons for entering the profession. The second section of the book examines the critical elements of what teachers need to know in order to teach and the conditions under which students learn. To teach well, a teacher must possess particular kinds of knowledge and understand how students learn best.

Creating stimulating learning environments is covered in the third section. In these chapters, you'll find information on forming effective relationships with students, planning for optimal learning experiences, and managing the lesson time and resources to best aid student learning. The fourth section takes a close look at the skills and knowledge a teacher needs to focus a lesson, maintain a dynamic instructional pace, communicate effectively, and maximize student learning with practice and feedback. You'll also discover options for varied instructional strategies and techniques for assessing student learning.

No matter how incompetent a teacher may seem or how successful a teacher may be, everyone can become a better teacher. The final section of the book is dedicated to making you a better teacher or coach. Program promotion ideas, ways to use technology to enhance instruction, strategies for improving teaching, and ideas for increasing expertise will provide you with a host of ideas for innovating and invigorating your teaching.

A good book should challenge your thinking, prompt you to engage the ideas presented, and lead you to improve the way you currently go about business. To make *Teaching Sport and Physical Activity* more useful, several features were incorporated into each chapter. Sidebar stories with insights from teachers and coaches I know will not only introduce you to some great teachers but also demonstrate the practicality of the ideas in this book. Time and circumstances have tested these concepts. Where appropriate, examples from actual teaching and coaching situations were included to stimulate ideas about how you might approach lesson plans, newsletters, teacher analysis, and so on. Discussion questions at the end of each chapter are intended to get you thinking and talking about the information presented. Your own opinions weigh heavily on who you are as a teacher and what you do as a teacher. Take a few minutes after reading each chapter and take a shot at the questions posed. They should help make a better connection between what you already know and what you just read.

A book takes time. This one took more than five years to write. That time was taken from other projects and other people in order for me to complete this work. It's appropriate, then, that I acknowledge my colleagues and students at the Sport Instruction Research Laboratory at the University of Georgia, who were generous and sensitive in time demands. A special thank you goes to the faculty and administration at the National Institute of Education, Singapore, who in granting me a six-month visiting professorship with terrific resources, permitted me the opportunity to complete this book. The many gifted and gracious teachers who allowed me to study them have taught me much and inspired me greatly, and I wish there were enough space here to acknowledge them all. Finally, I would like to express my gratitude to my students. Long did you suffer as I struggled to learn this craft called teaching. But in that process, you, above all those mentioned before you, taught me the most about what it takes to teach well. More important, in you I see the significance of teaching.

A special mention goes to Rainer Martens. We sat together several years ago in some long-forgotten conference city, and he asked what I was working on. I told him about this book, why I wanted to write it, and that I wanted to write it in my own time and in my own way. He encouraged me to do so and asked only that I give Human Kinetics a chance to review it when I sought a publisher. I did. The rest, as they say, is history. You now hold that book in your hand.

My journey of trying to become a good teacher is far from over. Looking back on my journey to date, I believe I've learned something about teaching, and much of that I share with you now. It thrills me to see my students learn, so my quest to be a better teacher continues. It is my hope that in reading this book, you will find ways to help your students learn better and, in that process, feel the thrill that comes from knowing you made a difference in someone's life.

Part I

Desire
Becoming a Teacher

Teaching Sport and Physical Activity opens with two chapters relevant for people considering a career in teaching and for those who are about to assume the role of teacher or coach. Chapter 1 begins with an examination of the factors that lead people into the teaching profession. The reasons a person chooses to become a teacher or coach are extensively examined at the outset because they strongly affect the kind and quality of teacher he or she becomes. Since the background experiences a person brings into teaching represent a lifetime of influence and information, they too are explored in chapter 1. For most people who wish to teach or coach, a certification or license is normally required. Therefore, chapter 1 continues by examining the preparation and certification programs common to teachers of sport and physical activity. Although much of this book is written for physical education teachers, it is not exclusive to this group. Options for teaching sport and physical activity that go beyond the school are discussed in the opening chapter. Finally, for someone entering the world of teaching or coaching, it's important to know the benefits they can expect to receive from their chosen profession. Chapter 1 closes with a description of the rewards to be gained from instructing students.

Teaching is inherently a social activity (i.e., you don't do it alone). Because learning so often takes place within an institution, politics inevitably play a role in teaching and coaching. Chapter 2 familiarizes teachers and coaches with the political environment of the teaching profession. Specifically, the chapter discusses the political conditions and social regulations of teaching. The politics of a profession, class, and school as they affect the activities and careers of teachers are examined and discussed in depth.

The road to excellence in teaching sport and physical activity will not be smooth, straight, or speedy. It will take time, effort, and understanding. To monitor your progress, it's important to know where you came from and why you have undertaken this journey. Part I examines these issues.

1

Chapter 1

Becoming a Teacher

Every calling is great when greatly pursued.

— Oliver Wendell Holmes

DESIRE

To enjoy sport and physical activity, people need special skills and knowledge. Teachers and coaches meet this need by helping people improve their skills and increase their understanding of the activity. Tennis instructors, for example, help their students develop better serves, groundstrokes, and game strategies. They also teach the rules, history, and etiquette of the game. What's more, a teacher's passion for the sport and student improvement can inspire students to practice and play. Physical education teachers have a broader mission. They teach a multitude of physical activities, ranging from team sports and individual activities to dance, gymnastics, and fitness. Sometimes they even teach health issues such as nutrition, drug awareness, personal hygiene, first aid, and safety. Regardless of what the subject is, the ultimate measure of a teacher is how much the students learn. Students of great teachers and coaches come away from the experience with skill, knowledge, and a desire to excel. This book was written to help you become one of those teachers or coaches.

Teaching demands both considerable knowledge and extensive skills. This is good news because it means no one was born a great teacher. There is always more to learn. Becoming a teacher is a life-long journey. Becoming a better teacher or coach is a challenge that never grows old. So what does it take to become a teacher? In this chapter, we will examine that process. Specifically, the issues of choosing to teach, the influence of a teacher's background, preparation and certification programs, options for teaching, and the rewards of teaching will all be considered.

The Decision to Teach

There are many reasons why a person decides to teach; it's important to examine these reasons because they profoundly influence satisfaction and success in teaching. Those who love sport and physical activity are most often attracted to teaching and coaching. The desire to remain in something they love is one reason people decide to become teachers and coaches. Other reasons for wanting to teach include remaining physically active, helping others, personal enjoyment, working with people, improving teaching quality, using athletic ability, job security, and easy entry into the field (Lawson 1983; Templin, Woodford, and Mulling 1982). Most teachers can usually identify several reasons for wanting

to teach (figure 1.1). The more reasons you have for entering the profession, the greater the chance of finding success and satisfaction in teaching and coaching.

Why Teach?
- Share rewarding experiences with others
- Continue attachment to a loved activity
- Re-create enjoyable experiences for others
- Help and encourage others
- Work with people
- Improve the quality of available instruction
- Use physical skills and abilities
- Attain job security
- Take advantage of easy entry into the profession

The Influential Role of a Teacher's Background

A person begins learning to teach the moment he begins learning. Learning to walk, talk, hold a pen, and read this book are skills that were taught to us. In learning those skills, we also learned something about teaching. Likewise, learning experiences on

Figure 1.1 Physical education teachers experience many positives in their job, including working with other people, sharing rewarding experiences, staying involved in a beloved activity, and the opportunity to stay active on a regular basis.

athletic fields, in workout rooms, and in physical education classes teach future teachers much about instructing sport and physical activity lessons. A teacher's history exerts a powerful influence over personal foundational beliefs, knowledge, perspectives, and instructional skills. In fact, a teacher's identity begins with her biography. A teacher's past continues to shape her decisions and practices throughout her career. Teachers should therefore examine these critical sources of influence to better understand the beliefs they embrace, the decisions they make, and the practices they adopt.

Three sets of experiences are particularly important in the development of most sport and physical activity instructors. These experiences include being a student or athlete, teaching or coaching, and education.

Experiences As a Student or Athlete

While still students, teachers begin identifying, selecting, and evaluating the instructional practices of their teachers and coaches. Previous teachers not only demonstrated the skills and duties of a teacher, but they also demonstrated a love of the subject matter, relationships with students, lesson content and activity ideas, and a professional demeanor. Your former teachers and coaches are role models for teaching practices and perspectives and, in many cases, provided the inspiration for choosing a teaching career. Their subtle influences remain powerful and pervasive over the duration of your career. When someone considers becoming a teacher, he compares personal characteristics with those of an admired teacher or coach. If a reasonable fit is found, a decision to teach is often the result.

Experiences As a Teacher or Coach

Teachers rely heavily on previous experiences that required the use of practices similar to teaching. For example, student teaching is often cited as the most beneficial aspect of teacher education because it represents actual time with the students. Athletic coaching, working in summer camps, and even child care experiences often give teachers practice interacting with children, organizing activities, and managing groups of people. Such opportunities serve the dual purpose of allowing beginning teachers to develop teaching skills and confirm their occupational choice. The experiences teach them "what works" when working with people, and they learn firsthand whether or not they like teaching or coaching.

Education

To gain knowledge of the subject; understand students; and prepare for designing, conducting, and evaluating lessons, teachers often undergo a formal educational experience. To build on background experience and acquire the necessary professional skills, orientations, and knowledge, prospective teachers enter a preparation or certification program.

For most professional instruction, a certification or license is either required or encouraged. Public school teachers must obtain their initial licenses through a state-sanctioned university degree program. Private school teachers are also normally required to complete an appropriate degree program that provides the knowledge and skills to teach competently. In the private sports industry, certification programs are often strongly encouraged and can lead to increased prestige, recognition, and income. Youth sports and sports federations also offer training and certification programs for coaches.

University Degree Programs

Teachers pursuing certification through a university program must meet two sets of requirements: state teacher certification and a university degree. Fortunately, coursework can be designed to meet both requirements simultaneously. It's quite possible, however, that someone in a teacher education program will take more courses than students in other majors simply because of the dual purpose of the program.

Prospective teachers enter university programs after observing many years of teaching practice during their time as students in schools. They go to university with a wealth of experience with teachers and strongly held beliefs about the educational enterprise. A prospective teacher's willingness to consider and adopt new practices and perspectives will, in part, determine the university program's success in developing good teachers (Graber 1991). Prospective teachers who begin with an open mind and are willing to learn have the greatest potential for learning to teach well. On the other hand, closed-minded people seldom learn much of anything.

The teacher education faculty is primarily made up of university professors who have experience in public schools and hold a doctoral degree. Faculty members, like other university professors, normally have an area of specialization and conduct research in their respective fields. Public school teachers traditionally serve as supervising or cooperating teachers for the student teaching experience.

A typical teacher preparation curriculum consists of three elements: coursework, field experiences, and student teaching (McCullick 2001). University coursework has its greatest value in supplying subject matter content. In particular, the activity, or "practical," courses allow beginning teachers to construct teaching routines and develop lessons fit for public school instruction. Prospective teachers find that practice teaching with students in public schools is among the most useful aspects of their preparation to teach.

Establishing relationships with students, subject matter knowledge, communication skills, classroom management, planning strategies, professional orientations, and legal responsibilities are but a few of the areas covered in a typical university-based teacher education program. The final learning experience is actual student teaching. In student teaching, a prospective teacher is paired with a mentor or cooperating teacher so she can apply this newly acquired knowledge in a "real world" setting under the guidance of an accomplished and experienced practitioner. Many teachers believe this to be the singularly most meaningful learning experience in the preparation process.

The press and grind of public school teaching requires beginning teachers to adopt professional perspectives that are practical rather than intellectual. In most cases, the university education brought to schools by new teachers cannot compare with the experience of their seasoned peers. Many veteran teachers believe they learned most, if not all, of their professional practice from the trial and error of classroom instruction rather than the lecture halls of universities. The low status of a university preparation often leads beginning teachers to suppress and devalue their education in favor of lessons gained from classroom experience or the stories and suggestions offered by their veteran colleagues (Schempp, Sparkes, and Templin 1993).

Professional Certification

Professional associations offer instructor certification programs in many sports and physical activities. Golf, skiing, scuba diving, tennis, martial arts, aerobics, and physical fitness are but a few examples of activities with instructor certification. These programs range from one-day training seminars to several years of classroom and applied practical experiences. The education faculty usually consists of association representatives and experienced instructors. Certification programs commonly require some classroom time, outside reading, applied practice assignments, and an evaluation process that ensures the teacher has the requisite knowledge and skills to safely and competently teach the particular sport or activity. Some of the better programs may also include an internship or apprenticeship period.

In many countries, certification is necessary to coach a sport (figure 1.2). A sports federation or organization often sponsors coaching development programs. Respected individuals with experience

Figure 1.2 Swedish national golf coach Peter Mattsson (kneeling) watches PGA pro Jesper Parnevik warm up prior to the final round of the 2002 British Open in Muirfield, Scotland. In many countries, certification is necessary to coach a sport.

Figure 1.3 With the development of programs such as the American Coaching Effectiveness Program, coaches have a means to extend their knowledge and skill.

and extensive knowledge serve on the educational committee and conduct the training sessions. Coaching certification often has varying levels depending on the age and skill of the participants as well as the experience and skill of the coach (Gowan 1992). In the United States, there is growing pressure to certify school sports coaches (Sisley and Weise 1987). With the development of such programs as the American Coaching Effectiveness Program (Partlow 1992) and the Program for Athletic Coaches' Education (Seefeldt and Milligan 1992), coaches seeking to extend their knowledge and skill can now find quality programs that meet their needs (figure 1.3).

Options for Teachers

More now than at any time in Western culture, many opportunities and avenues exist for teaching and coaching sport and physical activity. In years past, the only realistic option in North America for teaching and coaching was teaching physical education and coaching in public schools. While that remains a highly viable and attractive career option, other opportunities are available as well (figure 1.4).

Public Schools

The most traditional route for someone aspiring to teach physical activity is to prepare for and

Figure 1.4 Physical activity teaching opportunities extend far beyond mainstream sports in school gymnasiums, including scuba instruction in the Red Sea.

become a physical education teacher in public schools. Teaching public school physical education requires a credential from the state in which the teacher is employed. Completing an accredited teacher education program at a college or university normally meets the state's certification requirements. A teaching credential is usually transferable should a teacher accept a position in another state or province.

The preparation program includes a series of general education courses designed for an undergraduate or graduate degree, a series of courses specific to a physical education major, and substantial practical teaching experiences. The coursework for majoring in physical education traditionally includes the study of physical activity content, teaching methods, curriculum planning, motor learning, sport history, social issues, biomechanics, measurement and assessment, and exercise physiology.

Public school districts are usually committed to the professional improvement of their teaching and coaching personnel. To this end, many school districts allow for professional days (i.e., paid leave several days per year so the teacher can attend professional development activities). School districts may also cover the cost of in-service workshops, provide staff development opportunities, reimburse teachers' expenses for attending a professional conference, and provide a salary increase for obtaining advanced degrees.

The job requirements of a public school teacher vary slightly depending on the school, district, and state. Teachers are generally assigned to teach either elementary, middle, or high school students. Class sizes range from a few students to groups as large as 90 or more. The number of classes per day also varies. A teacher may be assigned as few as three classes in a block scheduled secondary school or as many as twelve or more in an understaffed elementary school. Facilities, equipment, and supplies also vary based on the support and funding levels of the school and district.

Private Schools

Much like public schools, private schools offer a viable option for someone wanting to teach sport and physical activity. Private schools vary in format and expectations for teachers and coaches. The obligations of a private school teacher range from part-time employment for teaching a seasonal activity to a full-time position that requires teaching, coaching several sports, and possibly even serving as a resident live-in counselor.

In many cases, private schools require their teachers to have preparatory backgrounds similar to public school teachers, but they often don't require that a teacher hold a state teaching certification. However, this does not mean that private schools are not interested in top quality teachers. Private schools may look for additional qualifications beyond university coursework. For example, schools with a strong educational heritage may

look for teachers who attended a similar private school themselves. Religiously affiliated schools usually look for teachers with similar religious convictions. Support for staff development also varies widely depending on financial resources and school goals. The job requirements for private school teachers depend on the school and its mission. Class sizes are normally smaller than in public schools, while facilities, equipment, and supplies vary based on the school, its resources, and the importance of sport and physical activity in the curriculum.

Professional Instruction

Instruction is a growth industry in sport and physical activity. As people pursue an increased number of physical activities, their need to learn and improve expands. This growth seems assured for years to come as an increasing number of senior citizens seek healthy retirement activities and children's sports continue to grow in both quantity and quality. Tennis, personal fitness, scuba diving, golf, rock climbing, softball, bowling, and fly fishing are just a few of the activities demanding more and better teachers to serve the needs of passionate participants.

Professional instructors may be on the staff of a school, such as a sailing or ice climbing school, or may be independent business owners whose prime service is instruction. Specialized summer camps and schools that offer top-level instruction in traditional sports such as baseball, basketball, hockey, and volleyball, as well as more extreme sports such as kayaking, hang gliding, backpacking, mountain biking, or parachuting, have created further opportunities for sport and physical activity instructors. If a physical activity requires skill and knowledge, someone needs to teach it to the newly initiated and improve the skill and understanding of those who already participate.

Most professional instructors receive certification from a sanctioned, recognized professional organization. For example, the United States Professional Tennis Registry certifies tennis instructors, the Professional Association of Diving Instructors trains scuba instructors, and the Professional Golf Association of America and the Ladies Professional Golf Association both educate and certify golf instructors. If you are interested in pursuing a career as a professional instructor, a professional association can help you become adequately prepared and properly certified. A love of the activity and a strong commitment toward helping others learn is essential.

Coaching

Coaching opportunities are extensive. Coaches range from volunteers coaching a Saturday morning youth sports team to million-dollar salaried coaches of professional teams (figure 1.5). The number of sports and the assorted performance levels in each sport have created a strong demand for good coaches at all levels.

In the United States, very few sports or states require a coach to be trained and certified. Preparation for coaching, in most cases, comes through observation as an athlete (Sage 1989a). Therefore, the level at which a person aspires to coach will depend largely on her level of competitive play. Coaching at the high school, college, or professional level normally requires playing experience at the respective level. Entry into coaching is traditionally done as an apprentice. That is, an aspiring coach usually functions as an assistant coach first, and after several years and multiple experiences, he is elevated to the head coach position. The length of the apprenticeship period varies depending on the sport and the level of competition. As a rule of thumb, the higher the level of competition, the longer the apprenticeship period.

Teaching Is Rewarding

There are many rewards, both internal and external, to be found in teaching and coaching. Internal rewards include those benefits that result in positive feelings about yourself and the job being accomplished. External rewards are the material and tangible benefits gained in teaching. Together, these rewards explain the satisfaction found in teaching and provide the motivation to teach well. For someone considering a career as a teacher or coach, it's useful to examine the benefits this decision brings. As the sidebar story of Tubby Smith demonstrates, understanding what you find rewarding about teaching and coaching can often be essential for gaining those rewards.

Figure 1.5 From teaching the fundamentals at an early age to teaching elite athletes at the professional and college levels, there are many possibilities for people who want to coach sport.

DESIRE KNOWLEDGE CONSTRUCTION DISCOVERY DEVELOPMENT

What's a Million Dollars Worth?

© AP Photo/Eric Draper

Tubby Smith

As I drove through rural Georgia with Tubby Smith, then head basketball coach at the University of Georgia, we discussed a recent offer he had received from a major midwestern University. We were on our way to Kenny Rogers' farm for a photo shoot as part of a charity event for the local Boys and Girls Club. Tubby was a longtime fan of the famous singer and was looking forward to meeting him. Knowing both men, I too was looking forward to the meeting as both are friendly, good natured, and down to earth despite their fame.

Tubby had been offered a million dollars to coach the Ohio State University basketball team. It represented twice the salary he was making in Georgia, but he had turned down the offer just the day before. I asked him why. "Do you know what a million dollars is to me?" Tubby asked. "No, what?" I replied. "Taxes. A lot of taxes. I can't spend what I make now. I love my job and work 52 weeks a year. My oldest son is on scholarship, so I don't have to pay for college, and the rest of my family lives very comfortably." Okay, then, if it isn't money, what rewards do you get from coaching? Tubby identified two dreams: to be head coach at the University of Kentucky and to coach his sons in college. One goal was being currently and partially met; his son G.G. was playing for him at the University of Georgia, and his second son, Saul, was about to graduate from high school and would also enroll at the University of Georgia.

By why Kentucky? "Tradition" was his answer. The University of Kentucky had, according to Tubby, the finest college basketball tradition in the country. It was, in his opinion, a tradition of excellence. He readily admitted that there were other fine schools and basketball programs—UCLA, Kansas, North Carolina, Georgetown, Duke, and others—but to his mind, Kentucky was college basketball at its best.

Two weeks after our conversation, Tubby was offered the head coaching position at the University of Kentucky. This offer he readily accepted. Saul was able to transfer schools and play for his dad like his older brother had before him. In Tubby's first year as head coach, he continued the tradition as Kentucky won the national championship. In his typically humble style, Tubby was quick to give credit to his mentor and predecessor, Rick Pitino. But Tubby Smith, by turning down a million dollars, had gained rewards that meant more to him than money.

Teachers often cite student relationships as highly rewarding (Templin and Schempp 1989). This makes sense because, after all, students are what teaching is all about. In addition to the good feelings that come from helping someone learn, teachers come to care for and appreciate their students. Chapter 5 explores the teacher-student relationship in greater depth.

Devotion to the subject matter, passion for the activities involved in teaching, and the sense of purpose that comes from helping others learn are also common rewards experienced by teachers. In short, teachers choose to teach because they love both people and the subject (Templin, Woodford, and Mulling 1982). Those who lack either of those passions are not likely to enjoy a satisfying career or remain long in the profession. As you grow in teaching, cultivating relationships with colleagues and other worksite personnel can also be sources of satisfaction.

Common external rewards for teachers include salary, status, agreeable work and vacation schedules, advancement opportunities, and workplace environment (Lawson 1983). Although external rewards are important components of the contentment equation, teachers usually identify the internal rewards of teaching as being more important to their overall job satisfaction. However, it's the accumulation of all these rewards that ignites the motivation to undertake the demands of teaching, kindles the desire to increase competence, and leads to the satisfaction that comes from a job well done.

Rewards of Teaching

Internal

Student relationships

Love of the subject

Love of teaching

Sense of purpose in helping others learn

Relationships with colleagues and staff

External

Income

Status

Pleasant work environment

Attractive work and vacation schedule

Advancement opportunities

Summary

This chapter examined the process of becoming a teacher. In particular, teachers' histories, education programs, career options, and rewards were discussed in an effort to analyze what motivates an individual to become a skillful and successful teacher or coach. The reasons a person chooses to teach and the experiences leading to that decision influence a teacher throughout his or her teaching career, because these reasons represent the foundational values and influential experiences that shape the type of teacher he or she becomes.

The process of becoming a teacher begins early and lasts a lifetime. Teachers begin learning their craft as students by watching their own teachers. It is the formal certification program that launches their careers. The most common form of teacher preparation is the university-based degree program. Certification programs are currently available for those who will teach outside of public and private schools. The education of teachers continues beyond the degree and certification programs; they learn from their experiences as well as from attending workshops, clinics, and in-services. Teaching sport and physical activity is ripe with options. The traditional choices of teaching and coaching in schools remain an attractive option, but sport and physical activity teachers are finding increasing opportunities in sports schools, camps, and private instruction.

Learning to teach is a lifelong process. Teachers can always learn something new about their students, their subjects, or teaching itself. The remainder of this book is dedicated to the knowledge and skills that can help anyone become a better teacher.

Discussion Questions

1. Who or what was most influential in your decision to become a teacher or coach?

2. Why did this individual or event have such a strong effect on your decision?

3. What characteristics, experiences, and knowledge do you currently possess that you believe will serve you well as a teacher or coach?

4. List those things that you believe will bring you the biggest sense of satisfaction in your teaching or coaching.

5. When your career as a teacher or coach comes to an end, what do you want to see when you look back?

Chapter 2

The Politics of Teaching

The social order is a sacred right which serves as a basis for all other rights. And as it is not a natural right, it must be one founded on covenants.

— J.J. Rousseau

Teaching is a social activity and as such requires a social order. Because of its social nature, teaching involves politics. The politics of teaching are found in the governing policies and the implicit principles that guide what people do and think in instructional environments. Ultimately, politics represent the struggle for what is valued in a group, society, or institution (Scribner and Layton 1995). On a practical level, the political tendency of a class or school shapes the relationships, rights, and responsibilities of teachers and students and influences the goals and directions of the educational enterprise. On a deeper level, the politics of teaching reflect and contribute to the covenants, or fundamental beliefs, of the larger social order to which teachers, students, and other members of the school belong.

The political climate in any social or institutional setting is highly contextualized. In other words, every school or class is a unique environment that is likely to generate a unique set of political dynamics. As people, time, location, and other factors change, so does the political climate. All teachers must be attuned to the political dynamics of the immediate teaching environment. In public schools, the politics become compounded by institutional and social demands. While reading this chapter, keep in mind that no two schools or classes will be identical in terms of its politics. This chapter is therefore offered as a guide for identifying factors that influence the politics of teaching.

In this chapter, the political conditions and social covenants of teaching will be discussed. The chapter focuses on the cultures of teaching in which social and political activities occur. Specifically, the politics of a profession, class, and school will be examined and discussed as they affect the activities and careers of teachers.

Cultures of Teaching

The cultural codes of teaching define what is and isn't important in the instructional environment. They also help us determine which actions are appropriate or inappropriate in a given situation. For example, it may be appropriate to discuss a student's learning disabilities with a group of colleagues in the search for professional guidance, but this same discussion would be inappropriate with a group of students present. It's through cultural codes of teaching that teachers learn how power and status are both distributed and achieved. In the process, teachers learn who has power (e.g., administrators, "involved" teachers) and how to gain the necessary political influence to secure and thrive in their teaching positions. Therefore, the politics of teaching are rooted in the cultural codes of the profession, class, school, and community.

Sparkes viewed the cultures of teaching as both contested and dynamic:

The patterns of understandings, which newcomers must grasp, make up the various cultures of teaching and form a process of reality construction that enable individuals to see and understand particular events, objects, language and situations in distinctive ways. Hence, teacher cultures are embodied in the work-related beliefs and knowledge that they share, which includes beliefs about the appropriate ways of acting on the job, what is rewarding in teaching, and the "craft knowledge" that enables teachers to do their work. Importantly, these patterns of understandings also provide a basis for making the individuals' behavior meaningful, and culture should be viewed as an active living phenomenon through which teachers create and recreate the worlds in which they live. (1989, 319-320)

Those new to teaching learn the cultural codes by watching their peers and gauging the reactions they receive from students, peers, administrators, and others they interact with in the school or community (figure 2.1). As discussed in chapter 1, teachers also rely on their biography to guide their practice. Experienced teachers are well versed in the cultural codes but can also resist and change those codes they find working against their goals as teachers. As vested and respected members of the school culture, these teachers are in far better political position to enact sensitive changes to the system. For example, if a change in curriculum, grading policy, or facility is needed, an experienced teacher is far more likely than a beginner to have the political power to stimulate the change.

Figure 2.1 One of the values of a student-teaching experience is learning about the atmosphere and priorities in a school's physical education program from a mentor.

The First Day

The following story was told to me by a first-year teacher during a study on the micropolitics of teacher induction. Marty was certified as a physical education teacher and, as often happens in public schools, was assigned to teach classes outside his area of expertise and certification. In high school, he had been an All-American track star and eventually went to college on an athletic scholarship. Marty taught junior high school in an affluent suburb of a large metropolitan city. In his own words, the community where he taught was "well-to-do," and he reported being satisfied with both his position and his students. The following story gives some insight into life in public schools as faced by first-year teachers.

The first day there was not much teaching going on. Our building has three levels. I have a basement class first period. Second period I have a class on the main floor. Third period I'm out in the gym. Fourth I'm back inside on the main floor. Fifth and sixth I'm in the gym again, and seventh period I'm back down in the basement. So this is my first day of taking attendance, learning the kids' names, laying down basic rules and regulations, picking up everything I need, and getting to all my classes. Kids have all sorts of questions on the first day: "When do I eat lunch?" and "When is this and when is that?" I'm still trying to figure out all those rules and regulations myself. My first class had 14 Spanish-speaking kids and 2 English-speaking kids. I was trying to explain class rules to a bunch of kids who didn't understand English. This is my introduction, and I'm thinking *Oh, great, I'm not going to make it!*

Fortunately, Marty did make it. In fact, he took a study leave to obtain his master's degree and then went back to teaching. He has since fulfilled his longtime dream of becoming a high school head track coach. The politics of teaching place extraordinary demands on teachers, particularly in public schools. Many of these demands have little to do with actual teaching. Therefore, it's important that teachers discover strong sources of support and revisit their reasons for being in schools. The rewards are there, but sometimes school politics make it a challenge to find them.

—Adapted from P. Schempp, A. Sparkes, and T. Templin, "The micropolitics of teacher induction,"
American Educational Research Journal 30(2):447-72. Copyright 1993 by the
American Educational Research Association. Adapted with permission of the publisher.

Politics of a Profession

A profession is defined by the services it provides and the tasks it undertakes. Regardless of the students, schools, clubs, communities, and subjects they serve, teachers are of the same profession. Therefore, physical education teachers share professional knowledge, skills, perspectives, and role demands. These commonalities form the professional culture of teaching. As professionals, teachers undertake particular demands and provide specific services to their students, schools, and communities. The professional culture of teaching offers teachers a guide for acting, thinking, and identifying the role demands they face.

Beginners most often learn the professional cultural codes by watching and mimicking other teachers. During this observation period, they learn appropriate forms of dress, suitable topics of conversation, acceptable and valued classroom practices, the importance of interaction with peers, the value of in-service activities, and perspectives for guiding their decision making (Lawson 1989). When

teachers step outside the conventional codes of acceptable behavior, their peers often inform them that their actions are "not professional." When teachers exemplify a professional cultural code, they can also be reinforced for it. "You look very professional today" and "You handled that very professionally" are examples of statements from peers or administrators that reinforce and promote the professional codes of teaching.

The codes of a professional teaching culture extend beyond a formal education and a set of acceptable skills and practices. A professional culture provides teachers with standards for dress, mannerisms, and behavior both in and out of class, along with ways of thinking about their duties as teachers. Although it's not possible to detail all the codes of professional conduct in this book, some examples may help teachers understand the importance and frequency of these codes in their practice. Two examples may be particularly helpful: dress and confidentiality.

Dress codes often play a part in defining a professional culture. To look professional, attorneys often wear business suits, doctors wear lab coats, and airline pilots wear uniforms. Like other professionals, teachers have acceptable forms of dress. The interpretation of and compliance with these codes is up to each teacher, but in the main, teachers are expected to dress neatly and appropriately for the activity they are teaching. For a physical education teacher, this might include athletic shoes, warm-up pants, khakis or dress shorts, a polo shirt, and a sport sweater or warm-up jacket. The way you choose to dress conveys important information to others about how you see yourself as a professional, the importance of your job, and the significance of your subject.

To teach well, teachers must know a great deal about their students (see chapter 5). At times, this information may be of a particularly sensitive or personal nature. For example, a student may find it difficult to stay focused on the subject because of a personal tragedy, or a student may experience difficulty mastering particular sport skills because of an unusual medical condition. Although it might be useful to discuss these issues with other teachers when searching for ways to overcome the obstacles and help the student learn, the teacher must not discuss this information with anyone outside the profession. Maintaining confidentiality is essential for maintaining a student's trust in a teacher.

The importance of a professional culture in teaching is realized in the status it gives teachers. Being a professional implies that you are skilled in the tasks of teaching and possess sufficient knowledge to make informed and reliable decisions relative to the instruction of students in a particular subject. Because of their skills and knowledge, professionals have a right to expect to make a reasonable living at their trade. They can also expect to have their skills and decisions respected by those who lack the education and experience in the subject area and in teaching. In the politics of teaching, professional status gives teachers the leverage to secure their jobs, promote their subjects, and help their students learn.

Understanding and operating within the teaching culture is not only necessary for teachers to make changes in the school, but it's also essential for their very survival in that school. Failure to understand what is appropriate and acceptable within that culture will soon have a teacher looking for a new place to work. The cultural codes for public school physical education teachers are played out on two levels: class and school (Zeichner, Tabachnick, and Densmore 1987). These contexts hold distinct tasks, expectations, and demands for teachers. The politics of teaching most often occur at these two distinct, yet related, levels.

Classroom Politics

The majority of a teacher's professional life is lived out in the classroom. Normally, a classroom is thought to be chairs, desks, four walls, and a blackboard. But a classroom is wherever a teacher and student(s) meet for instruction. For sport and physical education teachers, that can be a gymnasium, playing field, court, or even ski slope or whitewater river. What a teacher does, knows, believes, and values can easily be seen by the items in her classroom. Although teachers may be able to separate themselves from their classrooms, it's impossible for a classroom to be separated from the teacher who works there. Take a look around any classroom and you'll see the handprint of the teacher everywhere. What does or will your classroom say about you?

Establishing Order

As the primary authority figure, it falls to teachers to establish the social order that guides life in the classroom (Feiman-Nemser and Floden 1986). Administrators, parents, and even students hold the teacher responsible for establishing and maintaining the class order. To meet this expectation, teachers must quickly establish effective routines that constitute and regulate daily life in the classroom (figure 2.2). These routines represent established ways of performing repeated activities in the class. Experienced teachers develop routines for entering and exiting the classroom, securing equipment, starting and stopping instructional activities, and forming groups.

Novice teachers often find that the lack of comfortable, workable routines makes the burden of classroom demands heavy and at times crushing (figure 2.3). Telling a large group of diverse students how to act when they themselves are uncertain of what to do in the classroom is challenging, to say the least. Teachers unable to meet this expectation often find a class of students who, in the absence of clear guidelines for behavior, make their own decisions about what to do and when. Student sympathy for the plight of novice teachers is not a common scenario in the politics of a classroom. To adapt to their environments and establish social order in their classes, beginning teachers most often mimic the routines of their senior colleagues or rely on routines they remember from their days as students (Schempp, Sparkes, and Templin 1993). It normally takes a few

Figure 2.2 Physical education teachers learn quickly to establish routines for class management while working in large spaces with many students.

Figure 2.3 Though teachers meet as a department to set priorities within the physical education program, newcomers to the profession often find they have to establish routines that work for them and their students within their own classrooms.

years for teachers to feel comfortable establishing routines that best fit their practices and personalities.

Class Management

The first order of business and the primary classroom responsibility of teachers is clearly classroom organization and management. In a comprehensive review of research, classroom discipline was identified as the most serious and consistent problem among novice teachers (Veeneman 1984). Classroom management is so essential to teaching that it's often used to screen teachers in and out of schools. Devising and implementing classroom management strategies is an essential duty that no teacher can escape. Teachers able to manage students are well on their way to successful and satisfying careers, while those who cannot are doomed

to either miserable or short careers (Huberman 1989). Because of the importance of this topic to teaching, chapter 7 of this book examines effective management strategies for negotiating classroom life.

More than simply managing students, classroom management reflects the reality of teaching life and becomes part of the teacher's identity. Historically, teachers are expected to establish themselves as authority figures over students (Waller 1932). Further, teachers must demonstrate the power and authority they hold over students to those outside the classroom (Feiman-Nemser and Floden 1986). To put it bluntly, success or failure, especially in the early years, resides in the teacher's classroom management. The greater the level of control over students, the greater the level of success a teacher can expect in the classroom and the greater the status and recognition a teacher receives from peers, parents, and administrators.

Gaining power over students may be an important task and an essential part of the politics of teaching, but controlling and disciplining students does not bring teachers much personal satisfaction. It isn't the reason they became teachers. As discussed in chapter 1, forging meaningful personal relationships with students is far more rewarding for teachers. Although others in the school and community may define teachers in terms of their ability to control a class, teachers see the essence of their role in an almost contradictory fashion.

Rather than controlling students, teachers aspire to know, understand, and help their students. Teachers measure their success in terms of their students' success, not student compliance with classroom rules and obedience of teacher demands. Helping students master a skill or understand a game concept can stand right alongside motivating students to come to school, helping them control their anger, or planning their future. Therefore, the politics of the classroom demand that teachers establish themselves in multiple ways and through multiple roles in their students' lives: instructor, counselor, social worker, friend, and even surrogate parent (Schempp, Sparkes, and Templin 1993). Many teachers are sharing, caring people who feel deeply satisfied when the political environment of the classroom permits them to assume those roles.

Political Role of Students

Teachers spend more time with students than any other members of the school community. It is therefore logical to recognize that students play an important role in the politics of teaching. As Waller (1932) suggested long ago, winning over students' respect and gaining acceptance are critical to establishing yourself as a teacher. Teachers must master both instruction and management, and the more effective teachers find ways to fold the two together (Huberman 1989). Learning to manage student behavior and motivate student learning are two important tasks facing any teacher.

Students provide important input about a teacher's success; as such, they are critical players in the politics of teaching. Students give teachers immediate and continual feedback about their policies, practices, and perspectives. Besides reinforcing the primacy of classroom management, students convey their perceptions of subject matter importance. In the isolated confines of a classroom, this feedback strongly influences a teacher's sense of competence and professional value.

It's not uncommon, however, for students to convey a lack of concern and value for the subject matter in physical education. When this occurs, students' actions tell the teacher that what he teaches and who he is as a teacher is of little or no consequence to students. It becomes difficult for a teacher to stay motivated to improve either his program or his teaching skills in such an environment. This will be discussed in more detail later in the chapter.

Subject Expertise

The priority of management and the importance of interpersonal relationships in the political mix of the classroom have the potential side effect of marginalizing subject matter. In public schools in particular, classroom responsibilities facing teach-

ers may have less to do with teaching and more to do with keeping students controlled. Knowledge of the subject matter and ability to demonstrate this knowledge can, however, gain status for the teacher in the school, particularly among students (Schempp, Sparkes, and Templin 1993). Proving herself an expert in a subject area gives a teacher certain credibility and status. Unfortunately, subject expertise can be misused for political purposes if it's used to establish authority in the classroom rather than further the education of students (figure 2.4). Although important, subject matter expertise runs a distant second to the need for student control by teachers. The status of the subject matter and a teacher's mastery of it also play a factor in the politics of the school, as will be discussed in the next section.

School Politics

Teachers devote most of their time and energy to their classrooms, but they are also members of a larger school community. Skillfully undertaking duties of institution-wide consequence is, therefore, a serious consideration in the politics of teaching (Lawson 1989). A teacher's participation in institutional events and presence in the school are critical to the development of the teacher's identity and success.

Underlying school politics are the cultural codes that define the appropriate and accepted ways for a teacher to think and act. To become successfully established, teachers must determine the roles

Figure 2.4 Teachers must take care to make subject knowledge and the teaching of children a priority even while the politics of teaching at times demands other priorities.

played by other members in the school community and listen to the messages they convey. They must also adopt and devise strategies to gain the influence that promotes acceptance and success in the school. The major areas of political activity within the school culture include school functions, school members, value of the subject matter, and daily life in the school.

School Functions

Because their work in classrooms isolates public school teachers from peers and outside influences, school meetings and functions offer an opportunity to be seen by colleagues and administrators as part of the school culture (Schempp, Sparkes, and Templin 1993). Involvement in these activities may, therefore, hold serious consequences for career development and a teacher's social standing in the school. School functions give teachers a visibility they cannot achieve in the normal daily course of their duties. The tasks they undertake, their level of involvement in student activities, their committee work, and their interactions with staff, parents, and administrators are all platforms on which teachers establish themselves as respected, influential school members.

School staff meetings hold particular importance in the politics of teaching because this is where decisions of school-wide consequence are often made. Teachers attend numerous meetings with varying purposes (e.g., curricular, informational) and with various individuals (e.g., faculty, parents, administrators). In these meetings, teachers tell others who they are and what they do. Teachers also use these meetings to identify the roles they wish to play in the school culture. Teachers, particularly beginning teachers, need to give careful attention to what they say and to whom, how they dress, and how they present themselves, for they are judged by their peers based on their interactions in these meetings.

School Members

Teachers must learn to interact with established school members, including administrators, colleagues, support personnel, and students. The hierarchy of power in the school quickly becomes clear to new teachers. Principals and administrators are the most politically influential members of the school, followed by teachers and staff, and then students. A teacher's status is fixed within the teacher group, but teachers negotiate their identity with all three groups.

Administrators hold the most power in the school community. In public and private schools, the principal is often instrumental in obtaining employment for teachers. Maintaining employment and gaining promotion is usually directly dependent on satisfying the expectations of the administrators. Because teachers are often grateful for the position and because the principal is one of the keys to a satisfying work experience, teachers are normally loyal to their principals (Huberman 1989; Schempp, Sparkes, and Templin 1993).

Administrators use the codes of the school culture to select, retain, promote, and reward teachers. Teachers are made well aware of these codes and normally attempt to remain within these expectations for behavior, appearance, and attitude. Expressions of individuality and assertions of independence must fall within these boundaries in order for the teacher to be accepted by the larger school community. Often these codes have less to do with educating students and more to do with what Ginsburg (1987) termed the "ideology of professionalism" (i.e., looking and acting professional).

Feiman-Nemser and Floden (1986) identified "buffering" as a role administrators often play for teachers. That is, administrators serve as brokers between teachers and influences or regulations from outside the school. For example, administrators examine information or mandates from the school board, state educational agencies, and sometimes even parents and then pass them along to the teacher, usually with a comment regarding their relative importance.

Teaching colleagues and support personnel also represent influential groups in the politics of teaching. Peers in particular play active roles in helping newcomers make the transition into the school culture in ways that preserve their own sets of interests. Colleagues identify important tasks, support and guide curricular decisions, and inform beginning teachers of their status in the school. Experienced teachers must win and maintain the support and approval of their peers so that they can successfully negotiate their needs within the school. Establishing effective working relationships with peers is not only important for feeling a sense of acceptance and satisfaction in teaching, but it's also necessary for developing a curriculum, acquiring needed supplies and facilities, and stimulating professional growth.

Staff members transmit subtle and not-so-subtle messages that convey the importance of the teacher in the political dynamics of the school. Classroom teachers often give physical education teachers the impression that their work isn't worthy of appreciation and respect. This message manifests itself in several ways. For example, classroom teachers rarely seek professional advice or opinions from physical educators, and classroom teachers seldom, if ever, observe physical educators' work. Bringing classes early to the gym or picking them up late, punishing students for misbehavior in other classes by denying them attendance in physical education, and requesting help with unruly students are other ways classroom teachers convey the message that physical education is supervised play and not real academic work.

Physical educators must be on the alert for these negative messages and work in productive ways to overcome accepted views that physical education is unimportant. For example, if a classroom teacher attempts to prevent a student from attending a physical education class as punishment for something she did outside of physical education, the physical educator should make it clear that his subject is important to the student's education and another form of discipline is necessary. Communicating students' accomplishments in a physical education class to classroom teachers and school community members can effectively inform others of the significance of sport and physical activity in students' lives. Suggestions for promoting physical education programs are offered in chapter 13.

Veteran teachers have established traditions and perceptions that novices must accept, reject, modify, or accommodate as they establish themselves in a school. Teachers sometimes risk alienating other teachers when they inject their own brand of teaching or offer a professional opinion on a topic of discussion. For the most part, however, it seems new teachers find uncaring colleagues—teachers who are burned out or simply too busy for matters related to children's education. In the politics of teaching, finding effective and mutually satisfying ways of working with (or around) colleagues is an important consideration. Because other teachers are unique individuals, no easy or quick answers exist to guide this necessary activity.

The pressure of countless duties, the concerns of the classroom, and the isolated nature of teaching leave teachers much to their own devices when navigating the professional decisions and problems they encounter on the job. Although teachers may find it necessary to appease their peers and demonstrate a willingness to conform to institutional standards, colleagues don't seem to exert a powerful political influence in terms of educational practice or beliefs. The characterization of collegial relationships as "supportive but independent" is a consistent research finding (Zeichner, Tabachnick, and Densmore 1987).

Value of Subject Matter

In the politics of public schools, subject matter is not among the higher priorities. Classroom management, school activities, and the children's social and emotional needs all take precedence over subject knowledge. Lacey described this cultural norm as teachers' "emphasizing the welfare of the child above the interest of their subject" (1989, xv).

Although subject matter doesn't rate highly in terms of school priorities, it does play heavily into the politics of the institution. Distribution of funds, teachers' status, and time devoted to subject matter within a school day are all influenced by the perceived status of a subject area. Several research studies have shown that the status of physical education in schools is among the lowest of all school subjects (Evans 1988; Sparkes, Templin, and Schempp 1990). The marginalization of physical education in schools often leads physical education teachers to think *Who cares, anyway?* After several years of feeling that no one cares whether they teach well, offer innovative and responsive curriculum, or develop children's skills and fitness, teachers lose their motivation to improve both themselves as teachers and the program for students.

Subject matter is awarded status and prestige in accordance with the norms of both societal and school cultures (Evans 1988). A teacher's behavior and beliefs do, however, influence the opinions others hold of the subject. That is, the way teachers perceive their subjects and convey those perceptions influences how others perceive the subjects. As a teacher is identified with the subject she teaches, her identity becomes linked to how people in and out of school define that subject. If the subject is marginalized in schools and society, the teachers associated with that subject are also marginalized to the same degree (Sparkes, Templin, and Schempp 1990).

A subject that's marginalized in the politics of the school is often neglected by administrators and parents—two important elements in the political mix of a school. Consequently, students' respect for physical education diminishes as they realize that parents are unlikely to take an interest in their class performance or physical education learning and that other school members aren't likely to judge their social status based on physical education achievements. On the contrary, a student may actually jeopardize his social status if he identifies too strongly with physical education. In schools where physical education isn't graded on the same scale as other classes, or physical education grades aren't calculated into a student's grade point average, the message is clear: physical education doesn't count. Students are quick to adopt this perspective and act accordingly. They give little effort to studying game rules, history, and concepts or to practicing skills and developing fitness because it brings no academic rewards. Hence, physical education teachers are faced with an uphill battle to convey the significance of their subject to their often apathetic students (Schempp, Sparkes, and Templin 1993). Many teachers in contemporary schools face similar battles, but few must fight as long or as hard as those who teach physical and aesthetic subjects.

Although it's not a foregone conclusion that physical education must be a marginalized subject in schools, a teacher promoting sport and physical activity faces many obstacles, an unattractive tradition, and little support from students, parents, administrators, other teachers, or community members. In an environment of neglect and marginalization, it takes committed and determined individuals to maintain their motivation to teach well and provide a high-quality educational program. Well-taught physical education programs led by dedicated and talented teachers whose efforts are deeply appreciated by students, school, and community do exist in contemporary schools. Unfortunately, this is the exception rather than the norm.

Taking pride in their subjects, the instruction of those subjects, and the accomplishments of their students helps teachers overcome apathy and gain respect in their schools. To advance sport and physical activity, physical education teachers must attend staff meetings and professional development activities, stay updated on the latest trends in the field, promote their programs and student achievements, and serve as role models and ambassadors for their subject in the school and community. Physical education teachers are directly responsible for the perceptions of physical education and its value in the school.

Daily Life of a School

Teachers spend their days in the multidimensional and often frantic school environment. Pressed by time constraints, curricular demands, competing and contradictory needs of individual students, limited resources, and a relentless schedule, teachers must establish themselves amid constant fren-

zied activity. Duties outside the class and away from teaching make a teacher's life difficult. It's not one single duty that teachers find troublesome, but the multitude thrust on them. The number of decisions, the variety of tasks, and the immediacy of demands force teachers to use instinctive reactions, adopt time-honored traditions and management routines, and import lessons from related experiences (Schempp 1993). Because the pressures of school life are immediate and dynamic, teachers don't have time to reflect deeply on a problem before attempting a solution. There's little opportunity to recall lessons from teacher education programs, consult colleagues, or review pertinent professional literature. Instead, teachers must respond reflexively to maintain class momentum, satisfy the needs of a diverse student body, and adapt to school schedule and procedural changes. The demands of school politics can create a situation in which teachers feel they succeed or fail alone.

Teachers use several strategies to negotiate life in schools. A common strategy among new teachers is joining committees (Schempp, Sparkes, and Templin 1993). Curriculum committees are preferable because they allow teachers to influence the routines and requirements of classroom life while demonstrating their willingness to fit into the school culture. Dress is another social strategy teachers use to establish their identity and claim status in a school. While engaged in active instruction, teachers ensure that they are well groomed, physically fit, and dressed in appropriate sport clothes. At meetings, it's common for physical education teachers to change into business dress so they may be seen as equals as well as individuals who take pride in their appearance and profession.

By far, the most prevalent strategy is to remain silent. To exhibit their willingness to fit in and accept the status quo, teachers form a society of the silent. That is, they are often afraid to express opinions to peers and administrators that might be considered controversial and thus jeopardize their chances for success and survival in the school. This has the undesirable effect of not allowing these teachers to use or fully develop their talents for the good of the school. The society of the silent is also less likely to be targeted for additional duties by administrators.

As mentioned, the downside of remaining silent is that a teacher's talent and energy don't help the school. Also, the opportunity to be viewed as an active, contributing, and valued member of the school community is lost. Therefore, it is better for teachers to target areas in line with their instructional duties in which they believe they can make the greatest contribution to the school. In this way, the demands of both class and school are simultaneously met. An example of this occurs every spring in the classes of Mary Lynn Lane, an elementary physical educator. Mary Lynn teaches juggling to her fourth- and fifth-grade students. In the process, she also prepares them for the annual town spring parade. The parade committee requests that each school be represented by a group of students. Mary Lynn ensures that her school is attractively represented, while at the same time teaching her students a useful skill.

Teacher/Coach Role Conflict

Role demands are the expectations of what teachers will do and how they will do it. Some demands are explicit (e.g., lesson planning, classroom management), while others are more implicit (e.g., committee assignments, student relationships). A teacher has little choice but to meet the required demands; failure to do so means, at best, the loss of status and, at worst, the loss of employment.

In public schools, physical education teachers can be faced with multiple and sometimes conflicting role demands because it's often necessary for teachers to coach and coaches to teach (Sage 1989b). While it may appear to the uninitiated eye that coaches' responsibilities are part-time or supplemental to their teaching role, it would be more accurate to view coaching a school team as a full-time job. In certain sports, the time demands placed on a coach are indeed equivalent to a full-time position. As a teacher/coach, meeting the demands of both roles can place considerable stress on an individual (figure 2.5). Add personal responsibilities (e.g., parent, spouse, community member) to the mix, and it's easy to see that something has to give way. When numerous roles combine to place unreasonable demands on an individual's time, energies, and efforts, conflicts inevitably arise. Coaching along with teaching can put tremendous pressure on personal relationships, and family and friends are often neglected. Although the challenge of coaching and the love of sport often make a coaching position highly attractive, schoolteachers should carefully consider the time demands and the strain it will place on other professional and personal obligations.

The pressure to win and produce successful athletes, combined with the relatively low accountability of physical educators to demonstrate students' fitness or skill proficiency, normally means that the coaching responsibilities receive greater attention

Figure 2.5 People that combine teaching and coaching find they must make extra time to accomplish the tasks of both jobs.

and the students' instruction suffers (Sage 1989b). Success and accomplishment in a sports venue bring far greater reward and recognition to a teacher/coach than is found in the physical education classroom. The politics of the school and community place a much higher value on a sports team's success than on the success of students in physical education.

Summary

The politics of teaching can be a challenging dimension to the professional life of a teacher. Teachers experience classroom and institutional politics in different ways. The conditions of the school, the individual variations of students, and the unique expectations of each teaching position create a singular world for every teacher. Likewise, each teacher embodies a distinct collection of personal factors—background experiences, education, beliefs, motives, and so on. It is in the conflict between external factors unique to the school and internal factors unique to the teacher that a teacher searches for identity within the political climate of the profession, school, and classroom.

Each teacher in each school is a distinct individual, but commonalities exist among all teachers. Understanding the politics of teaching is important for teachers who want to make the most of their talents, experiences, and energies. Although the problems teachers face are many, solutions and support do exist. Those able to successfully navigate the tricky waters of school life can develop programs that will be appreciated by their students, schools, and communities.

Discussion Questions

1. What constitutes the "look" of a professional teacher? What constitutes the "look" of a professional coach? Discuss appropriate and inappropriate dress, language, and activities.

2. Teachers and coaches are often called upon to play different roles as they carry out their professional obligations. Which of the following roles do you see yourself assuming and which do you believe to be inappropriate: instructor, counselor, social worker, spiritual advisor, friend, surrogate parent, legal advisor, role model.

3. Is sport and physical activity important to the lives of your potential students? Why? If you believe sport and physical activity is important for people, how will you convey this message to your students and others?

4. When do you choose to fit in with the status quo of a school, and when or how do you voice a contradictory opinion?

5. Those who both teach and coach often face role conflict between teaching, coaching, and personal life. If you find yourself in role conflict, what will be your priorities? How will you attempt to solve the conflicts brought about by competing role demands?

Part II

Knowledge

Determining What Teachers Know and How Students Learn

In part I, the reasons for setting out on the road to excellence in teaching and coaching were examined. In this section, it's time to begin acquiring the information and understanding needed for a successful trip. In the most fundamental sense, teachers use their knowledge to promote student learning. Therefore, part II includes two chapters that address these two critical issues: teachers' knowledge and student learning. Chapter 3 describes the knowledge teachers need and use to undertake their instructional responsibilities. The diverse forms of knowledge teachers rely on to efficiently and effectively teach students meaningful subject matter are identified and described in this chapter. To acquire this extensive knowledge base, teachers make use of several resources, which are also de-

tailed. In short, this chapter describes what teachers need to know and how they learn that information to continually improve the quality of their instruction.

The purpose of teaching is to help students leave the learning experience with new knowledge or improved skills. If a student leaves the classroom knowing something she didn't know before, learning has occurred. If a student's performance of a sport or physical activity improves during a lesson, he has learned something. For teachers to conjure this bit of magic, they need to know exactly how their students learn. In chapter 4, the three phases every student must pass through in order to learn are examined, followed by an exploration of the factors that affect student learning.

Chapter 3

Anatomy of a Teacher's Knowledge

Knowledge is power.

— Thomas Hobbes

KNOWLEDGE

Teaching takes knowledge. In fact, to teach well, a teacher must know a great deal. It would be convenient if a teacher's knowledge could be slotted into independent categories. If this were true, all you would need to do is stock these categories with information to become a superior instructor. The more you know, the better you can teach. Rather than a tidy collection of knowledge areas, however, teaching demands what Donald Schon (1983), referring to professionals in their work environment, described as "knowing-in-action." That is, teachers make judgments and take actions that are spontaneous and situational. Developing knowing-in-action requires both knowledge and experience. In other words, teachers must have the knowledge to make sound decisions and the experience to recognize when and how to use what they know.

In this chapter, the knowledge all good teachers must know will be identified and described. Subsequent chapters will focus on the action side of instruction. Ultimately, teachers combine knowledge and action to form their own special blend of instruction. Because each teacher is unique, there is no magical formula that applies to knowledge for all teachers. There are, however, areas of knowledge that help you teach well. Although these knowledge areas are not separated when teaching, recognizing the kinds of knowledge required to teach helps teachers identify areas that may need improvement. This chapter discusses the various types of knowledge necessary to teach and the sources teachers use to accumulate and construct that knowledge.

Knowledge Areas of Teaching

In making decisions and judgments before and during instruction, teachers draw from several types of knowledge. Most people realize the value of a teacher with a strong command of the subject he is teaching, an understanding of his students, and an array of strategies for teaching that subject. But several other knowledge areas also supply teachers with information that helps them create dynamic, purposeful, and effective lessons. These include knowledge of curriculum and learning environments and a special brand of knowledge unique to teachers called pedagogical content knowledge. These knowledge areas are explained in this section.

Subject Matter Knowledge

If "subject matter concerns permeate the task of teaching" (Feiman-Nemser and Parker 1990, 42), it logically follows that a teacher's knowledge of the subject is vital for both the students' and teacher's success. Subject matter knowledge is the *what* of teaching. It includes the facts, concepts, and skills that characterize the sport or physical activity. The greater a teacher understands the subject, the better she is able to teach it. An in-depth understanding of the subject permits teachers to "elucidate knowledge in new ways, reorganize and partition it, clothe it in activities and emotions, in metaphors and exercise, and in examples and demonstrations" (Shulman 1987, 13).

Teachers with only a rudimentary understanding of the subject are destined to teach the subject in simple ways. Teachers who have an extensive understanding of what they teach can find more ways to present the subject to their students. For example, a teacher with only the faintest idea about basketball might begin teaching by explaining a few points on basic skills such as dribbling, shooting, and passing. A greater understanding of the

game brings about greater analytical skills, and so a teacher with extensive basketball knowledge may begin the class or unit by having the students play three-on-three games to analyze their skill level, rule knowledge, and understanding of the game strategies. This teacher's extensive knowledge base would thus allow him to target specific areas for instruction that would best serve these students. Subsequently, the teacher is then able to design appropriate lessons to speed along the students' understanding and competence. With insufficient or limited knowledge of the sport, this would simply not be possible. A teacher with a hearty knowledge of the subject is in a far better position to teach well than a teacher who knows little of the subject. As will be seen in chapter 16, expert teachers do all they can to learn more about the subjects they teach.

Knowledge of Students

Pia Nilsson, the famed Swedish golf coach, once described her role as a coach as being much like a gardener. She saw her athletes as a gardener might see flowers—they come in all varieties and each requires special and particular conditions to bloom. The gardener must have an extensive knowledge of the flowers and their needs to properly tend the garden. Likewise, a teacher or coach needs an extensive knowledge of her students to teach effectively.

To know your students and their characteristics, you must understand how different individuals might think, feel, and interact with others, as well as understand their potential as movers, performers, or athletes. Although there will be similarities among students, there will also be individual differences in learning styles, capabilities, behavior, attitudes, dispositions, and aspirations (figure 3.1). As discussed in the first two chapters, teachers find getting to know their students one of the best rewards of teaching, so most teachers enjoy the challenge of understanding the people they teach.

Skillful teachers make use of information they can acquire about their students, but particular areas of knowledge are essential for teaching sport and physical activity. Understanding human growth and development characteristics permits the teacher to select activities that are challenging but not overtaxing for students (Broekhoff 1985). Knowledge of the effects of physical activity on the human body lets teachers know when the student

Figure 3.1 Knowledge of their athletes' individual differences has helped head coach Suzanne Youclan and assistant Doug McAvinn win five NCAA national gymnastics championships at the University of Georgia.

can sustain more activity or when the limits of exertion are close at hand. A grasp of the students' learning patterns and preferences helps the teacher choose between a verbal explanation or a demonstration and judge the appropriateness of certain forms of feedback (Magill 1990). To make the learning experience positive and rewarding for the students, a teacher must understand the role of such factors as personality, motivation, and self-esteem in learning (Gruber 1985). There are social and cultural motives for participating in physical activity, and understanding each learner's perspective for engaging in movement helps a teacher present information to students in ways that have greater relevance to their lives (Oliver and Lalik 2000). Most teachers will agree that you can never know too much about your students, and the really good teachers know how to use that knowledge to create purposeful and appropriate learning experiences. The sidebar story makes this point quite well.

Know Thy Students

Courtesy of Golf Magazine.

Laird Small

Laird Small is the director of the Pebble Beach Golf Academy in Monterey, California, and one of *Golf Magazine*'s Top 100 Golf Instructors in America. His competence and reputation as a teacher have brought him into contact with a great many accomplished and high-profile golfers. But the following story, told in his own words, reveals one of the essential characteristics that has made Laird such an outstanding teacher: his knowledge of his students.

To me, measuring success in golf is not done on the scorecard. The students I am most proud of are two young boys, both part of our AT&T junior program, who have used golf to overcome difficult times in their lives. Casey, 9, began taking clinics and lessons from me after suffering through his parents' agonizing divorce. He would come out after school to take lessons and hit balls on our driving range, and he began to regain his confident, outgoing personality after he discovered a "safe" place in which he could escape from the stress at home. Casey's "golf therapy" was so effective, he and his mother recognized it could help his friend Micha, 8, who had suffered a catastrophe of his own. A year ago Micha's father was killed in a bicycle accident. Micha, naturally, sank into a horrible depression, so as diversion therapy, Casey's mother brought Micha to the golf course. I built Micha a set of golf clubs and gave both boys a series of lessons. At first, Micha was reserved and "shut down" emotionally. He and Casey formed a close friendship with each other through golf. Micha regained his confidence and started opening up. He is lively and jovial again. . . . Their swings and scores continue to improve, but the most important improvement has been in their personalities. Golf has given them a mental diversion from the heartaches of their everyday lives. Succeeding at golf has restored their confidence. But most important, golf has helped them forge a fast friendship with each other. And those things are what the sport is all about.

—Laird Small, director, Pebble Beach Golf Academy, Monterey, California

Instructional Knowledge

In addition to knowing their subjects and students, teachers must also know how to convey knowledge to their students. In other words, a teacher must be able to communicate what she knows about the subject in ways that help students learn easily and efficiently. Instructional knowledge refers to the skills, strategies, and principles teachers use to convey information so that students can learn it (figure 3.2). Knowledge of students is the *who* and instructional knowledge is the *how*. Lee Shulman believes this knowledge category "incorporates the more generic capacities for lesson and unit planning, classroom organization and management, teaching techniques, student evaluation and grading and the like" (1986, 9). This is a particular form of knowledge that teachers share; it transcends subject matter, student age level, and other contextual conditions.

The numerous ways of teaching, often called teaching styles or methods, represent a large segment of teachers' instructional knowledge. Chapter 11 details several effective instructional teaching methods. More specific topics such as opening class, presenting information, giving feedback, and closing class are also within this category of knowledge and have been shown to influence what and how well students learn. The students' time in class, who makes what decisions during instruction, and classroom management represent topics in the realm of instructional knowledge. The more a teacher or coach knows about instruction, the greater the op-

Figure 3.2 Teachers take care of instructional knowledge in any spare moments they can find.

tions he has for helping his students learn. Two ways that teachers learn instructional techniques are recalling methods used by teachers they have observed and creatively searching for new ways to present familiar ideas. Don't be afraid to experiment or to copy other teachers. The name of the game is student learning—play it any way you can. Because this represents so much of what a teacher needs to know, part IV of this book covers several topics related to instructional knowledge.

Curricular Knowledge

With curricular knowledge, teachers can fit content topics, instructional materials, learning activities, and outcomes into instructional programs. Being able to effectively select and organize the most important items from a body of knowledge for a particular group of students is a special form of knowledge. Curricular knowledge represents the *when*. That is, curricular knowledge helps teachers decide what students need to know first, when they are ready to learn more, the progressions to follow to best learn the sport or activity, and what students should know at the conclusion of the instructional program.

Information sequencing and management is one way to view curricular knowledge. The range of skills and activity knowledge (e.g., rules, history, strategies) to be learned and the sequence in which the information will be taught are fundamental decisions made using curricular knowledge. Lesson plans, unit plans, and yearly plans help teachers map these decisions. Without good planning, it's difficult for a teacher to organize and sequence the information students will learn in an instructional program. Planning skills and knowledge are topics for chapter 6.

Curricular knowledge goes beyond subject matter selection and organization; it includes conscious decisions regarding all aspects of student learning. The dominant beliefs of teachers often define their instructional philosophies, which in turn influence the subject areas they select for instruction as well as the method by which they teach (Jewett, Bain, and Ennis 1995). As a result, students learn much more in a lesson than just a skill or concept. Although most attention in curriculum is devoted to subject-oriented information, students learn many implicit messages as well. Implicit learning is often termed the "hidden curriculum" because teachers are often unaware of the messages they convey to students about the status of the subject matter, power relations and social status of students, and other attitudes and beliefs. For example, the practice of having children choose sides with one "captain" picking a particular team often conveys an unintended message to children picked last that they are unskilled and largely unwanted. A seemingly small event, such as dividing a class for an activity, can have profound and long-term effects on learners. For this reason, a thoughtful and caring teacher or coach gives close attention to all instructional activities.

Knowledge of Learning Environments

The learning environment consists of the social and physical factors in and around the classroom. According to Shulman (1987), knowledge in this domain ranges from understanding the social dynamics of a class to recognizing the character of the community. The degree to which a teacher can create an environment that supports, sustains, and promotes student learning is largely dependent on the teacher's knowledge of learning environments (figure 3.3). The greater the knowledge of the environmental factors, the better a teacher can manipulate and maximize the learning environment to the students' benefit.

Equipment and facilities are important components of the environment. To good teachers, facilities can perform a variety of functions. Walls can become target areas or places to post motivational slogans or student accomplishments. Courts or fields can be rearranged to allow greater participation or more effective use. Bright colors, natural light, and fresh air all create a positive learning environment. Look around any instructional facility and you learn much about who the students and teachers are and what they value.

Knowledge of equipment also serves a teacher. The more a teacher knows about the supplies and equipment that can be used in teaching, the more instructional options she has to help students learn. A sawed-off handle makes a shorter racket that can help someone learn a forehand stroke faster. A bigger ball is easier to hit. A boundary cone can be used as a field marker, a target, or a ball support. Creative teachers are constantly in search of devices and designs that can alter a learning environment in ways that promote better learning.

The learning environment also includes the social climate. Creating a social environment in which learners feel free from ridicule or embarrassment is an important prerequisite for learning. Students who are afraid of trying or who fear failure are not likely to learn. The learning environment must be-

Figure 3.3 No matter where teaching is to take place, instructors must get their learning environment in order with thorough knowledge of their equipment and facilities and a sense of purpose.

come a place where students feel support for their efforts, experience success, and work for the success of others. Research has shown that students who share in meaningful instructional decisions actually learn more than students who have all the learning decisions made for them (Mancini et al. 1983). To promote such a climate, teachers must know how to create an environment with a sense of purpose that is rich in mutual respect, trust, and cooperation.

Pedagogical Content Knowledge

Lee Shulman, a distinguished professor of education, introduced the term *pedagogical content knowledge* (PCK) to describe that "special amalgam of content and pedagogy that is uniquely the province of teachers, their own special form of professional understanding" (1986, 8). From her research, Grossman (1990) identified the four categories that form pedagogical content knowledge: curricular knowledge, general pedagogical knowledge, knowledge of learners, and knowledge of educational ends, purposes, and values. PCK represents an integration of various teachers' experiences into a unique and very useful form of knowledge.

Rovegno (1992) conducted one of the few studies of pedagogical content knowledge in physical education. She found that as future teachers begin shifting their focus from a general conception of content to a more detailed level, they begin to break content into progressive instructional steps. She also found that aspiring teachers recognize the difference between knowing a subject and being able to teach it. PCK is more than applying knowledge to a particular problem. It's knowledge that comes from teaching a particular subject along with experience teaching that subject to different students under different conditions. It is, in a sense, knowing what works with a particular group of students learning a particular topic.

According to Housner and Griffey (1994), PCK lets teachers adapt information about a topic or skill to match variations in a learner's background and abilities. This knowledge allows teachers to represent the subject in ways that students will comprehend it. Analogies, metaphors, examples, simulations, demonstrations, instructional cues, learning aids, drills, and other applied knowledge representations all bring new knowledge to students in economical and efficient ways that go beyond the simple explanation.

Teachers Need to Know

- Subject
- Students
- Instruction
- Curriculum
- Learning environments
- Pedagogical content knowledge

Constructing Knowledge

Knowledge isn't simply a commodity you collect or pick up as you move along. Rather, teachers build knowledge by blending new information with knowledge gained from previous experience and study. Teachers weigh the merits of new information based on its potential to improve teaching and enrich student learning. Several factors influence the construction of a teacher's knowledge. Among these are teaching experience, sport experience, teacher education, personal biography, teaching expertise, knowledge sources, and workplace constraints (Schempp 1993).

Teachers rely on an extensive variety of sources to select and construct the knowledge necessary to teach (Schempp, Templeton, and Clark 1999). In fact, the more expert the teacher, the greater the number of resources he relies on to find new ways to freshen and develop his instructional practices. Perhaps that may, in part, explain how he became an

expert in the first place. Beginners and lower skilled teachers tend to see little need for improvement; they therefore rely on few resources for information and are heavily dependent on their own experiences as students and fledgling teachers. Beginners prefer practical examples and their own observations, while higher skilled teachers learn to use and value a significant number of knowledge sources. Regardless of the expertise, experience, activity being taught, or location of the instruction, teachers overwhelmingly depend on experience as the primary source of their knowledge. Other significant knowledge resources include students, other teachers, teacher education, workshops and clinics, and publications.

The Importance of Experience

In noting the importance of experience to knowledge, British philosopher John Locke observed that "No man's knowledge can go beyond his experience." It's little wonder that teachers find their experiences invaluable for constructing teaching knowledge. Experiences cited by teachers as most influential reside in three domains: experiences as students, experiences as sport participants, and experiences as teachers. In some form or another, experiences in these areas affect and

Courtesy of Gonzaga University.

Figure 3.4 Even the most successful coaches and teachers, including Gonzaga University men's basketball coach Mark Few, had to learn the trade through years of experience.

influence teachers' behavior and conceptions of practice (figure 3.4).

Experiences As a Student

As noted in chapter 1, biography is a critical factor affecting the knowledge and skill teachers acquire. Early sport and schooling experiences remain a career-long influence over teachers' practices and development. Dan Lortie (1975) described the 12 years traditionally spent as a student in elementary and secondary schools as an "apprenticeship of observation." That is, students serve an apprenticeship for teaching through their observations of the duties undertaken by their teachers. Activities such as participating on athletic teams, personal training, and attending or working in summer camps also provide apprenticeship opportunities for teachers.

During this time, potential teachers not only make decisions about being a teacher, but they also formulate opinions about the type of teacher they will become. These early experiences form a screen through which all subsequent information about teaching must pass. As students, teachers observed four important areas: student learning, class operation, interpersonal relations with students, and desirable personal qualities.

By observing countless teachers and coaches, teachers learn much about motivating students, selecting content, using a variety of teaching styles, giving feedback, demonstrating and explaining skills or concepts, and evaluating students. Particularly important for physical education teachers is the chance to observe strategies for operating and orchestrating a class. Lessons learned at this time also include lesson planning, administration duties, and safety regulations. Practices like starting class on time, giving time-outs, using groups or squads to organize students, and establishing rules such as "No talking while the teacher talks," "Move only on the teacher's command," or "No horseplay" are carryovers into the teaching career from the apprenticeship period. Ask any teacher about what she learned from previous teachers, and be prepared for a long list of critical teaching skills and perspectives.

It must be emphasized that teachers became *acquainted* with these tasks during their apprenticeships, they did not *master* them. Unfortunately, many beginning teachers and those entering teacher education programs fail to realize that seeing a lesson through the eyes of a student is very different from seeing it through the eyes of a teacher. These teachers often believe they already know most, if not all, of what there is to know about teaching because they've watched many teachers for many years

(Hutchinson 1993). This attitude, as you can imagine, prevents many potentially good teachers from ever getting better. These teachers, who are destined to teach in ways they were taught, are inclined to spurn meaningful innovations and only accept new knowledge that fits with old ways of thinking (Lortie 1975). Poorer teachers tend to see their early experiences as the blueprint for their careers. Better teachers see their early experiences as a firm foundation on which to construct new knowledge and build a future as a great teacher or coach.

Experiences As a Participant

Sport and physical activity experiences provide a useful source of knowledge for teachers. It's from personal sport experience that the love of physical activity developed, and for many teachers it represents an important commonality they have with their students, enabling them to better relate and express information to them. Playing experience gives teachers knowledge about what students feel when learning—both the joys and frustrations. Teachers can find within their own experience a wealth of activities that helped them master skills and concepts. Drills and practice scenarios that teachers found enjoyable and effective are likely to provide a similar benefit to their students. A high school teacher I once worked with was very knowledgeable about basketball but knew little about soccer. However, when teaching soccer passing, Steve was able to modify basketball passing drills such as the star drill, line passing, and the three-person weave all to good effect in his soccer instruction.

Additionally, teachers' attitudes and experiences with the subject matter influence what they teach, how, and to whom. People teach best what they know best. It was in their own experiences with activity that the love of movement developed in sport and physical activity teachers. The love and enthusiasm a teacher has for her subject is contagious and, once caught by students, provides a powerful motivation for learning. A class led by a teacher who loves the subject is more likely to be responsive and willing to learn, as can be seen in this example:

Growing up in Hamburg, New York, had not given Shelly Agnew (figure 3.5) much experience working with street-hardened, at-risk high school youth. On one clear May morning, this diminutive blonde found herself in front of a group of tough, resistant, and often violent high school males from inner-city Boston who were being forced to participate in a "last chance" educational program in rural Maine. The subject was field hockey. To say that those boys

Figure 3.5 Shelly Agnew's passion for her favorite sport encouraged her students to treat field hockey with respect when she introduced them to it.

didn't want to be there would be an understatement. Shelly, however, was undaunted. Having played field hockey for her college team and successfully competing at the national level, Shelly not only knew the sport well, she also held it dearly. She was not going to see "her sport" mistreated or disrespected by anyone. As the group reluctantly and defiantly surrounded her, she slammed her hockey stick on the ground and said in a steady, firm voice: "I love this sport and no one is going to screw around with it." She then looked each of those boys in the eyes to let them know she meant it. They were silent. …She had their attention. She then said quietly, "Ok, let's get to work," and the lesson proceeded.

Experiences As a Teacher

In several studies, teaching experience has been identified as among the most important sources of knowledge for teachers (Fincher and Schempp 1994; Schempp, Templeton, and Clark 1999). As teachers accumulate years of service, they gain an important resource for determining the *how* and *why* of what they do. Shulman (1987) described the knowledge teachers construct from in-class experiences as the "wisdom of practice." It's only through the practice of teaching that teachers are able to test innovative ways of teaching subject matter to different students under varying conditions. Teaching experience also helps teachers learn to communicate effectively with a variety of students. There seems no substitute for experience in learning to teach.

For this reason, beginning teachers often find their student, or practical, teaching to be among the most useful experiences in teacher education. This often leads to the complaint that rather than more classroom time, teacher education should include more practical experiences. What these teachers fail to realize, and what most good teachers recognize, is that it takes both experience and classroom time (or any other form of study such as reading, seminar participation, or workshop attendance) to develop the knowledge necessary to teach well. You cannot become a great teacher simply by undertaking a teacher education program, nor can you become a great teacher simply by acquiring many years of experience. It takes both.

Learning From Students

Students are a source of knowledge for teachers, and the particular importance of students in the teaching and learning process makes their contributions to teachers' knowledge unique (Schempp, Templeton, and Clark 1999). Students provide the most direct feedback regarding a teacher's success or failure. From students, teachers learn which teaching styles and learning activities are most motivating, enjoyable, and effective. When teachers see students making progress, asking questions, and showing interest in the subject, they know they've done something right. Bored, frustrated, or underachieving students tell a teacher that something isn't working and it's time to look over their instructional practices and activity selections.

A teacher's communication effectiveness is directly mirrored in the actions and responses of the students. Blank stares or misperformed skills are a good indication that the message was not received. Good teachers find ways to connect and communicate with their students. Good communication usually begins by knowing your audience and understanding how they best receive a message. Because every student is unique in some way, interactions with a variety of students offer teachers an encyclopedia of personalities and learning styles. The very best teachers are able to use that knowledge to good effect in getting the message across.

Effective teachers realize that communication isn't a one-way process of a teacher talking and demonstrating to passive students who listen and observe. Good communication demands that teachers and students maintain a two-way flow of information. Good communication, therefore, requires students and teachers to exchange ideas, thoughts, and feelings. Teachers who are good communicators thus learn a great deal from their students. When knowledge is shared, teachers can help their students to more effectively learn and students can help their teachers to more effectively teach.

Other Teachers As a Source of Knowledge

No other source of information is as attuned to the problems, concerns, and needs of teachers as other teachers (Schempp, Templeton, and Clark 1999). Although firsthand experience may be the best source of knowledge, other teachers with similar experiences provide "field-tested" solutions to real-world problems. Teachers all face comparable challenges and responsibilities. Learning how another teacher has solved a particular problem or met a similar challenge can make a significant contribution to a teacher's knowledge base.

Other teachers are often preferred workshop leaders, because they speak from wisdom rooted in practice (Schempp 1993). From colleagues, instructors gain information about new and different teaching aids, drills, skill progressions, technologies, and communication strategies. Other teachers provide models of teaching success and offer an outlet for discussing new ideas and collaborative efforts. Unfortunately, meeting other teachers and coaches for these fruitful conversations is often a challenge because the daily duties of teachers and coaches don't bring them into regular contact with their professional peers (Lawson 1989). Workshops, seminars, education programs, and coaching clinics are generally the most useful avenues for establishing valuable and mutually beneficial links with other teachers.

Teacher Education Programs

Teacher education programs face a dilemma. On the one hand, these programs receive some students who believe they have little to learn about teaching. Having spent so many years in schools observing teachers, prospective teachers often believe they know most, if not all, of what they need to know about teaching before they enter a teacher education program. These individuals see teacher education as simply a rite of passage so they can acquire the necessary credentials to receive teaching posts. People who believe they have little to learn, learn very little. On the other hand, teacher education programs are expected to produce competent teachers. To become a competent teacher, however, takes knowledge and experience. Because of time and degree requirements, most teacher education programs only provide a fundamental knowledge of teaching and limited teaching practice. For the inexperienced teacher, the most a teacher education program can offer is a preparation to teach. There is still a great deal more to learn after a teacher leaves the university and begins teaching.

This isn't to say that teacher education programs are worthless or of marginal value. On the contrary, they provide the essential knowledge and structured introductory teaching experiences that prepare teachers for successful careers (Schempp and Graber 1992). The knowledge sport and physical education teachers receive in teacher education cannot be acquired from just teaching experience. In preparation programs, teachers learn the latest information relative to teaching and the subject areas of sport and physical activity as well as related discipline areas. Physical education teachers are schooled in such disciplines as exercise physiology, sport sociology, biomechanics, psychology, human development, anatomy, health, and motor learning. They also learn instructional strategies, assessment procedures, student learning styles, classroom management, lesson planning, adaptations for special populations, and curriculum development. Physical education preparation programs also naturally include sport and physical activity courses. Teachers become proficient in a multitude of activities and also learn to teach these activities to a variety of learners.

The final learning experience in teacher education programs is generally an application or apprenticeship experience in which fledgling teachers exercise their newfound knowledge and previous perceptions in front of students. Some sport education programs require an apprenticeship with a seasoned or certified professional. In physical education, field experiences are often integrated into selected coursework so that prospective teachers develop knowledge by testing classroom lessons and information from books in field-based settings. For example, if the topic is "guided discovery" in a teaching methods class, a field experience might be arranged where prospective teachers venture to a public school physical education class and teach third graders an overhand throw or a twelfth-grade class a "give and go" soccer pass using guided discovery as the teaching method.

The pinnacle of education programs for physical education is the student teaching experience. In student teaching, prospective teachers take the lessons learned at a university to a public school and undertake the full-time responsibilities of a teacher under the guidance of an experienced mentor. The power of this experience significantly shapes teachers' understanding and perspectives of their work as teachers and thus remains an influential source of knowledge for the remainder of their careers.

Publications

As experience and expertise accumulate, the information gained through preparation programs, first-hand experience, and conversations with other teachers is simply not enough. Good teachers want to learn more, and to do so they begin turning to other sources of knowledge (Schempp, Templeton, and Clark 1999). Books, professional journals, and magazines offer information on virtually any topic of interest or concern to teachers (figure 3.6). Not surprisingly, teachers find books on the sport or activity they teach helpful because of the easy transfer of information from the book to instruction. Books can also explore topics more in-depth than a magazine article or an Internet Web site.

The advantage of journals and magazines is that they provide up-to-date information from leading people in the field. Journal articles are also concise and to the point, so they can be read quickly and easily scanned for critical information. Professional associations often publish journals in an effort to keep their members on the front line of innovation and new information. In physical education, the *Journal of Physical Education, Recreation and Dance; Strategies;* and *Teaching Elementary Physical Education* are all journals teachers find useful as sources of new ideas and professional information.

Unfortunately, many sport and physical activity instructors, particularly beginners and those with lower levels of teaching expertise, often do not use these sources of knowledge. It's interesting to note, however, that one of the major differences between expert and average teachers is the size of their personal and professional libraries (Schempp, Templeton, and Clark 1999). One method for quickly assessing a teacher's competence is to take a peek at his library. The library of an expert instructor is full of books and magazines. Most experts are voracious consumers of knowledge relative to teaching and their subjects, and printed materials are a resource they heavily depend on for new information.

Workshops and Clinics

Workshops, conferences, and clinics offer a means of sharing a range of information on new equipment, different instructional methods, assessment techniques, and more effective communication skills (Schempp, Templeton, and Clark 1999). Related topics also include warm-up routines, drills, technology, budgeting, and injury prevention and rehabilitation. Aside from the formal agenda of the workshop, informal interactions with workshop leaders, teachers, and other participants are beneficial for expanding any teacher's knowledge base. A presentation by a leader in the field can be informative, entertaining, and inspiring. At times, workshops offer perspectives and insights of someone outside the immediate field. Speakers on motivation, planning, personal growth, and other such topics offer useful information not accessible through other means.

Figure 3.6   There are many publications that allow teachers to continue improving their abilities and staying on top of innovations in the field.

Sources of a Teacher's Knowledge

- Experiences as a
  - Student
  - Participant
  - Teacher
- Students
- Other teachers
- Teacher education programs
- Publications
- Workshops and clinics

Summary

This chapter identified the knowledge skillful teachers need to help students learn as well as the sources used to construct an extensive warehouse of knowledge. There are many sources teachers can tap to build a substantial knowledge base for teaching. Among them are experience, students, other teachers, teacher education, workshops and clinics, and publications. The greater a teacher's understanding of the subject, students, and teaching process, the better equipped he or she will be to meet the challenges of helping someone learn a sport or physical activity. Good teachers are good learners who pursue knowledge that enables them to maximize their abilities as teachers and grow as individuals.

Discussion Questions

1. What did you learn from your previous teachers or coaches about
   a. motivating students?
   b. conducting a lesson?
   c. managing a class?
   d. student relationships?

2. To become a better teacher, which of the following areas of knowledge do you believe you need to learn more about and why?
   a. Students
   b. Subject matter
   c. Teaching

3. What might be some of the "hidden lessons" or "hidden curriculum" issues in a typical sport lesson? In particular, what social values (both positive and negative) might be conveyed in a sport or physical activity lesson?

4. Identify one thing you have learned about teaching from the following resources:
   a. Experiences as a student
   b. Experiences as a participant in sport or physical activity
   c. Experiences as a teacher or coach

Chapter 4

Learning Sport and Physical Activity Skills

Learning is but an adjunct to ourself.

— William Shakespeare

KNOWLEDGE

The purpose of teaching is learning. A simple maxim but one that gets surprisingly overlooked by instructors who are pressed for time, worried about equipment, or preoccupied with student fun. Good teaching begins with a teacher who clearly identifies student learning as the goal. The lessons of these teachers will produce students who are more knowledgeable, higher skilled, and eager to participate in sport and physical activity. For those who measure their teaching success in student learning, understanding how people learn is important information.

Although not all students learn in precisely the same way, there are characteristics common to the way most people learn. A skillful teacher manipulates these characteristics to accelerate and expand student learning. Every physical skill ever learned required a three-step process. In other words, a person passes through three distinct phases in the attempt to understand, acquire, and master a motor skill. An adept teacher not only recognizes these phases but also uses them to accelerate learning. In addition, several factors affect the acquisition of physical skills. In this chapter, we will first examine the phases of learning and then explore the factors affecting skill learning.

In sport and physical activity instruction, the primary learning focus is traditionally placed on mastering a skill or series of skills. Rules, etiquette, strategies, history, and the like are also taught and equally important for students to learn. The stock-in-trade of a sports instructor or teacher/coach, however, remains the activity skills. The performance of these skills determines the satisfaction and success learners experience in participation. Skills, by definition, are learned and, therefore, can be taught.

In learning skills, students strive for mastery so that they can perform sport skills on demand with ease and proficiency. When a student can perform a skill that she could not perform previously, or she can perform a previously learned skill better, learning has occurred. By definition then, learning happens when students are able to perform at a consistently higher level than was previously possible. In the next section, we will examine the steps students take in learning sport and physical activity skills.

The Steps of Learning

Teachers who understand how students learn have a distinct advantage: they can teach in ways that maximize student learning while reducing the time needed to learn the new information. If you were told that next weekend you were to bowl a cricket match, what would you do? If you are North American, there is a good chance that the first thing you would do is find a cricket match in order to see what a bowler does. Perhaps you might seek out books on cricket or talk with people who know the sport. After you understood a bit about the game and the responsibilities and skills needed to bowl, you would most likely want to practice. Practice would continue until you felt relatively comfortable bowling with proper form and satisfactory outcome. Then come game day you would, for better or worse, bowl your first cricket match. As you did for every motor skill you can perform, you just completed the three phases of learning a motor skill. Although you may not have mastered the cricket bowl, you likely learned to perform it at some level of proficiency. The steps in learning this skill were (a) understanding, (b) practice, and (c) performance. These three steps (Fitts and Posner 1967) will be examined more closely.

Step One: Understanding

Human movement skills hold two characteristics: sequential action and temporal execution. In other words, a skill represents a series, or sequence, of actions that are performed with a degree of timing. If the actions are performed with mechanical efficiency in a smooth and progressive order, the results are usually a reasonably performed motor skill. For students to learn these skills, teachers must focus the students' attention on both the critical movements in the skill and the smooth transition from one movement to the next (Magill 2001).

In walking, a person swings the left arm forward while bringing the right foot forward. As the left arm reaches full extension, the right leg is extended and the right heel contacts the ground. Next, the left arm begins to move back toward the body as the body weight is shifted from the heel to the ball of the foot. If any of those actions are performed inefficiently (e.g., the left arm fails to come fully forward or the outside of the foot contacts the ground before the heel), then the skill isn't being performed efficiently or accurately. Similarly, if any of the movements are performed out of sequence (e.g., the front of the foot contacts the ground first and weight is shifted to the heel), the skill isn't performed well.

When learning a new skill or refining a previously learned skilled, the learner must clearly understand the movements to be performed and the timing of those movements. Put another way, the serial components of the movement task must first be understood before the learner can deliberately practice the skill to mastery (Kluka 1999). Students need to form a picture in their minds of the essential components that make up the skill and the order in which those activities are performed. For example, if the student doesn't understand that a forward step with the foot opposite the throwing arm is necessary for throwing a ball, there is little chance he will ever be able to throw a ball successfully enough for any ball game.

In this stage of skill learning, teachers need an arsenal of knowledge and activities that may help students better understand the skill. As the point was made in the previous chapter, the more a teacher knows about the subject matter, the better she is able to teach it. For tasks new to the learner, a teacher may begin the lesson with an introductory explanation of the skill. Demonstrations are an effective strategy for getting someone to understand the mechanics of a movement. Asking students to describe their conceptions of the skill is another method of helping them gain a better understanding. Videos, movies, pictures, and other visual aids also convey the essential information regarding the skill and its performance. Sometimes teachers can find effective blends or combinations of these strategies. These and other techniques are discussed in greater depth in chapter 9.

Regardless of the presentation strategy, you must keep two factors in mind when helping students understand the skill being learned: (a) convey only a few points to the student at a time (pick the most essential), and (b) make those points precise, concise, and memorable. A problem common to many beginning teachers is the tendency to "over-teach." That is, they overload the student with so much information that the student cannot possibly remember the important points to carry into the practice phase of learning. Effective teachers, in contrast, identify the skill components most needed to be mastered given the learner's present skill level and ability. With a concise and appropriate picture of skill performance firmly rooted in the student's mind, she is now ready for the next phase of skill learning: practice.

Step Two: Practice

Teachers often believe their job is completed after they explain or demonstrate a skill, but nothing could be further from the truth. Once the students understand what needs to be done, a crucial step in the learning process now begins. Students must practice what they know until the skill is mastered (Magill 2001). Without practice, a skill simply can't be learned, or at least not retained for long. Michael Jordan didn't learn to play basketball because someone gave him a good explanation or demonstration. He learned to play basketball by spending a great many hours practicing putting the ball through the hoop. A good teacher recognizes the importance of adequate, purposeful practice for learner success and will not only search for appropriate practice activities but also attempt to find ways to motivate and reinforce the learner during practice. The importance of practice and feedback for learning and improving cannot be overstated. An entire chapter in this book (chapter 10) is devoted to this vital segment of the teaching and learning process.

Step Three: Performance

Combining sufficient understanding of a skill with a healthy amount of practice prepares a person for the final learning stage: performance. At this stage,

the skill is executed in a game or activity. When executing the skill, the student should focus on the purpose of the activity and not the process. In other words, when stepping up to the free throw line in basketball or into a starting block, the student should focus on making the shot or getting to the finish line, not on the technique or mechanical aspects of performance.

Because results are more important than technique during performance, the performer should no longer think about the skill itself but rather rely on the skill having become a comfortable habit through long hours of practice. If a player taking a penalty shot in the final minutes of an important soccer game thinks more about where he is going to plant his non-kicking foot than about his target, it's likely he will get a good foot plant but unlikely that the ball will hit the back of the goal. Although thinking about one or more aspects of a skill is vital for understanding and practicing, when it comes to game performance, students must trust that they've sufficiently learned the skill and just let it happen as a natural response to the game or activity.

When a skill is being performed in a game, sport, or activity, conscious thought is replaced by automaticity—that is, the skill is performed from motor memory and not by conscious control (figure 4.1). In fact, thinking while performing a motor skill can be detrimental to the performance, what people who

Figure 4.1 Great athletes practice so much that automaticity occurs when they compete in the activities they excel in.

study motor skill learning call "paralysis by analysis." Consider how awkward walking would be if you consciously attempted to recall and control every aspect of a step. Automaticity provides the aesthetic linkage that permits maximum control and power to be combined into a smooth, progressive, cumulative action.

For most motor skills, this phase of learning occurs after long hours of practice (Schmidt, Wrisberg, and Wrisberg 2000). Extended and deliberate practice leads to a familiarity with the skill that allows the learner to detect performance errors and to make corrective adjustments. One distinguishing characteristic of the automaticity stage in skill learning is consistency: there is little variation from one performance to the next. The student no longer concentrates on the aspects of the skill performance and is now free to concentrate on the conditions of performance. For example, a tennis server no longer needs to carefully consider the grip, toss, or follow-through during the performance and can now focus on where and how she wants the ball to go.

As learning progresses, the student or athlete performs the required skills accurately and repeatedly with fluidity, elegance, and ease. This unconscious attention to the mechanics of the skill has the added benefit of allowing the student to focus on other information pertinent to the skill performance (e.g., time on the clock, gaps in opponent's defense, changes in wind direction). Extensive hours of practice are an important prerequisite for developing the automatic aspect of top-level performance.

Being able to perform the skill does not, however, signal the end of learning. A student can always learn to perform better, and if practice isn't continued, it's unlikely the performance level will remain very high. This last step in learning simply means that the skill can be performed without conscious effort, leaving conscious thought for more immediate concerns of the game or activity. Continued improvement in skill performance depends on increased understanding and additional practice. In other words, students must continually reenter step one to get new information, step two to practice, and step three to perform the skill to improve and develop as a player or participant.

Summary of the Learning Process

Skill learning is a cyclic process: learning always continues. It is the rare student who can hear an explanation or see a demonstration, practice once or twice, and have the skill mastered. For the majority of learners, learning a skill is a gradual process that requires continual information and repetitive practice. Once the student masters the fundamentals of the skill, it becomes a matter of refining and improving as the student moves along the road to mastery. A learner, therefore, needs to constantly revisit each phase of learning—understanding, practice, and performance.

Factors Affecting Learning

An astute instructor recognizes the factors that affect learning and manipulates those factors in the search for ways to advance learning. A student's ability to remember and draw on past experiences and her desire to learn are influential factors found in each stage of learning (understanding, practice, and performance). Put another way, a learner's retention, learning transfer, and motivation affect both the speed and amount of learning. Good teachers can use these factors to create effective, efficient, and meaningful learning experiences.

Retention

Retention refers to memory. It represents the trade-off between how much is remembered versus how much is forgotten. A student who remembers more learns more. Helping students retain information begins by understanding the nature of what they are trying to remember (Kluka 1999). Most sport and physical activity skills represent a series of movements that are both sequential and temporal. The sequential order of the actions seems to be easier for students to remember, whereas the timing, or temporal portion, of the skill seems more difficult to retain (figure 4.2). Someone who has not practiced a skill for a while will usually discover his "timing" is off. It's difficult, for example, to maintain the required fluidity of a swimming stroke, dance step, or gymnastics skill without continual practice. Renewed and continued practice of the activity is the only way to restore the timing of the performance. Teachers must encourage continual practice to promote retention of the temporal aspects of the skill.

The sequential components of the skill appear easier to retain, but their retention can still be enhanced by good teaching or coaching. In the understanding phase of learning, clearly identifying, demonstrating, and explaining the sequential components promotes retention. Teaching only a few components at a time also promotes retention because it's easier to recall fewer items than more

Figure 4.2 Physical activities require coordinating several temporal skills in order to function properly.

items. A common problem for most beginning teachers is the temptation to tell the students all they know about a particular skill. This does more to confuse the students than to enlighten them. When teaching fewer points, a teacher needs to consider carefully which points are most critical to the particular student's performance success and provide only those to the learner. As the learner gains in proficiency through practice, she will be ready for more information. In addition, effective teachers almost always summarize the important points of a lesson at its conclusion. They want the students to leave the lesson with a clear understanding of what they learned that day. The information covered last in a lesson is often remembered best, so end your lessons with a summary of the most important points.

If the information never gets into memory, it can never come back out. In the practice phase of learning, providing feedback and reinforcing correct performances help the learner retain and recall the critical skill components covered in the understand-

ing phase. Finally, encouraging and providing opportunities for the automatic performance of the skill help the learner ingrain the kinesthetic sense and develop a motor memory for the skill. As they close a lesson, expert teachers like to leave the students with a positive, successful memory of their skill performance. Let the last performance a student makes in a lesson be a good one. Retaining a positive image of skill success will bring the student back for more.

Learning Transfer

Transfer in learning occurs when previously learned lessons influence a new learning experience (Magill 2001) (figure 4.3). Transfer can be positive or negative. In positive transfer, the student learns a new skill quickly and easily when he see similarities to a previously learned skilled. For example, a tennis player may perceive a volleyball serve to be like a tennis serve in terms of body position, ball toss, weight transfer, arm movements, and follow-through. Negative transfer occurs when a previously learned skill interferes with the development

Figure 4.3 Transfer in learning occurs when previously learned lessons influence a new learning experience, such as when a tennis player takes up racquetball, a sport that is similar but also has fundamental differences.

of a new skill. That same tennis player may have difficulty learning racquetball because it requires a powerful wrist action, and years of tennis have ingrained a pattern of a firm wrist throughout the stroke.

One way instructors can promote positive learning transfer is to investigate the learner's background. If you can identify skills the learner already has, pointing out similarities between learned skills and the new skill speeds along the learning. A second method is to ensure that the fundamental principles of the new skill are fully understood. By understanding the principles of the movement, the learner may recall similar principles from other skills she has learned. Someone learning to kick a field goal in football may see the importance of planting her non-kicking foot alongside the ball because it's the same principle used in shooting soccer penalty shots.

Transfer occurs in all three phases of learning a motor skill. The lessons learned in the understanding phase of skill learning must transfer to the practice setting, and in turn, gains made in the practice phase of learning must transfer to skill performance in the sport or activity. To promote interphase transfer, teachers should attempt two strategies. First, the key points acquired in the understanding phase must be the same points that are practiced; these points must also be reviewed with the learner during or after the performance. Reviews and reinforcement help students transfer skills from the chalkboard to the practice field to the big game. Second, making the practice activities and environment closely resemble the conditions under which the skill will be performed in the automatic stage encourages transfer from practice to performance.

Motivation

Motivation is a person's drive to accomplish and achieve a goal. Motivations help explain what people do and why (figure 4.4). In learning motor skills, motivations influence students' selection of skills to be learned and the commitment they make to learning those skills. Two dimensions of motivation are particularly important for a teacher trying to stimulate learning: level of aspiration and goal setting.

Level of Aspiration

According to Ralph Waldo Emerson, "Nothing great was ever achieved without enthusiasm." That sums up rather nicely the role of aspiration in learning. A person's desire to learn is a major determiner of his potential to master a skill. Aspiration is measured by

Figure 4.4 Students use many different motivations to learn motor skills and strive for expertise in physical activities.

a person's expectations of performance. A learner's aspiration is a personal matter primarily based on self-concept and prior success and failure. With respect to self-concept, if a person believes she can learn and can picture herself performing the skill, learning is likely to follow. Without that picture of "self as successful performer," there is little chance that the student will put forth much effort or dedication to the task. The story "Realizing a Dream" at the end of this section is an example of a person who, despite limitations, firmly believed he would develop into a premier performer and professional athlete. No one likes to work hard if he believes his efforts will end in futile failure. This brings us to the second element of aspiration: prior success and failure.

Students' self-concepts are strongly influenced by past successes and failures. Again, the perception of success or failure is personal. A score that Tiger Woods might consider failure would dramatically exceed the average recreational golfer's wildest dreams of success. Regardless, people who perceive themselves as being successful in past experiences will hold higher performance and learning expectations than will people who believe their attempts at physical activities have resulted in a miserable record of embarrassing and inadequate performances. Positive perceptions and belief in success also motivate a learner to seek new information and to practice (Roberts 1992).

A skillful teacher pays strong attention to the learner's level of aspiration. Recognizing that each person is unique with differing needs, self-concepts, and performance histories, good teachers find ways to motivate learners and make them feel successful.

Bolstering self-concepts by recognizing successful performances and hard work in practice is one method. Structuring practice activities geared to the student's abilities so that success is a likely outcome is another. Providing positive feedback is still another method designed to focus the learner on successful performances. Setting realistic goals, planning for their achievement, and celebrating their attainment has also proven effective in motivating people to learn, practice, and perform sport and physical skills. For substantial learning and accomplishment to take place, a teacher or coach must help students see themselves as successful performers. Although seeing yourself as a winner doesn't always guarantee that you will win, seeing yourself as a loser almost always guarantees the outcome.

Realizing a Dream

© Sport The Library

Terrell Brandon

Every summer, a collection of college students and faculty find their way from the United States to the far reaches of the globe as part of Camp Adventure. Dr. Christopher Edginton began the program to give the recreation and leisure students at the University of Oregon experience in conducting summer camps along with the opportunity for international travel. One summer, Chris asked me to help out by organizing a Camp Adventure sport camp for military dependent children stationed in Korea. The camp was to be held on an Army base a few miles from the DMZ in the northern part of South Korea. I never found an effective way to say no to Chris, so off I was to Korea for two weeks with a couple of recreation students to teach sport skills to Army kids. Among the staff was a student named Terrell Brandon. When we began the trip, all I knew about "T" was that he was a sophomore recreation major who played basketball and was a generally all-around nice guy who was easy to talk and joke with.

We'd finish our instruction around 4:00 every afternoon, and there isn't much that civilians with free time can do on a military base. Most of the staff would head back to the barracks for some "down time" before dinner. T would head for the gym to practice basketball. I was more "up" than "down," so I joined him. He spent most of his time practicing a few selected skills. First, he would practice his shot release, what he called "touch." He'd begin nearly under the basket and would flip the ball with his fingers and wrist, making the ball touch nothing but the net as it cleanly passed the rim. The ball would time and again just drop through the hoop. He would slowly work his way out from the basket in different directions, taking delight in swishing the ball through the net. When he got too far to simply use his fingers and wrist, he began taking jump shots. He kept working his way out to about mid-court. He then began some dribbles, making a move or two and then gracefully elevating and releasing the ball. The ball seemed to float to and through the basket, just tickling the net as it dropped. After mid-court, he would spend a few minutes working on his breakaways. "There isn't anyone who can catch me in an open court," he once told me. He seemed to relish the supreme control he had over his body and the ball as he moved down the court and up to the basket to gently lay the ball off the backboard and through the net. The hours and hours T spent practicing could be seen in his smooth, powerful, and confident moves.

It was during these times that we talked because we were both relaxed and the activity was more about "minimum effort with maximum results." He told me about how he got into basketball (to avoid gangs) and his biggest accomplishments (he isn't a braggart, so it took me a while to discover that he led the Pacific Ten conference in scoring that year. You would have thought that as someone in physical education, I would have known that, but T was undisturbed by my lack of knowledge of his prowess). He talked of his love and respect for friends and family (particularly his mother) and his firm belief that one day he would play in the National Basketball Association.

It was during one of these practice sessions that he told me about one of his strongest motivations for reaching the pinnacle of his sport—his high school English teacher had told him he was too short to ever

(continued)

(continued)

be good. T believed with all his heart that he could be good and set out to prove the teacher wrong. The first thing he did was practice, practice, and then practice some more until he could dunk the ball. From there, he just kept on practicing and getting better.

Terrell Brandon's motivation to be among the very best propelled him to his dream of playing in the NBA. He has played in more than 600 NBA games, scored more than 9,000 points, and received the NBA Sportsmanship Award. As only the eighth player in NBA history under six feet to be selected as an NBA All-Star, T certainly proved that English teacher wrong. He also proved what is possible if someone has a dream and the faith and drive to pursue it.

Goal Setting

Goals represent what we want to happen. They are the intended consequence or outcome of our efforts and activities. They represent our dreams and aspirations. In goal setting, the learner identifies the level of skill performance she would like to see result from practice. Typical learning goals in sport and physical activity include wanting a more accurate serve, a more consistent swing, a faster lap time, reduced body fat, or increased muscle tone. Goal setting is also intimately tied to motivation. Someone with clear and purposeful goals is far more motivated and prepared to learn than someone with a general idea of what he would like to see happen (Weinberg and Gould 1995).

Setting goals helps the teacher or student plan the practice intensity, duration, and activities (figure 4.5). Objective goals are the most effective. Practicing free throws 15 minutes every day until the athlete is making 8 out of 10 is a superior goal to practicing free throws until the athlete gets better. Goals must also be realistic; goals that are set too low or too high do not stimulate learning. Furthermore, the goal must be attainable but must also present a challenge. Because students come with varied activity experiences, motivations, personalities, abilities, and lifestyles, consideration must be given to the individual differences of the learners. Finally, when setting goals, communication and understanding between the teacher and student is critical because goals must have personal significance and meaning to the learner if the learner is to put forth the effort, time, and commitment necessary to achieve them. Goal setting provides a powerful teaching and learning tool that must be given careful consideration by both teacher and student.

Figure 4.5 At a very young age, children show great effort and enthusiasm for physical activity when teachers and coaches present it as fun and encourage goal setting.

Promoting Learning

Retention

Encourage continual practice.

Identify, demonstrate, and explain the most important points.

Give feedback and reinforce good performance.

Encourage performance opportunities.

Learning Transfer

Use previously learned skills when teaching new skills.

Use the same information for both explanations and feedback.

Practice in game-like conditions.

Use actual experiences as examples in explanations.

Motivation

Recognize successful performances.

Focus feedback on the positives.

Set realistic, challenging goals.

State goals clearly and objectively.

Make goals personally meaningful.

Factors Affecting Performance

The fundamental purpose of learning a motor skill is to improve performance in a game or activity. But skill learning is not the only performance factor. Physical attributes, maturation, environmental conditions, and motivation all influence the performance level of a skill (Kluka 1999). Learning a skill and performing a skill are not the same. Although a teacher or coach has little or no control over these factors, understanding the factors affecting performance helps teachers and students set realistic and pertinent learning goals. It also lets teachers discuss a student's game or activity performance beyond just the degree of satisfaction with the skill learning.

Physical Attributes

Physical attributes include the physical make-up of the person—strength, weight, height, endurance, and so forth. These attributes affect the physical functioning of the person and consequently the ability to perform motor skills. Therefore, changes in physical characteristics can alter someone's performance. Increases in cardiovascular endurance influence performance in many activities such as swimming, running, and soccer. Increases in strength affect performances in football, weightlifting, or field events. Increases in physical fitness take many skill performances to higher levels and reduce the deterioration of skill in the later stages of a game or activity when fatigue becomes a factor.

A good teacher can supply students with appropriate fitness activities that will enhance the students' ability to perform the skills they are learning. When learning a new set of skills, learners should assess their present fitness levels and seek appropriate, healthy methods of increasing the physical attributes that will contribute to better skill performance. Teachers and coaches need to be aware of physical attributes when selecting activities and skills for students. Skills that are physically too demanding for a student should not be taught, but neither should skills that are too simple. Proper preparation and stretching for both practice and performance sessions should also receive consideration from both the student and teacher. It goes without saying that practicing skills while exhausted not only increases the chances of injury but is also likely to result in bad habits and performance decreases. Practice skills when fresh and alert.

Maturation

As a person physically matures, the ability to use various muscle systems changes. Many skills cannot be properly learned until a certain level of maturation is achieved. For example, catching a fly ball in baseball can prove impossible for a child who has not yet developed the visual skill of tracking and eye-hand coordination. As humans grow older, their physical performances begin to deteriorate. Signs of degeneration begin to show shortly after puberty when flexibility decreases. As a person matures, reaction time slows, metabolism slows, and even strength begins to wane. The degeneration process can be slowed by exercise, but it cannot be completely arrested. Maturation and the principles of human growth and development directly influence physical activity and motor performance.

Environmental Conditions

The specific requirements of the skill and the conditions in which the skill is performed also affect performance. Equipment innovations, changes in rules, and playing conditions (e.g., weather, officials, opponents) are examples of environmental conditions. A performer has little influence over the weather or rules, but she can maximize her performance by learning to adapt to various circumstances. Ensuring that equipment is in top condition and of proper fit, thoroughly understanding the rules, studying opponents, and training in a variety of weather conditions are methods used by top performers as they prepare to do their best. Teachers would do well to consider environmental conditions as they organize and structure the learning environment. Proper equipment and facilities not only are necessary safety considerations, but they can influence learning as well. Practicing a skill in conditions similar to those a student may encounter during game or activity participation is also something a teacher should consider. For example, if a game isn't canceled because of rain or snow, practice shouldn't be, either.

Motivation

Motivation is a key element in both learning and performance. The desire to achieve greatly affects the ability to perform a skill or physical task. Someone who doesn't care if he performs well will not likely do well. Stories of great athletic achievements often tell of a person with an iron will to succeed and excel. Although it takes more than desire to perform any physical activity at its highest level, it's impossible to achieve such heights without the hunger to do so. In a recent study, experienced physical education teachers identified student motivation as their single largest problem (Schempp, Manross, Tan, and Fincher 1998). They believed they could teach anyone the subject matter *if* the student was motivated to learn. If there was no motivation, they contended, there could be no learning. The teachers therefore saw their first task as motivating the student. The same holds true in performance. Participants lacking the belief or desire to perform at their best will not likely perform at their best.

What a person is thinking or feeling while performing can greatly affect the ability to perform For this reason, a teacher would do well to review the student's thought process and motivation factors when discussing a recent game or activity performance. Because thinking and emotional control are so critical to performance, an industry in sport psychology has emerged. A practicing sport psychologist teaches athletes particular ways of thinking that will help them to achieve. Imagery is one technique a sport psychologist teaches athletes (Martin, Moritz, and Hall 1999). The athlete is taught to imagine a successful performance immediately before attempting the task. Some examples include a pole-vaulter seeing himself gracefully clearing the bar, a basketball player envisioning her free throw falling smoothly through the basket, or a baseball batter imagining making solid contact with the ball.

A pre-shot routine is another technique a sport psychologist will teach an athlete. A pre-shot routine prepares the athlete for taking a shot and represents a set of practices that are repeated time and again. A typical pre-shot routine includes properly setting (or aligning) the body, focusing on the target, and immediately beginning the shot or action. A tennis player may have a pre-shot routine for serving the ball that might include pointing a shoulder at the service court and setting the feet (alignment), bouncing the ball several times to get the body in motion, locking the eyes on a specific target in the service court, and then tossing the ball—all with no break in the activity. Archers, golfers, bowlers, and free throw shooters can all benefit from a pre-shot routine because it covers important factors for a successful performance (e.g., body alignment) and allows no time for negative thoughts to enter the mind just before performance. Mental sport skills do improve performance, and they can be taught like any other sport skill. The following books offer additional information on this topic for interested teachers and coaches: *Frameworks for Sport Psychologists: Enhancing Sport Performance* (Karen Hill, Human Kinetics, 2001), *Doing Sport Psychology* (Mark Anderson, Human Kinetics, 2000), *Mental Training for Peak Performance: Top Athletes Reveal the Mental Exercises They Use to Excel* (Steven Ungeleider, Rodale Press, 1996), and *In Pursuit of Excellence: How to Win in Sport and Life Through Mental Training* (Terry Orlick, Human Kinetics, 2000).

Summary

This chapter examined the steps used for learning physical skills, factors influencing student learning, and factors influencing skill performance. Teachers who understand the learning process are better able to plan instructional activities that maximize student development and achievement. When helping students learn and improve skills, it's important for teachers and coaches to explain and demonstrate the skills so students have a firm understanding of how the skill is to be performed. Practice activities must be structured so students can refine and master both the important skill components and the rhythmic patterns necessary to perform the skill with ease and competence. Finally, teachers must provide or suggest ways for students to apply the learned skills in an actual game or activity. In sport and physical activity learning, the proof is in the performance.

Retention, learning transfer, and motivation all affect skill learning. Teachers who use these factors to their advantage find ways of promoting greater learning. Physical attributes, maturation, environmental conditions, and motivation all influence the level of physical performance. Skillful teachers and coaches use these factors to set realistic learning expectations and offer insightful analyses of student performance. Teachers who identify student learning as their primary mission in teaching will find the information in this chapter indispensable.

Discussion Questions

1. The first phase in learning a skill is understanding. Identify and discuss at least four different methods you might use to convey critical information about a skill you are teaching to students.

2. Describe three skill drills you have found helpful in developing your sport or physical activity skills. Why were they effective for you?

3. As a teacher, how will you help students retain or remember the information you present to them in a lesson?

4. Motivation is a key factor in both learning and performing sport skills. Do you have particular motivation techniques you like to use in your own sport participation? What techniques do you think will be effective for motivating your students or athletes to both improve and perform?

Part III

Construction
Creating the Learning Environment

With the knowledge discussed in chapter 3 and an understanding of student learning (chapter 4), teachers can now establish a caring, creative, and effective learning environment in which they can teach and students can learn. With this in mind, this section provides strategies for developing effective relationships with students, planning and organizing for student learning, and managing the learning environment. Teachers able to apply these strategies are well along in their journey to excellence in teaching and coaching.

Part III opens with chapter 5, Building Relationships, a critical keystone to creating a positive, productive learning environment. Suggestions are given for developing empathetic relationships with students that serve as a basis for good teaching and learning. Enthusiasm is important fuel for both a relationship and good teaching, and thus ideas for increasing enthusiasm are offered. Finally, equity issues in sport and physical activity are critical for

building relationships, and they receive significant attention in this chapter.

In chapter 6, the essential skills and knowledge to plan and organize a learning environment are presented. The chapter opens with a discussion of the effect the number of students has on a learning environment. Procedures and skills for planning lessons and units, as well as for long-term planning, are presented next. Finally, the chapter ends with a checklist of questions that can help any teacher or coach plan and organize the instructional environment.

The final chapter in part III, chapter 7, covers information necessary for managing the learning environment. Effective management practices, guidelines for establishing rules and procedures, and specific topics related to management issues form the content of this chapter. This information is essential for beginning teachers, but experienced teachers and coaches will also find some new ideas here.

Chapter 5

Building Relationships

Teaching is a developing emotional relationship.

— Jacques Barzun

CONSTRUCTION

Most people choose to teach sport and physical activity for two reasons: a love of the activity and a love of people. Much of this book focuses on ways to effectively teach activities, but it is of equal importance that teachers develop interpersonal skills and build relationships with their students. Not only will these relationships serve teachers and learners in reaching their learning goals, but they also will be a significant and continued source of satisfaction for both the teachers and the pupils. All who teach or coach can fondly recall at least one memorable mentor. At some point in time, your students should recall you as both a skilled instructor and a caring human being.

The Power of Caring

Four elements must be present for a relationship to grow and develop in ways that permit one person to influence the life of another. Teachers who establish relationships with students based on these principles are often those whose influence extends far beyond the classroom or activity area (Teven and

McCroskey 1997). The first element is respect. Teachers must respect and protect the fundamental rights of each student. Ralph Waldo Emerson believed that "the secret of education is respecting the pupil." The abilities of students should also be respected and never used as a source of ridicule.

Respecting students' dignity is crucial for establishing trusting, human relationships. This was a lesson I learned early in my teaching career. Responsible for a physical education program at an institution for mentally challenged adults, I was teaching basic balancing skills one afternoon. My praise for my students was positive and profuse. As I helped Irving, a middle-aged man, along a low balance beam, I gushed words of praise and encouragement for this rather simple task. When Irving finished, he turned to me, looked me straight in the eye and in a low, clear voice said, "You know, Paul, I may be retarded, but I'm not stupid." That day, Irving taught me a great deal about the dignity of learners.

Empathy, the second element, requires teachers to take the student's point of view from time to time. Attempting to view a situation from another's perspective can often reveal solutions to problem situations. A skillful teacher or coach can then plan lessons that lead to significant learning and satisfaction for the student. For example, sometimes a physical activity instructor may find it hard to understand a student's struggle to learn a new skill because such learning always came rather easily for the teacher. But learning motor skills isn't always easy for someone lacking a certain amount of strength or coordination, or someone who might be a bit overweight, or someone who has experienced a long line of failure in physical activities. At such times, a teacher must be patient, accepting, and encouraging. Empathy is the door through which understanding shall pass, and it is through understanding their students that teachers are best able to help them learn.

Caring relationships are characterized by warmth, the third element. A warm relationship requires the teacher to be positive, optimistic, encouraging, and supportive of the students' efforts to learn (figure 5.1). Considering the conditions some teachers face today, particularly in public schools, exuding warmth can sometimes be a challenging task. It's no secret that teachers in schools often face disrespectful, apathetic, and self-absorbed students. But those who make continual efforts to find the good in someone can usually find it. Teachers are also role models, and as such, it's their responsibility to display the attitudes they expect in their students. Warm relationships, therefore, begin with the teacher. Those who

Figure 5.1 Teachers use many positive personality traits to help students learn, including patience, persistence, and humor.

see a little good in everyone see a different world than those who cannot or will not see.

Finally, a caring relationship is genuine. Being sincere and honest with students removes doubt from the relationship. Teachers are there to help students learn. Teachers who genuinely measure their success in the achievements of their students find success many times over. In addition, teachers and students both have needs. Those teachers who attempt to meet the needs of their students usually find the efforts returned (Teven and McCroskey 1997).

Building Relationships

Human relationships are the product of the care, concern, and efforts of at least two parties. Relationships lacking in these qualities are doomed to be dysfunctional. Relationships that celebrate these qualities are likely to be mutually rewarding and satisfying. Because they are the primary authority figures in the learning experience, teachers must do at least half the work in building effective, functional relationships with students. The techniques and suggestions offered in the following sections can help teachers establish and maintain relationships by expressing concern and feelings for their students.

These skills cannot, however, disguise feelings of apathy, distrust, or insincerity if those are the true feelings of the teacher. After all, if a teacher doesn't have the best interests of the students at heart, there is little reason for him to be a teacher and virtually no chance that he will find either satisfaction or success in the teaching profession. However, teachers who strongly wish for students' lives to be better through their learning experiences will likely experience success in teaching.

Focus on the Important

Consider carefully the learning environment you wish to foster. Identify the behaviors and attitudes that are most critical to this environment. For example, which of the following student characteristics best represent the qualities you wish to see in your class: effort, performance, cooperation, peer support, leadership/followership, improvement, risk-taking, humor, discipline, achievement, or compliance? When students exhibit the qualities a teacher deems valuable, the teacher should let the students know these qualities are valued. By reinforcing and supporting the activities and actions you most cherish in your students, you will most likely see those qualities emerging more often and in more students.

When a student displays sporting behavior, recognize it by letting students know that it was both noticed and appreciated (figure 5.2). Depending on

Figure 5.2 Teachers and coaches should make sure to praise sporting behavior among their athletes.

the student and circumstance, you can make your proclamation public so others are aware of it, or you can speak privately with the student. In this way, students gain insight into what you most value. Teachers who focus only on what they don't want to see or who point out student behavior only when it violates rules convey negative feelings to students, not positive ones. Promote relationships based on the positive qualities you wish to see in your students, and you will likely see more of those qualities in your classes.

It's equally important that a teacher understand the qualities a student seeks in a teacher or coach. Which behaviors are most important to the students? For example, nearly all students admire a teacher who is fair, organized, confident, flexible, knowledgeable, and caring. They don't necessarily want a teacher who holds low expectations for either the students' performance or in-class behavior. Students appreciate teachers who help them learn and who model the behaviors they expect of their students.

Although teachers cannot be all things to all students and should not attempt to be someone they are not, they can develop and model the behaviors and characteristics students most value in a teacher. Teachers can learn what is important by listening to students. However, it may take some students a while before they reveal what they most value in a teacher. John Hichwa, a National Teacher of the Year, once received a note from a former student who at 26 years of age wrote, "I have an apology to make to you. I am sorry for all the trouble I caused you when I was in middle school. I thank you for understanding me, being patient, and never screwing me to the wall" (Hichwa, 1998, 8).

Consistency Counts

It isn't possible to treat everyone the same, but it is possible to treat particular behaviors or actions in a similar manner. We all find some people easier to like than others. However, teachers must look past their personal likes and dislikes and treat students' behavior with a level of consistency. If an action by a student gains praise one day, it should not draw criticism the next. Likewise, when an action of one student draws either praise or rebuke from the teacher, a similar action by another student should receive the same reaction.

Teachers who praise the activities of students they like and criticize the actions of those they least favor are deemed unfair by students. It's more important to students to be treated fairly than it is for teachers to like them. Ideally, a student would prefer both. But if one student receives praise for improving fitness or mastering a drop shot, then the next student who does the same or better should also receive similar recognition.

When disciplining a student, teachers need to convey a feeling of "I like you, but I don't like what you just did." It's easier to be consistent and fair when teachers punish or reward the behavior rather than the person. The behavior is appropriate or inappropriate, not the student. Beginning teachers often take unruly behavior by students personally, although students seldom intend it to be so. Emotions, therefore, take over, and novice teachers begin to react to the students. This leads to a no-win situation. Teachers who can respond to inappropriate behavior in an unruffled, rational way can often defuse the situation and still emerge with the student relationship intact. Calmly saying, "Peter, I need you to listen to this if you are going to understand how to hit this shot" is often more effective than harshly yelling, "Peter, when I talk, you listen!" Although there are situations that try a teacher's patience, the teacher who searches for ways to like and love his students is well on his way to building effective and satisfying relationships.

Maintain Balance

Responses to students should fit the situation. Don't go overboard with reactions, but don't react too lightly, either. Stating the criteria for your approval often helps regulate your reactions. For example, quietly telling a student after a particularly strenuous practice "Your effort and commitment were terrific today. You helped everybody get the most out of this practice—including me. Thank you," conveys to the student your sincere appreciation for her efforts. What's more, you will likely see those qualities again, and not in that student alone.

Teachers who balance their reactions to students sometimes ignore off-task behavior to offset the fact that they sometimes ignore on-task behavior. Strategically ignoring off-task behavior also keeps the students' attention on the more important learning activities rather than redirecting it to the less productive and unwanted off-task behavior. However, if the off-task behavior continues and begins to distract other learners, the teacher should deal with it quietly and effectively.

Balance can also mean not getting too carried away with praising students' accomplishments. It's important to recognize someone's achievement, but seldom is an achievement in a sport or physical activity class front-page news. So don't treat it as such. Let the students know that the achievement is recognized and important, but then refocus your attention on setting and reaching the next goal. I once witnessed a student teacher attempting to be supportive when his student made an ill-fated attempt at a jump shot. The teacher said "Nice shot," to which the 12-year-old turned around with an incredulous look and said "That was an air ball, dude."

Pupils Are People, Too

To establish meaningful relationships, a teacher must view students as whole persons (Hichwa 1998). Like teachers, students have interests, aspirations, rights, responsibilities, and enterprises outside the confines of the gym or practice field. Taking an interest in students' lives demonstrates a sincere concern for students as people, an important prerequisite for a developing relationship. Although it's not recommended that students and teachers form close, personal friendships, showing appreciation and respect for the students' world allows teachers to better understand the people they teach. As the relationship develops, students enjoy moments when teachers share their personal interests and activities. Teaching is meaningful human interaction, and seeing each other as people goes a long way toward making the learning experience more satisfying, productive, and enjoyable for teachers and students alike.

Knowing and Understanding Your Students

A difference between expert and less expert teachers can be found in the amount of information presented in a lesson. Interestingly enough, expert teachers promote more learning with less information. In part, this occurs because better teachers see themselves teaching students, not subject matter (figure 5.3). Therefore, they convey only the information they believe the students need and present it in ways they believe the students will best understand it (DeMarco 1997). These teachers will continually revisit and revise particular points until the students understand and master the concepts being taught. On the other hand, less expert teachers see themselves teaching a subject. To these teachers, the content is taught in a logical progression, regardless of whom they teach, and the more information they can spill out of their mouths, the more teaching they

Figure 5.3 Larry Satchwell, who was honored as a NASPE national elementary teacher of the year, knows that a teacher must convey to students that they are more important than the subject matter.

are doing. Butch Harmon, Tiger Woods' golf instructor, perhaps best summed up the difference between these two approaches when he said "I don't teach golf. I teach people who want to play golf" (McCullick, Schempp and Cumings 1999).

A number of years ago, I watched a student teacher attempt to teach basic basketball dribbling to a high school physical education class. One student posed a discipline problem; as the lesson was being taught, he would continually dribble to one corner of the court and shoot a perfect jump shot into the basket. Despite repeatedly being told "We'll learn shooting next week," the boy couldn't resist the temptation. Later, as I sat with the teacher and discussed my observations, I found out that this boy was an All-State basketball player. The teacher realized that the boy already knew the dribbling lesson of the day and was bored, but she was at a loss as to what to do. Her lesson plan called for dribbling to be taught that day because that was how she structured the progression in her basketball unit. As we talked about the problem of this skillful but bored student, she began to see ways to restructure her lesson to meet this student's needs as well as the needs of the other students.

She hit upon the idea of having the student help her teach the unit. After all, this boy loved basketball and was popular with his classmates. He wasn't usually a behavior problem, but standing in line waiting to dribble a ball was beyond restraint for

him. In lessons that followed, the teacher reviewed the day's lesson with the student and asked him to demonstrate some of the skills. Then, while she instructed the majority of the class, the student devoted individual attention to some of the lesser skilled students. The boy enjoyed sharing his love of the game with others and felt responsible for helping his peers develop their skills. By the end of the unit, it seemed everyone came out a winner: the teacher, the basketball player, and the rest of the students. Taking a little time to know and understand this student not only eliminated a class problem but also made the class a better learning experience for everyone—including the teacher.

Reveal Feelings and Emotions

For a teacher to influence a class, the teacher must convey to the students that they are more important than the subject matter. Communication is key here. If classes and teams are made up of people who feel free to express their feelings and emotions, the group members form connections and develop a sense of acceptance. Teachers who are honest and open with their reactions and feelings gain the respect and understanding of their students.

This doesn't mean you have to convey every emotion or feeling. There are times when a teacher may harbor particular feelings about a student or other individual, and it would not serve to improve relationships should those feelings be made public. But demonstrating concern and care for the students, the class, and the subject must come from the teacher first before it can be expected of the students. Therefore, expressions of genuinely positive feelings can improve and cement positive relationships. At times, negative feelings need to be aired in order to overcome them. But this needs to be done cautiously and with the intent of building relationships rather than further deteriorating them.

> ### Building Relationships
> - Focus on valued actions and personal qualities.
> - Maintain consistent behavior.
> - Balance your responses.
> - See your pupils as people.
> - Know and understand your students.
> - Reveal your feelings and emotions.

Figure 5.4 Regardless of the activity, skill level, or age of the students, a teacher is influential in fostering a positive attitude toward the activity among learners.

The Power of Enthusiasm

Enthusiasm improves instruction and promotes interpersonal relationships. The teacher's level of enthusiasm has been firmly linked with student performance. Enthusiasm is, after all, contagious. Students who perceive their teacher as intrinsically motivated show more enthusiasm and innovation and enjoy the lesson more than students taught by a teacher thought to be unenthusiastic (Wild 1992). Students in classrooms of enthusiastic teachers display intrinsic motivation and greater vitality (Hisley and Kempler 2000).

Teachers' enthusiasm can be directed in one or more of the following directions: the topic of instruction, learning and skill improvement, and the students. Teachers who love their subjects soon infuse their students with affection for the topics (figure 5.4). Celebrating students' learning and skill improvement results in the whole class or team pulling for each other as new skills are acquired and old ones refined. And teachers who feel enthusiastic about their students' learning often find those feelings returned several times over.

Get in Touch

A teacher's enthusiasm begins by getting in touch with his feelings about the subject, students, and teaching. Teachers who remind themselves why they enter classrooms and who take time to enjoy the things that brought them into teaching find it easy to become and remain enthusiastic. It may be the love of a particular activity, the curiosity of a child, or the act of creatively sharing knowledge that brings joy in the process of teaching. Identifying your source of happiness, satisfaction, and passion in the classroom is a necessary first step in promoting enthusiastic teaching.

Teachers who make the effort can often find many aspects of the instructional process that bring them joy and provide fuel for their enthusiasm. Sometimes in the day-to-day pressures of a tight schedule, teachers can lose sight of bright spots in their teaching. The many and varied demands and distractions deflect attention away from the sources of satisfaction and joy for a teacher. It's therefore important that teachers revisit their reasons for entering the profession (see chapter 1), identify those things that ignite their enthusiasm, and refocus attention and energies toward those activities. In practical terms, this can mean something as simple as devoting as much (or more) attention to the student who discovers a new skill in your class as to the unmotivated or disruptive student. Skillful teachers can build their passions into powerful teaching tools. Get in touch with those passions and use them to be a happier, more enthusiastic teacher.

Show Your Enthusiasm

Once the sources of enthusiasm have been located, a teacher must now make this enthusiasm public. Personality plays a factor here. Gregarious people seldom have difficulty expressing enthusiasm (or any other emotion, for that matter). More reserved individuals are less practiced in the art of conveying passion for a subject or student success. Nonetheless, a teacher must check the behavior displayed before the students and ensure that it somehow communicates positive feelings for the unfolding events in class.

Enthusiastic teachers often smile and move about with vitality and a bounce in their step. Varying your tone of voice and using rapid speech peppered with adjectives also conveys enthusiasm. Eye contact is critical because it sends the message that your full attention is on your students; the commitment and care of good teachers are often reflected in their eyes.

Enthusiastic teachers are usually extensive planners who habitually devise ways to improve their classes and the class environment. In their search to promote a positive, learner-centered environment, they cover the walls of their gyms or lesson areas with posters, signs, and pictures. Finally, enthusiastic teachers take an active role in the class. At times, that might mean participating along with students, and at other times that might mean leading the cheers and applause for a significant student achievement.

Enthusiasm Is Contagious

Students are quick to perceive their teacher's feelings. A teacher showing enthusiasm toward the subject at hand or the success of the class is recognized and appreciated if the enthusiasm is genuine. The animated activity and the lively, passionate voice of an enthusiastic teacher is often, unfortunately, a novelty for the students and they tend to take notice.

When students find a teacher who is concerned about their learning, the students' feelings toward learning often turn positive. In response to seeing a teacher display love for a sport or activity, students can't help but alter their own feelings. When a teacher expresses sincere pleasure at being in the class, students find themselves enjoying the experience as well. It may take a while for students to warm up to the subject or their learning, but often this is a testing period in which the students attempt to "wait and see" if the teacher is sincerely enthusiastic or simply putting on a good show. If the enthusiasm is rooted in a teacher's passion, it will endure, and over time that enthusiasm will spread to the students—and beyond.

With the fostering of enthusiasm toward the subject, class, or learning, a teacher will begin to detect changes in students' behavior. The first change is the attention paid by the students. Enthusiastic people are interesting to watch, and enthusiastic teachers capture the attention of their students. Students' enjoyment will also be reflected in their smiles. Their movements become more animated, with prompt responses after directions or questions. Students remain more focused on the activities, practice with greater intensity, begin volunteering answers and responses, and celebrate, along with the teacher, their accomplishments and the accomplishments of others. The instructional session becomes a positive, enjoyable experience for all. Enthusiasm can transform the routine and mundane into the exceptional and memorable.

Jimmy Williams loves being physically active and fit. He also loves his students and finds great joy in sharing his unbridled passion for physical activity with them. In a day and age when adolescents shy away from physical activity and are becoming increasingly unfit and overweight, students at Jackson County Comprehensive have to earn the right to a place in Mr. Williams' physical education classes. Mr. Williams' classes are so popular that the school cannot accommodate all who wish to take them. In a typical physical education class, Mr. Williams participates along with his students, sharing information, demanding they give their best—he is!—and supporting every serious effort at learning. From time to time, I visit Mr. Williams to observe student teachers. His enthusiasm captures even me. On my last visit, Mr. Williams invited me to join the class in plyometrics and to try a new skating activity in my stocking feet (everyone is invited to participate in Mr. Williams' classes). Despite my dress clothes, off came my tie and my shoes, and soon I was exercising with high schoolers to the beat of heavy metal music. The sweat, smiles, and supportive atmosphere felt great. I left thankful that we have teachers like Mr. Williams, whose enthusiasm for physical activity and children instills the knowledge, attitudes, and feelings that help his students establish and maintain a healthy, happy life.

Issues of Equity and Understanding

Respect for human dignity resides at the heart of every effective, functional, prospering relationship. Human relationships cannot survive, let alone thrive, if respect does not go both ways. Teachers who demand respect but are unwilling to return it have little hope of having a significant, long-term influence on students. Teachers and students must develop relationships characterized by respect, trust, and understanding. Although it's not humanly possible to hold a universal affection for all students or even to deal with all students equally, it is possible to treat all students equitably and seek to understand the needs and aspirations of each student.

Forming equitable relationships with students based on respect, trust, and understanding isn't a particularly easy task. Often, barriers to these relationships were put in place long before the teacher arrived on the instructional scene. In this section, several social issues that form historical and pervasive roadblocks to effective relationships will be discussed and explored. These issues include sexism, racism, heterosexism, and socio-economic class distinctions. The purpose of this section is to help teachers identify and overcome these social barriers so that they may form fair and just relationships with their students.

Kids With Compassion

Tina Hall

Respect and caring seem automatic for most young children. It's generally only after they've been in the world of adults that some are socialized into being disrespectful and uncaring toward other individuals or groups. As teachers, we play a key role in promoting respectful and caring attitudes. For example, if you do not tolerate put-downs in your classes, most children will follow this expectation once it is firmly established, and all will begin to feel safe in your gymnasium. One way of fostering acceptance in the gymnasium is for the teacher to post expectations and positive consequences on the wall instead of listing negative rules and consequences.

One of my posted expectations is "All students will treat others with respect." In kindergarten and first grade, respect for others is generally the practice and takes little if any prompting on the part of the teacher. Gender, color, and body size differences don't seem to influence peer groups until about second or third grade. When asked to find a partner, a five- or six-year-old child quickly joins hands with someone nearby. If someone is left out, all groups generally encourage that individual to join them. However, there are always exceptions to the "norm."

One morning I was teaching a lesson on kicking. I invited the students to come in close for directions and a demonstration of our initial task. On the way, they were to choose a partner and sit together. All quickly chose a partner and had a seat in front of me. In the middle of my demonstration, Jessica came in late. I asked the class to invite her to join a group as all had a partner. Not one child said a word. I assumed I was unclear and repeated my suggestion. Still no one responded. I obviously looked puzzled, and LaToya thought she should explain, "We don't want Jessica in our group because she gots the lices" (she pronounced it "lie seas"). Before I could jump in with a great teachable social moment (at the same time thinking I didn't want lice, either), Jessica reacted with a smile and said, "No, I don't. They checked me with the pencil and said I was okay." Again, before I could speak, all the children offered her a place with their groups. I continued the kicking lesson.

—Tina Hall, 1994 Tennessee Elementary Physical Education Teacher of the Year

Sexism

Perhaps no other issue raises greater barriers in sport and physical activity than gender. From preschool games to professional sports, there are "boys'" teams and "girls'" teams. The divide based on gender appears to many—both females and males—as natural and normal.

Although biological differences between males and females suggest separation for the sake of fair competition in some sports, sexism appears when *social* and *cultural* gender differences are used as reasons for denying access or opportunities. To deny access or opportunity in sport or physical activity based on gender differences is unfair and, in many cases, illegal if public funds are involved.

Perceiving someone as physically inferior or superior based on social differences in gender is also unfair and unjust. It's all too common to hear terms such as "throwing like a girl" when, in reality, the demonstrated throwing pattern is underdeveloped rather than gender specific. Most of the differences between boys' and girls' performances of sport skills are attributable to social, not physical, factors. Teach a girl to throw properly, and she is every bit as capable of performing a mature throwing pattern as a boy. Because of strength differences, some boys may throw farther or faster than some girls, but that doesn't suggest that girls can't throw or learn other sports or physical activities (Thomas and French 1985). To deny girls instruction in throwing because of the belief that "girls can't throw" or that "girls shouldn't throw" is where misunderstanding leads to inequity.

For the instructors, it may be all too easy to unconsciously perpetuate the myths of masculinity and femininity as they influence participation in sport and physical activity. Letting students "joke" or carrying personal prejudices into the instructional setting does little to spread the conviction that sport and physical activity offers healthy and wholesome experiences for everyone. When one male student says to another, "You throw like my sister," the intention may be humor, but the statement betrays the message that girls are competent sport participants. A heightened sensitivity of how gender roles are defined in sport and physical activity is a must. Unfortunately, sport can become a place where the myths of gender superiority or gender weakness are guiding principles. For example, all too often a boy with a sports injury is told "Be a man and take it" or "Don't act like a sissy, get back in there." Not only do such slogans devalue the individual who is the target, but they also perpetuate sexists myths about who is and isn't able to adequately participate in physical activity.

But beyond preventing sexist activities, teachers need to proactively work toward creating an environment of acceptance and inclusion in physical activity (figure 5.5). Dispelling myths that certain activities are "boy" activities and other activities are "girl" activities is one place to start (Griffin 1984; 1985). Pat Griffin makes an important point in stating that there may be as much variation in patterns of activity participation between people of the same sex as there is between the two sexes. In other words, a teacher cannot stereotype participation patterns and activity preferences on the basis of gender. For physical education teachers, this means teaching a range of health-related activities inclusive of both boys and girls.

Figure 5.5 One positive trend in physical education over the past quarter century is understanding that it is important to teach physical activity to both girls and boys, and that both girls and boys are capable of learning those skills.

Coed instruction may provide a more supportive, effective learning environment, but at times it might be appropriate to teach boys and girls separately. Activities dependent on close contact or being stronger than one's opponent (e.g., wrestling, self-defense) may be better taught in single-sex environments, while activities more dependent on skill, individual fitness, or knowledge may be best taught together (e.g., swimming, weight training, or tennis). Activities that give an advantage based on size or strength (e.g., basketball, volleyball) can be appropriately taught in a bi-gender setting. If competition is a necessary part of the instructional process, some games may be single gendered, but it would be better to have coed games based on activity competence, not segregated by gender (Treanor et al. 1998).

Research suggests that adolescent boys and girls prefer same-sex physical education classes to coed classes. Both boys and girls believed they performed skills and played team sports better, received more practice opportunities, and were less fearful of injuries in same-sex classes (Treanor et al. 1998), although the girls perceived that they competed harder in coed settings. These preferences, however, may be short lived because another study revealed that high school students preferred coed classes (Lirgg 1993). Therefore, age may play a factor in preferences for same-sex or coed classes. The important points for a teacher are as follows: sports and physical activities are not exclusive by gender, both genders can and should participate in a wide range of activities, and sport and physical activity learning environments should not perpetuate harmful and inaccurate gender stereotyping.

Racism

Racism is a difficult issue for most people, and teachers and students in physical activity settings are not immune to the problem or its difficulty (figure 5.6). Racism is a complicated and emotionally charged process that is fraught with fear, anxiety, distrust, denial, and misunderstanding. In contemporary cultures, race assumes a far more social significance than it does biological. Minor physical differences, such as skin or hair color or anatomical shapes of the eyes or nose, lead to exaggerated and inaccurate assumptions regarding everything from intellectual and physical abilities to work ethic and morality.

To transcend racism and develop healthy, productive relationships with students, you must first

Figure 5.6 The University of Georgia Sport Instruction Research Laboratory is an excellent example of breaking down barriers among races, ethnicities, and national boundaries. Teachers at the institution include Chinese, African-American, and French women.

examine your own racial heritage. It is from that heritage that your assumptions and beliefs regarding other racial groups are rooted. Racial stereotypes are, after all, not products of our imagination but rather are taught to us by those around us and solidified in the experiences we share.

Once you identify the images and perceptions your own heritage has for other racial groups, the process of identifying your personal prejudices, biases, and stereotypes can begin. This is not an easy process; these beliefs may represent years of experience and reinforcement. Racial biases are often unconscious, making them all the more difficult to detect. But becoming aware of racial biases is an important step in removing barriers between teachers and students. As Louis Harrison suggested, "a more thorough understanding of the stereotyping process will be a deterrent to the perpetuation of maladaptive stereotypes" (2001, 97).

Although examining and understanding personal heritage is critical for building effective relationships with students, it's equally important that teachers seek to understand the racial heritage of their students. Being aware of the traditions and values embedded in students' racial backgrounds helps teachers understand students in critically important ways. Standards of dress, language (particularly slang terms), personal characteristics, social interactions, celebrations, icons, and leisure activities are all keys to the values and perspectives underlying a culture. In examining the cultures of their students, teachers may find a common ground for more effective communication, and effective teaching is not possible without effective communication.

Because most people recognize the debilitating effects of racial stereotyping, providing a nonthreatening forum for discussing race-based perceptions and prejudices is one method for addressing these issues with students. To make discussions nonthreatening, they should be issue-based rather than personal in nature. In a practical setting, when teaching a sport or activity that has stereotypical myths, these myths might be discussed during the lesson. For example, when teaching basketball, myths such as "Basketball is a black person's sport" or "White people can't jump" might be raised and discussed with the students. Questions such as "How do you think these myths came into being?" "Are these myths accurate?" and "How can we dispel these myths?" will lead to more fruitful discussions than questions such as "How many people here believe this is true?"

Teachers can also be sensitive to racial issues when identifying sport role models in their teaching

(Harrison and Worthy 2001). Tiger Woods (African American/Asian) in golf, Ichiro Suzuki (Japanese) in baseball, Serena and Venus Williams (African American) in tennis, John Stockton (European American) in basketball, Rudy Galindo (Hispanic) in figure skating, and Saudi Arabia (Arabic) in World Cup soccer are all examples of successful athletes/teams who don't fit the stereotypes for their sports. When citing examples of successful athletes and their traits, identifying individuals like these helps dispel stereotypical racial biases. For example, to talk of Stockton's passing, Suzuki's batting, or Williams' serve not only provides the students with an appropriate motor pattern but also offers evidence that athletic success and performance are not based on race. Placing posters or pictures in the learning environment of athletes representing a diversity of racial groups further reinforces this point.

Social Class

Identifying a person's social class isn't an easy task, yet selecting, practicing, and participating in sports is strongly influenced by social class. Sport and physical activity have long been viewed as a means by which advantages and disadvantages that might stem from social class can be somewhat equalized. Sport holds the potential for social equality that other human activities may not. Within concepts such as fair play and teamwork, sport can often erase the privilege and disadvantage created by social class. When stepping into the starting blocks or onto a wrestling mat, a person's social status will have little influence on the outcome of the race or match.

Like gender and race, social class is often characterized by myths. Rich people are snobs, young men from inner-city projects are criminals, religious people are out to take away our freedoms, immigrants bring disease, and people on welfare are lazy are but a few examples of the many social class myths. Not all or even a majority of individuals in a particular social class possess the characteristics that the myths attribute to them. Social class is defined not by myths but rather by relationships, labor, and material goods.

According to social philosopher Max Weber (1964), social classes are formed and defined in terms of the division of labor (i.e., what you do is fundamental in identifying your social class). Further, Weber believed that it was in social institutions (e.g., schools and churches) and recreational activities that social classes were formed and defined. To understand a particular group, it's necessary to understand how the individuals within the group form their relationships with one another and with the world. By understanding the formation of social relationships based on the actions of teachers, coaches, and participants, insight into how, what, and why sport contributes to society can be gained.

If gyms and playing fields are places where basic units of society (Weber 1964) are formed, teachers and students must ask themselves what roles they play in the formation of social relationships. If social class is based on the division of labor, then the work tasks and interactions of teachers and students need careful attention. Connections between relationships in sport and social relationships outside sport need to be understood.

The distribution of material goods (e.g., equipment) and services (e.g., instruction) also needs to be examined. Analyses of funding patterns, equipment distribution, staff selection and support, and participant services are all vital for identifying how economic factors affect access to knowledge and privilege in sport and physical education. Although it might be difficult, for example, for teachers in a working class school to match the equipment and facilities of an elite private school, there is no reason their efforts to provide the best instruction possible should be any less than at the private school. Teachers without the financial power to purchase necessary equipment often have the equipment donated, have it made by a community-minded individual or by students, or make it themselves.

Social class can even influence the expectations teachers have for students. It was disheartening for me to recently hear a middle school teacher say "You can't expect much from these kids. Look where they come from." Teacher expectations are often formed based on impression cues (Martinek 1996). That is, a teacher perceives particular student characteristics, such as body type, dress, speech, attractiveness, or disabling condition, and then forms expectations based on interpretations and impressions from these cues. Many of these characteristics (e.g., dress and speech) are products of social class. When teachers hold low expectations for students, they give the students less praise, ask them fewer questions, give them less content-related information, and criticize them more (Martinek 1996). In general, teachers teach less to students for whom they hold lower expectations. The tragedy lies in that students often learn a great deal more when teachers hold higher expectations for both the learners and for themselves as teachers. For these reasons, teachers must analyze the expectations they hold for their students' learning and revisit those beliefs from time to time to see if they are indeed justified.

Teachers and participants in sport and physical activity must begin to not only recognize the power of social stratification by examining their own beliefs and behavior patterns, but they must also work toward promoting equal opportunity through their sports. Sport and physical activity should not be a place where social class and economic privilege biases are created or endorsed.

At-Risk Youth

It appears that sport and physical activity programs can make a difference to youth who are at risk. At-risk youth are potentially unable to negotiate the social system and its institutions in a manner that lets them become contributing members of society. For a variety of reasons, these children are at risk of dropping out of school and engaging in criminal and socially deviant activities. Martinek (1997) believes that the gym can be used to teach life values and effective decision-making skills. It may also provide potential resources for cultural, physical, educational, and social enrichment. More important, he feels that sport and physical activity may provide an environment of hope by surrounding these young people with positive and constructive activities. But it takes more than just a place or a program.

According to Martinek and Hellison (1997), promoting resiliency in troubled youth helps provide them with the necessary skills for success in mainstream society. Resiliency requires social competence, autonomy, optimism, and hope. Social competence is the act of being responsive to others. At-risk youth need to learn to be flexible and caring and must acquire a sense of humor (Martinek and Hellison 1997). When children develop these traits, it helps them develop positive relationships with others. They become more responsive and form stronger bonds with individuals who may help them move forward with their lives. Some of these people may include family members, classmates, teachers, and community leaders.

Developing social competence may be the first step in nurturing self-respect (Martinek and Hellison 1997). A person without self-respect has difficulty respecting others or even understanding why he should respect others. Without self-respect, or the means of giving respect to others, it's difficult to be a productive member of a community. When a troubled youth feels he doesn't play a productive role in his community, he often pushes himself away from those who can help him most. This situation, of course, makes it even more difficult for an individual to create a "normal" way of life.

The second key element needed to create resiliency is autonomy (Martinek and Hellison 1997). At-risk children need a clear sense of who they are. They need to learn to act responsibly on their own, think for themselves, and be independent. Troubled youth who can successfully adopt these traits are more able to reject negative pressures from peers or gangs. A positive personal goal for an at-risk youth may simply be attending school on a regular basis or getting to work on time.

The last of the key elements needed to instill resiliency are optimism and hope. Without hope, most at-risk children fall into a sense of learned helplessness. According to Martinek and Hellison, "learned helpless children feel they have little, or no control over social and academic outcomes" (1997, 38). These particular individuals will tend to give up when faced with an adverse situation. Their attitude is that no matter how hard the sun tries to shine through, the clouds will never clear.

Research indicates that at-risk youth who are optimistic view their bad situation as temporary and believe they will overcome it (Martinek and Hellison 1997). In other words, although it may be raining today, someday soon the sun will shine. Optimism and hope allow a child to set goals and to persist in tough life situations. More important, at-risk children who establish optimism and hope believe that a prosperous future lies ahead of them. Of the key elements, optimism and hope have the greatest impact on at-risk youth. As teachers and coaches, providing opportunities where effort, hard work, and ability are rewarded with success in sport and physical activity gives children just cause in being optimistic and hopeful that they have some control over their future and who they are.

Sexuality

Considering the wonderful social, emotional, and physical benefits to be gained from sport and physical activity, it's unfortunate that contemporary society often sees sport as a masculine domain. In particular, contact sports and activities requiring strength are seen as male sports (e.g., football, ice hockey, baseball), while activities requiring balance, coordination, flexibility, and fine motor control (e.g., dance, gymnastics, tennis) are seen as more acceptable for girls. The characterization of sport as a "boys' thing" or the attitude that "real men play sports" is fine for skillful young men and boys. But for those outside that classification, the "masculinization of sport" places them in the margins and even at risk when it comes to sport participation. For teachers and coaches dedicated to promoting the benefits of sport and physical activity, this is clearly an obstacle that needs to be overcome.

Despite the common cultural myth, sport does not make men from boys or turn the feminine into the masculine, nor do sport and physical activity develop character. Yet, the selection of an activity for a boy or a girl is often made based on perceptions of social acceptability for the student's gender. Selecting a sport associated with the opposite gender often brings with it the chance that the student's sexuality will be questioned. That is, boys who participate in "girls' activities" may be labeled gay, while girls who choose "boys' activities" may be labeled lesbian. This labeling further reinforces heterosexism. Rather than having sexual orientation a private matter, it can become public, derided, and turned into a form of oppression that prevents someone from participating in a healthy, enjoyable, and enriching activity.

History is rich with athletes, both male and female, who were or are openly homosexual. Roy Simmons was a guard for the Washington Redskins football team, Greg Louganis won multiple Olympic gold medals in diving, and Bob Paris captured both the Mr. America and Mr. Universe titles; these are but three examples of successful gay athletes. Similarly, successful lesbian athletes include Wimbledon tennis champion Martina Navratilova, golf champion Muffin Spencer-Devlin, and Commonwealth Games gold medalist Lisa Marie Vizaniari. Sport success is not influenced by sexual orientation. However, an individual's sport experience can be enormously influenced by a coach's, teacher's, or teammate's attitude toward sexual orientation (Griffin 1998).

Homophobia, or the fear of homosexual individuals, results in unfounded fears regarding gay, lesbian, and bisexual people. In sport, parents might fear that a gay coach will influence their son into a deviant lifestyle, a lesbian physical educator will seduce a young girl, or playing a sport against a bisexual individual carries with it a high risk of contracting HIV. These fears usually result in avoidance of homosexuals, ridicule, and denial of participation and job opportunities for people with nonheterosexual orientations.

If a teacher discovers she's homophobic, it's important to realize that this is a common cultural bias that has been socially indoctrinated. Homophobia can be overcome, but it takes time, effort, and understanding. The teacher must first understand the destructive consequences of homophobia—for both heterosexual and homosexual individuals. Next, the teacher must become familiar with stereotypical images and impressions of homosexuals. It's then necessary to identify personal behaviors and attitudes that might promote homophobia. This might include language or slogans, dividing boys and girls in physical education activities, or playing games with names such as "Smear the Queer." Recognizing these perspectives and practices is a prelude to finding ways to offer a more just learning environment. Finally, the teacher must identify personal actions to address homophobia. Like many types of stereotypes and biases, homophobia is steeped in ignorance. Seeking out an individual who is gay to discuss homophobia or reading material designed to address these issues are two strategies of overcoming personal biases that may inappropriately influence professional behavior. The reward for undergoing this change can lead to increased opportunities for allowing sport to become a meaningful part of someone's life, and that, after all, is why most people aspire to teach and coach.

Summary

The ability of a teacher to make a difference in a student's life is largely based on developing a healthy and positive relationship. The power of caring for their students is a defining trait of distinctive teachers. A teacher who respects, empathizes with, and warmly and genuinely cares for his or her students conveys the message that they are important people. Equity issues in sport and physical activity are critical for building relationships because teachers and students enter the instructional process carrying cultural myths and biases that work against positive relationships. Caring teachers take the time to build empathetic relationships with students by recognizing that students deserve to be understood and treated fairly. In large part, this requires recognizing biases and stereotyping behaviors that prevent an equitable learning environment for all students and athletes and then seeking strategies and activities to overcome those biases—a simple statement to make but an enormous challenge for most teachers and coaches. The chance for effective teaching and personal satisfaction for both teachers and students is, however, greatly enhanced when the instructional process grows from meaningful human relationships.

Discussion Questions

1. Describe three strategies you might use to foster an atmosphere of caring in your learning environment.

2. Identify a sport or physical activity that you feel very passionate about. Considering your personality, how would you convey your love of this activity to your students or athletes?

3. You have agreed to coach a high school wrestling team. Wrestling is not a particularly popular sport in this high school, and the team has amassed a mediocre record over the last several years. On the first day of practice, you face five wrestlers returning from the previous year and four new wrestlers—one of whom is a freshman girl. The team has never had a female wrestler, and the boys are very surprised when she announces that she wants to join the team. What do you do?

4. One morning while I was teaching physical education in a Boston elementary school, a boy from a refugee family came to my class wearing tennis shoes that were a size too large and without laces or socks. The family was new to the United States and dependent on local charities for their food, clothing, and housing. These tennis shoes appeared to be all they had for this boy's feet. He found it difficult to walk in them (he actually shuffled his feet), and it was impossible for him to run in them. If you were the teacher, what would you do?

Chapter 6

Planning and Preparation

Failure to prepare is preparing to fail.

— John Wooden

CONSTRUCTION

Preparation is a key to success in any endeavor, and sport and physical activity instruction is no exception. There is no substitute for preparedness; there is also no excuse for not being ready to teach well. Good teachers are constantly planning and preparing. Novice teachers often wrongly believe that teaching requires no preparation because they don't actually see the thought process that constitutes planning by good teachers. A study by Housner and Griffey (1985) showed that experienced teachers expressed much more concern for their planning than did novice teachers. Poor teachers seldom, if ever, prepare because they either don't believe it to be necessary or simply don't want to expend the effort. However, knowing what and how to prepare can make the instructional process efficient and enjoyable, and it's essential for good teaching.

Preparation takes effort, knowledge, and some skill, and it begins long before the start of any class. The most effective teachers are those who capitalize on what they know when preparing for a class and who search for new information in areas where they feel they have knowledge gaps. The years spent engaged in physical activity and sport provide the foundation on which to prepare effective lessons. Personal experience offers a teacher a vast store of useful knowledge for instructional planning. In addition, colleagues and experienced teachers are an important source of information when devising instructional programs and lessons (Fincher and Schempp 1994). Expert teachers also depend on extensive professional libraries and stay current with new developments by attending workshops, seminars, and conferences (Schempp, Templeton, and Clarke 1999). Coursework in a teacher education program or a certification program offers another valuable cache of knowledge. Magazines, newspapers, videos, and television programs all offer ideas from which clever teachers can craft effective lessons.

Good teachers are always in a state of preparation. Being alert to new approaches and fresh ideas, turning over old ideas to see a new perspective, and searching for ways to refine and polish good ideas into great ones are all methods of finding new and better material for constructing lessons. As a teacher assembles ideas for an upcoming lesson, it's important to consider the subject, students, and facilities; consult with peers for feedback and ideas; research new information; and reflect on previous lessons and experiences. There is no singularly proper way to prepare a lesson, but the guidelines presented in this chapter have proven valuable for many teachers.

Creating a Learning Environment

In learning a sport or physical activity, the quality and quantity of the experience are often measured by the opportunities students have to freely explore ideas and beliefs, gain new insights, and practice useful skills. Creating an organized and thought-out learning environment to promote these activities is critical if students are to receive the greatest benefit from the available instruction time. This requires carefully guiding the instructional activity, the students' actions, and the use of the equipment and learning space.

One factor that strongly influences the creation of a learning environment is the number of students to be accommodated. If a lecture is deemed appropriate, then it matters little if 1, 100, or 1,000 students are listening as long as all students can see and hear. But sport and physical activity lessons are not intended to provide learners with information they can only see and hear. In most cases, they are in-

tended to improve the learner's performance by providing time to practice movement skills and interact with other learners. The number of students standing before the teacher, therefore, will strongly influence the creation of a positive and progressive learning environment.

Individual Instruction

Individual learning focuses attention on the needs, interests, abilities, and motivations of a single student (figure 6.1). Individual instruction holds several advantages and a few disadvantages for both the teacher and student. On one hand, serving the needs of a single learner makes the organizational part of the lesson relatively easy depending on the content to be taught. Large amounts of equipment, paperwork, and other details associated with conducting classes are unnecessary. With one student, a teacher has less demand for large spaces, expansive facilities, or extensive supplies, and a single student permits more flexibility in making changes once the lesson begins. The full attention of the teacher can be focused on the learner's particular needs.

On the other hand, teaching a single student holds some restrictions. Partner and group activities are not feasible, so a teacher needs to plan for an

Figure 6.1 Individual learning provides the student the opportunity for specific instruction.

extensive number of individual activities. A single student will also lack the comradeship that accompanies group learning and cannot derive motivation or a sense of collective achievement that comes from being with others. The teacher represents the sole source of social and emotional support for the student during the learning process. Lessons with a single learner are best reserved for students with exceptional needs so that a teacher may devote full attention to the learner's special requirements. Individual sports and activities, such as swimming, golf, bowling, fencing, gymnastics, and skiing, are good candidates for teaching using individual instruction.

Group Learning

Small group instruction or dividing a large class or team into smaller groups has several advantages as well as disadvantages. First, small groups allow students to use one another as resources. Students supporting, encouraging, and assisting one another in the learning process builds a community of learners that may propel learning in ways the teacher is simply unable to accomplish alone. Group learning involves students more personally in each lesson because, as part of a group, the learning of others will, in part, depend on their involvement (figure 6.2). A teacher is supposed to help a student learn— that is a given. But when students help each other learn, it goes beyond the expected in most cultures and into the realm of an extraordinary learning experience.

Second, group learning demonstrates the independence of learning. That is, students discover that it's not only the teacher who can play the role of instructor—students can, too. Third, teachers may find it easier to organize and manage several small groups than one large group. The Tactical Games Approach (Griffin, Mitchell, and Oslin 1997) is one instructional model in which sport concepts and skills are taught to large classes purposefully divided into smaller groups.

In coaching situations, each coach can capitalize on the expertise of other coaches through group learning (figure 6.3). In football, for example, defensive players can work with defensive coaches while offensive coaches work with offensive players. It's also possible to have athletes rotate to different instructional areas during the practice. A baseball or softball team could be divided into three smaller groups. One group might begin the session with batting practice under the direction of the batting coach, then move to fielding practice supervised by a fielding specialist, and then finish the practice with base-running drills organized by a base coach. Another group would begin the practice with fielding, move to base running, and finish with batting, while the third group would begin with base running, move to batting, and finish with fielding. The

Figure 6.2 Group learning allows the teacher to cover fundamentals with a large group when an activity is first introduced.

Figure 6.3 Coaches that obtain expertise in a specific skill provide a valuable function.

small group setting allows the players to receive the benefit of each coach's expertise in a more individualized environment.

Using small groups does present some challenges for the teachers and students. In small group instruction, a teacher may have to do more planning to accommodate the individual and collective nuances of the group members. Not all groups will progress at the same rate or work on the same tasks. When a teacher devotes her attention to one group, it may mean leaving the remaining groups without supervision or support. Finally, procedures need to be in place for students to get needed assistance and guidance when the teacher's attention is with another group.

When organizing small group lessons, teachers must pay attention to the students' skill level. Students who are near equals in terms of skill and fitness levels, motivation, and experience are more likely to find a better fit in small group instruction than a group where the abilities and interests of the students vary widely. Small group instruction may be best suited for learners who are beyond the beginner level in learning and who have more advanced levels of maturity, motivation, and independence. Sports or activities that are normally conducted in small groups, such as basketball, tennis, cheerleading, sailing, or dance, are well suited for small group instruction.

Large Classes

Public school teachers usually have little choice or control over the number of students placed in a particular class. In larger classes, everyone performs the same learning activity at the same time and at the same rate. The advantage is that the teacher can efficiently explain or demonstrate the skill or concept to 50 students or more as if he were explaining it to 5. With all students practicing the same skill or activity at the same time, the teacher can also monitor the class with greater focus, allowing him to identify common errors among several learners and offer one correction that applies to many. Feedback to one student may also help another student struggling with a similar problem.

Large classes require a great degree of management and organization. One student being off-task or one unclear direction can derail the learning of several, if not all, students. It is therefore essential that a teacher instructing a large group give careful attention to the positioning and movement of students as well as the rules and procedures to guide in-class behavior. Where students will be for instruction and how they will relocate from one area to the next should be carefully planned. Novice teachers often underestimate the importance of relocating students.

A clear signal should also be planned and reviewed with the students so that transitions from one area or activity to the next can be made with a minimum loss of instruction time. Routines can be helpful here. If a teacher makes the students routinely meet or warm-up in one area at the start of a lesson, students will naturally go there for each lesson opening. If the same signal (e.g., voice command, musical instrument, or whistle) is used to start and stop activities, students in large groups will become accustomed to the signal and respond more appropriately.

Although having many students in a class may often prevent teachers from giving each student individual attention, there are some benefits to large classes. The most obvious benefit is economy. One teacher with many students is cost-efficient—provided the instructional quality is sufficiently high so that the students are indeed learning. Large groups also lead to a sense of "team," and motivated students can help spur the learning of the less motivated. The Sport Education instructional model (Siedentop 1994) is one approach to teaching sport that incorporates the skills, abilities, and interests of many students into the singular goal of thoroughly learning a sport. Activities that require or incorporate many people, such as soccer, aerobics, hockey, lacrosse, volleyball, or rowing, find this instructional climate useful.

Steps for Planning a Lesson

Planning is a key ingredient in the development of a good lesson. To varying degrees, teachers plan before, during, and after a lesson. Planning before class generally involves identifying potential lesson goals, selecting topics to be taught, designing interesting activities to promote student learning, organizing equipment and supplies, and giving the evaluation process some consideration (Yinger and Hendricks-Lee 1995). During class, teachers continually monitor the flow and focus of the lesson, gauging the progress of the students toward the learning goal. As they make adjustments and direct the lesson, teachers constantly weigh alternatives and plan the next series of actions and activities. At the conclusion of a lesson, teachers—particularly very good ones—assess the merits of the lesson, make decisions about activities that will best serve the next lesson, and take mental or written notes on student troubles and triumphs. Although the actual process of instructional planning varies from teacher to teacher, this section of the chapter presents the steps common to most teachers' planning.

What Will They Learn?

Preparation for any lesson begins with identifying a purpose or goal. What do your students need to learn? What will your students know when they leave the lesson that they didn't know when they arrived? In sport and physical activity settings, these goals are usually physical skills (e.g., serving, passing, striking) or activity-related knowledge (e.g., game rules, fitness facts, strategies). Without a clear purpose, it is difficult to offer meaningful instruction. This point cannot be overemphasized. Teachers or coaches who step before students or players with no purpose in mind will simply waste their students' time and their own. As Yogi Berra put it, "If you don't know where you are going, you might wind up someplace else." In other words, the only way to get somewhere is to know where you are going. Similarly, the only way your students can learn or your players can improve is if they know what they have to learn.

A variety of resources can help you identify instructional goals. Written plans such as curriculum guides, yearly plans, or teaching manuals are one way to identify goals (Yinger and Hendricks-Lee 1995). These sources usually suggest progressions in skill and knowledge development and are particularly useful when teaching something for the first time or two; they are also helpful when

lessons are given in a series or unit on a particular sport or topic. For example, the goal for a single lesson may be selected based on goals achieved in the previous lessons and goals desired to reach through future lessons.

Many experienced teachers like to begin with their knowledge of the students' abilities and current skill levels (Sardo-Brown 1990). Through observations and conversations with students, or reflections on experiences with similar students, a teacher can identify pertinent goals that will lead to both worthwhile learning experiences and significant student achievement. Because of this, teachers commonly watch the students play or practice a skill in the first few minutes of class and then decide the goal for the instructional session. If the teacher has observed the students many times before or is required to follow a scripted curriculum, then objectives can be determined before class.

A third source of learning goals is the student. Often students know precisely what they need to learn or improve. An advantage of student-identified learning goals is that students are often highly motivated to achieve them. Because they have had input into the direction and purpose of their learning experiences, they usually work harder to reach their goals. Don't hesitate to ask students what they would like to learn and why they would like to learn it. The answers may surprise you, and they will certainly help you plan useful instruction for your students.

Regardless of the sources used to select and define instructional objectives, among the most critical factors in identifying learning goals are the student's aspirations, present skill level, and physical abilities. If these three factors are considered when determining the lesson goals, both the teacher and the student have a greater chance for instructional success.

Selecting Learning Activities

Once the purpose of the lesson is determined, the next step is to select or create appropriate learning experiences so that the instructional goals can be achieved. Learning experiences can include lectures, skill drills, videotape viewing, discussions, or any other activity that provides the learner with the information to be learned. The prime consideration when selecting these activities is efficiency of learning. What activity will best teach a student the information or skill at hand?

Learning activities are derived from many resources (Sardo-Brown 1990). The teacher's personal experience as both a student and teacher of the subject matter is a good place to begin. Sometimes learning activities from one sport or activity are easily transferred to another sport with only a few minor adjustments. For example, a basketball dribbling drill might be easily adapted for practicing the soccer dribble. Discussions with other teachers about activities they have found effective are also helpful. A favorite source for most teachers is books that include sport-specific skills, drills, and learning activities. Expert teachers are book collectors, and they rely on them heavily for new ideas and activities for their lessons. Finally, one of the best sources for learning ideas resides in the fertile imagination of the teacher. Knowing the subject, the students, and the resources available can often give a creative teacher the necessary platform for designing excellent activities for her students.

Organizing the Lesson

Having determined both the goals and learning activities, the instructor must next organize the learning experiences to achieve a maximum cumulative effect. This requires the teacher to consider the sequence and length of the selected activities. Once again, the students play a critical role in determining the order of the experience. For beginners who are perhaps tentative and need reassurance that they can indeed learn, selecting activities in which they experience success early in the lesson is crucial. The lesson activities can then be made increasingly more challenging as both skill and confidence increase.

Consideration should also be given to the equipment needed as well as the location of the instruction and practice areas. Placing equipment in close proximity to the learning activities will save time that can be devoted to learning. Conducting learning and practice activities in close proximity will reduce transition and relocation time, again permitting more time for instructional activities. If it's not possible to locate the instructional activities close together, then teachers need to plan easy and efficient routes from one location to the next so that learning time isn't wasted.

Are We There Yet?

Ask any parent who has taken a child on a long drive, and he or she will invariably tell you that somewhere along the route, a small voice from the back seat will ask "Are we there yet?" The child is growing tired of the journey and wants to know when the destination will be reached. Although it's

a question that often annoys a parent, it's a good question for a teacher. As the lesson progresses, and particularly when the lesson concludes, a teacher must evaluate the quality of the experience. Have the students learned yet? If not, is there a better route or alternative activities that might get them there faster? If they are already there, then it's time to plan the next learning destination. Asking these questions during the lesson helps the instructor make the necessary adjustments to promote greater learning (Yinger and Hendricks-Lee 1995). Asked at the conclusion of the lesson, the answers will provide insights for revising future lessons and lead to long-term improvement in teaching.

Steps in Planning
- Set a goal.
- Select activities to meet the goal.
- Organize selected activities to achieve a maximum cumulative effect.
- Evaluate the lesson and student learning.

Mapping Instruction

Whether teachers choose to write down their plans or simply carry them in their heads is often a matter of both experience and personal preference. However, it's recommended that beginning teachers make at least a few notes, if not a complete plan, before beginning instruction. Many experienced and successful teachers and coaches attribute much of their success to thorough, written planning.

Teaching a class can often be like finding your way through a city. Like travelers, teachers use maps to plan where they would like to go (goals) and how they would like to get there (activities) (Yinger and Hendricks-Lee 1995). Teachers' maps also help them decide precisely when they've arrived at their intended destination (evaluation). If you journeyed through a city many times before, you're familiar with the major routes and acceptable alternatives to accommodate unforeseen circumstances that may divert you from the planned primary route. Experienced teachers, like experienced travelers, will often make a mental map of their journey, picturing primary routes and acceptable alternatives (Sardo-Brown 1990). If you're not familiar with the city, you'd better have a written map to guide your progress. Novice teachers, similar to inexperienced travelers, benefit greatly from a written map and often lose their way if they simply rely on a mental map.

The type of maps teachers need largely depends on the length and breadth of the instructional journey. For one-time lessons, a single lesson plan is sufficient. Tennis, golf, and ski instructors may see a student once or twice. When the instruction is focused on a longer period, however, it's important to sequence the information and skills to be learned: an instructional unit plan is in order. Instructional camps, certification programs, seasonal activities, and recreation programs are examples of instructional units. For programs lasting a year or longer, such as a typical public school physical education program, a curriculum guide or long-range plan is recommended.

Lesson Plans

Lesson plans offer a flexible guide for conducting a class (figure 6.4). The plan may include one or more of the following: goals, lecture notes or key points, practice activities, equipment list, and evaluation criteria. The lesson plan ensures that thought has been given to the lesson and that the activities are organized in a purposeful, sequential pattern to maximize student success, interest, and learning. Exactly what and how much goes into the plan depends on the needs of the individual instructor.

A plan is not a script in which every detail must be precisely executed with nothing added or modified once the lesson begins. Rather, the plan serves as a reference and guide for the instructor's multi-faceted decision making during the lesson (Yinger and Hendricks-Lee 1995). Because there are so many decisions to be made in a lesson, ranging from equipment selection to student performance evaluation, a lesson plan helps teachers by guiding them to make many key decisions before the lesson even begins. And just like any map, if a teacher or coach encounters unanticipated obstacles or conditions, a good lesson plan contains a few alternative routes or activities (see appendix A).

Unit Plans

When instruction is carried out over several lessons with a unifying theme, a unit plan is recommended. A unit plan represents the comprehensive planning of a sequence of lessons. Skills and knowledge can be scheduled in a progressive fashion to achieve a maximum cumulative effect from the instruction. This type of planning gives teachers an overview of what will be taught and when. From the unit plan, the teacher can then draft plans for each lesson. Unit planning also aids in administration because equipment acquisition, student evaluations, and facility scheduling can all be accommodated.

Like lesson plans, the contents of a unit plan are tailored to the particular needs of the teacher. In most cases, the unit plan contains a combination of the following: general goals for the unit, specific goals for each lesson, sequential listing of skills and concepts to be taught, facilities and equipment needed, and evaluation criteria and procedures (see appendix B).

Figure 6.4 Lesson plans ensure that thought has been given to the lesson and that activities are organized in a purposeful, sequential pattern.

Long-Range Plans

Instructional programs that run a year or longer require long-range planning. Long-range plans allow program goals to be directly translated into a progressive, comprehensive, and workable instructional program. The needs, abilities, and interests of the learners; the strengths of the instructors; and environmental conditions such as equipment, facilities, and even weather can all be accommodated in long-range planning. Planning over an extended period ensures that instructional activities are progressively presented; this lets students or athletes build from one success to the next as they assemble a body of knowledge and gain useable skills. Variety in activities, information, and experiences can also be planned long term to keep student interest high. Like unit and lesson plans, long-range plans serve as instructional guides. They provide a thumbnail sketch of the program, making change readily visible and possible.

Considerable variation can be found in the format of long-range plans owing to the different needs of instructors and institutions. Long-range planning should, however, include the following: a statement of the program's purpose and goals, a list of key skills and knowledge to be learned, a timeline as to what will be taught and when, a list of necessary equipment and facilities, and an outline of evaluation procedures (see appendix C).

Be Prepared: Five Questions to Answer

A teacher can never precisely predict what will happen in any given lesson. The students may or may not be motivated on a particular day, an outdoor activity may be met with rain, a piece of equipment may turn up missing or broken, or a host of other unanticipated events may unfold. When a lesson does not go according to plan, a skillful teacher is prepared to accommodate the change and meet the new challenges. Research suggests that experienced teachers give thought to selected and unpredictable aspects of the lesson and have contingency plans ready (Housner and Griffey 1985). Some of these plans are prepared before class, and some are formulated as the class progresses. If you can answer the following questions before the start of each lesson, you should be prepared for most contingencies and be well on your way to an organized, purposeful lesson.

Whom Am I Teaching?

Analyzing and identifying student backgrounds, interests, and lifestyles allows teachers to tailor activities and teaching styles to fit the particular personalities in class and to select activities better suited to students when changes are deemed necessary. As changes develop in students (e.g., frustration, boredom, skill mastery), the activities or teaching style can be altered to accommodate the learners' traits. In teaching sport and physical activity, it's particularly helpful to understand the students' previous experiences and knowledge in sport and physical activity, personality traits and motivations, current fitness levels, and personal interests.

Where Am I Teaching?

The facilities and location of instruction may significantly affect the lesson. Construction work near an outdoor court has a way of distracting students' attention and drowning the teacher's words. Knowing the size and condition of the learning area helps in selecting class activities. Recognizing the possibilities of rearranging facilities to accommodate learners is also useful information. Locating alternative areas for teaching and knowing how to quickly get there can often salvage a lesson when the primary teaching station becomes unavailable.

Student comfort and safety should be prime considerations. It's difficult to learn new skills with the sun in your eyes or while shivering from cold. And knowing how an injured student can be treated or evacuated and the location of the nearest phone to call for assistance are two pieces of information possessed by every prepared teacher.

What Do I Have to Teach With?

Skillful teachers find novel and clever ways of using equipment and supplies to help someone learn a new skill. Taking a mental inventory of available equipment gives a teacher an advantage when selecting alternative activities during the lesson. For a novice teacher, a beanbag is something to be tossed and caught. For the experienced teacher, a beanbag isn't just for learning to throw and catch; it can also serve as a boundary marker, a target, a tool to teach balance, or a host of other options depending on the needs of the teacher and students. Many experienced teachers have found ways to make needed equipment and have discovered imaginative learning devices in such places as kitchens, garage sales, and storage rooms. Charles Sorrell, a National PGA Teacher of the Year, loves to visit toy stores in search of new ideas for teaching familiar subject matter. Larry Satchwell, a NASPE Elementary Physical Education Teacher of the Year, uses his imagination and a workbench to create innovative equipment to help his students learn. Those who make the most of available resources are generally able to find solutions to any teaching challenge.

How Much Time Do I Have?

Knowing the time available for instruction is an important element for keeping the lesson well paced and moving toward the established goal. When deciding to make a change, consider the time remaining so that a class can maintain balance between its opening, main body, and closing. Changing activities with only a few minutes left in the lesson may not be a wise choice. If changes are needed in the lesson, they are better made sooner than later. If the current activity is in need of changing but little time remains, perhaps a discussion with students may be a better option than prolonging a failing activity. Experienced teachers will always reserve a few minutes at the end of the lesson for a review and summary. A lesson is orchestrated, and in order for the flow and momentum to build, teachers need to be aware of time.

What Am I Trying to Accomplish?

Perhaps the most important question when preparing a lesson is what you are trying to accomplish. When the lesson fails to accomplish its original intent, have a clear vision of the lesson's mission to make appropriate in-class decisions. In determining the quality of the lesson or the appropriateness of a particular activity, first check to see whether the activity is moving the lesson toward the intended goal. If not, changes are needed for the lesson to be successful. When things begin to unravel in a lesson, your first question should not be "What do I do now?" but rather "What are we trying to accomplish here?" The answer to the second question will often lead to an answer to the first.

Answer These Questions and Be Prepared

- Whom am I teaching?
- Where am I teaching?
- What do I have to teach with?
- How much time do I have?
- What am I trying to accomplish?

Success in Sydney

Jack Bauerle

Jack Bauerle earned his place as an assistant coach for the U.S. women's Olympic swim team in 2000. As head coach at the University of Georgia, his squad had won three consecutive NCAA championships. Also, six of his swimmers had qualified for the U.S. Olympic team on its way to Sydney.

When I asked Jack to describe the role of planning and organization in his coaching, he laughed: "It is a joke on our coaching staff that we don't tell the kids what I've written down for practice because it will change." I asked him to explain.

"It is imperative," he said, "to have a plan written down. But it is also imperative to change the plan as the practice develops. The biggest change in my coaching, however, came when I got organized. You have to have an idea of what you want the team to do that day, week, or season if you are going to accomplish anything. We break our planning down by the season: daily practice, meet weeks, and the championships. We wouldn't have won (three national championships) without being organized."

I asked him if the planning and organization was the same in Sydney during the Olympics. "Definitely," he said. "In Sydney, we broke down the training groups into the coaches' strengths. I had

(continued)

(continued)

middle distances because that is where I had the most success as a coach. There was a lot of trust among the coaching staff. I would have trusted my swimmers with anyone there. We had three weeks of training and eight days of meets in Sydney. The chemistry of the coaching staff was incredible and absolutely critical to our success. This led to a lot of camaraderie and the kids knew the coaches all communicated. Everyone was on board and it impacted the athletes. Going into it, we weren't satisfied with where we were. Yeah, the swimmers had all qualified, but it wasn't enough. We needed to be faster if we were going to win and we had only a small window of opportunity. Because the coaching staff was always together, we didn't have many formal meetings, but we were analyzing and planning constantly. Because we were such a close group, we were always communicating. The planning was time-consuming because we looked for every edge we could find.

"We had computer read-outs from the coaches at home for every swimmer, so we were able to sprinkle something into the practices for every individual so we could make each kid feel taken care of. The training programs were similar for both the men and the women. Coaching kids who were this motivated was like dying and going to coaching heaven. It is not a bad way to come to the pool: with national and world record holders.

"The practices were intense. The training level goes up with people this competitive. We sold them on training against each other rather than training independently. This brought the intensity way up. I'm 100% convinced that this made our team successful in Sydney: training together and against each other. It was the most exhausting experience I've ever had, but also the most exhilarating."

The six Georgia swimmers competing for the United States at the Sydney Olympics captured four gold medals and one silver.

—Jack Bauerle, head coach University of Georgia men's and women's swim teams,
U.S. women's team assistant coach at the 2000 Olympic Games

Summary

This chapter presented the essential skills and knowledge needed to plan and organize a lesson. Much of the energy teachers devote to planning and organizing a lesson focuses on creating an environment in which students can learn. The number of students has a strong influence on the shape and feel of that environment. Teaching one student is quite different from teaching 40 or 400 students. Equipment and facility needs, learning tasks, and management concerns all shift with the number of students to be accommodated in a lesson.

A well-planned lesson has a far greater potential to prove satisfactory to both students and teacher. To this end, identifying the purpose of the lesson (what will the students learn?), selecting learning activities (what will the students do?), organizing the lesson procedures (how will the students conduct themselves in class?), and specifying the evaluation procedures (how will I know what students have learned?) are all essential components that should be considered by the teacher before the lesson. Good planning provides a guide for the teacher to navigate the lesson as well as options to select from should a deviation from the original plan be called for.

Planning can take several forms. Planning for a single class, planning for a series of classes around a central theme or subject, and long-range planning are common strategies found in the arsenal of good teachers. Having several types of plans lets teachers focus on today's goals while keeping an eye on the intermediate and long-range purposes of their instruction.

In addition to having a plan, a teacher needs to give attention to several key areas of concern before class so that necessary changes and deviations in the lesson can be made smoothly and purposefully. Understanding the students to be taught, the location of instruction and potential alternatives, available equipment, available time, and a review of the lesson goals all help a teacher enter a class prepared to provide meaningful instruction. It is more common to hear teachers lament that they were unprepared for a lesson than it is to hear teachers complain that they were too prepared. Thorough preparation goes a long way toward creating a satisfying learning experience for both a student and teacher.

Discussion Questions

1. Select a sport or physical activity and discuss the ways you might teach that subject using (a) individual, (b) group, and (c) large class learning environments.

2. Select a sport or physical activity and plan a yearlong program. Specifically, briefly identify (a) the program purpose and goals, (b) key skills and knowledge to be learned, (c) a timeline as to what will be taught and when, (d) necessary equipment and facilities, and (e) an outline of evaluation procedures.

3. In a group discussion, address this question: Should a teacher or coach write out a lesson or practice plan? Justify your position.

Chapter 7

Managing the Learning Environment

Effective leadership is putting first things first. Effective management is discipline, carrying it out.

— Stephen Covey

CONSTRUCTION

According to the eminent educational scholar Walter Doyle,

teaching has two major task structures organized around the problems of a) learning and b) order. Learning is served by the instructional function. Order is served by the managerial function, that is by organizing classroom groups, establishing rules and procedures, reacting to misbehavior, monitoring and pacing classroom events and the like (1986, 395).

Managing a learning environment refers to how teachers and coaches prevent and solve the problems of order so that teachers can teach and students can learn. Research suggests that the greater the amount of student movement and choice in a learning environment, the greater the need for management. Sports and physical activities are full of movement and choice. The teacher must, therefore, develop a strong set of management skills. Experienced physical education teachers believe that a precursor to effective teaching is effective class management (Parker 1995). These teachers believe

Figure 7.1 Teachers can maximize time by keeping students occupied while they take roll.

that before student achievement can occur, you must establish goals, organize classes, and develop a management scheme.

In this chapter, effective management practices will be identified and described, as will the guidelines for establishing rules and procedures that assist in maximizing learning (figure 7.1). Specific topics related to management issues are also addressed in the chapter and include achieving order, dealing with major and minor rule infractions, handling situations in which no rules exist, and identifying potential management problems.

Establishing Order

The first task of any teacher is to structure the learning environment so that teaching and learning can take place without confusion or distraction (Fink and Siedentop 1989). Whether you are teaching in a gym, in a classroom, or on a playing field, some minimal level of order is necessary. The lessons or practices must be sufficiently constructed to capture and sustain the attention of the learners. A mutual understanding of the purposes, practices, and principles is required if the class is to proceed to the satisfaction of everyone.

Set the Tone Early

The first several meetings are critical for class organization and management. In the early sessions, students become oriented to the learning environment, begin establishing relationships with the teacher and fellow students, learn rules and procedures, and understand the expectations for their personal performances in the class. Research reveals that a skilled teacher will use the first several meetings with students, and the first few minutes of every class, to create the desired atmosphere by clarifying goals, reviewing rules, and making expectations explicit (Fink and Siedentop 1989). With everyone understanding what they are supposed to be doing and why, the class can proceed efficiently and effectively (figure 7.2).

Figure 7.2 When teachers post class rules, guidelines, and procedures at the beginning of the school year, students get the message that they are important.

Good class managers verbalize and model the behavior they expect to see because behavior is often contagious. If a teacher expects students to enjoy the lesson, he must not only tell students that enjoyment is the desired goal, but he must also demonstrate his enjoyment of the activity. If the teacher demands maximum effort from her students, she must not only inform the class of this expectation, but she must also exert effort herself. Demanding that students give maximum attention and effort to a class that is ill prepared or poorly conducted is hypocritical and not likely to result in the satisfaction of either the students or teacher.

The teacher must hold students accountable for their in-class behavior during these early sessions. If you want the rules and routines of the class to be adopted quickly by the students, you must show a commitment to these procedures by not only modeling the desired behavior but also expecting the students to conform to the established social guidelines. Providing feedback on students' behavior during the early sessions establishes the desired routines and reinforces the behavioral expectations.

Effective managers operate a class using a system of practiced routines. That is, there are certain methods of conducting a class that, once established, put the class operation on autopilot so that the teacher spends less time on managerial duties and more time actually teaching. Routines vary from teacher to teacher but can usually be seen in the way students enter the class, warm up for an activity, secure equipment, receive instruction, and exit the class. These routines are best explained and then rehearsed in the first several class meetings. In fact, a teacher may initially sacrifice some instructional time so that these routines can be well rehearsed and ingrained in the class operation. In the next section, guidelines for establishing rules and procedures will be offered.

Establishing Rules

Life in a sport or physical activity class, like anywhere else, is governed by rules and procedures—both implicit and explicit. Implicit rules are those that are unstated; they are generally borrowed from the wider culture. For example, most teachers and students see the teacher as the dominant authority figure in a class. That usually doesn't need to be made explicit. Explicit rules are exclusive to the class and, as such, must be established and made public through a statement of some sort.

Establishing class rules and operating procedures is one of the most critical aspects of teaching. Because these serve as guidelines for regulating the actions of the lesson, they represent the building blocks, the foundation of all activities that will follow (Evertson and Harris 1992). Some teachers feel more comfortable designing the rules themselves, while other teachers prefer a more democratic style and involve the students in establishing the rules and class procedures. Regardless of who devises them, workable rules and operating guidelines require thought and careful consideration.

Rules are the formal codes of conduct (Doyle 1986). They offer a clear statement as to what an individual is expected to do and not do. They guide behavior that is visible to other class members and prevent actions that are likely to distract the class from the task at hand. In selecting and establishing rules, consideration must be given to behavior that disrupts learning, is likely to cause injury, or damages property. In other words, rules must be designed to promote learning, ensure safety, and preserve the facilities and equipment. For beginning and experienced teachers alike, these three principles should form the foundation of any set of established class rules.

To be most effective, rules should be concrete, clear, and functional. Concrete rules are particular to a specific activity. For example, "No horseplay" is vague and open to interpretation (assuming there are no horses in your class!). A rule such as "Listen while others are speaking" provides a concrete guide to acceptable classroom actions. Public posting of rules and frequent repetition by the teacher are two ways to make rules clear. Functional rules directly address activities that are fundamental for making the class operate. Necessary activities in the class revolve around issues of safety, information exchange, equipment, and personal interactions and rights.

Rules are intended to guide behavior, not control it. Rules should therefore be stated in positive ways; they shouldn't simply form a list of "don'ts." For example, "Be supportive when someone is learning" tells a student what they should do as opposed to the negative "Don't make fun of others." A good set of rules for a learning environment obviously takes time to develop and implement. But because they are so essential for creating a productive, healthy learning environment, it is time well invested by a teacher or coach. The following list offers several general suggestions for establishing effective rules.

Guidelines for Establishing Rules

- Keep rules short and to the point.
- Use the fewest rules possible (no more than seven) so students can remember them.
- Whenever possible, state rules in positive terms.
- Establish clear and fair consequences for rule infractions.
- Review the rules often, especially during the initiation phase.
- Remind the class of rules at times other than when they are broken.
- Write and discuss rules in language that is appropriate for students.

For rules to be effective, there must be consequences for breaking them. Consequences should be presented at the same time as rules so that everyone clearly understands the severity of rule infraction and their penalties. They should be structured not so much to be punitive but rather to ensure that following the rules is a more attractive option. Consequences should also permit a degree of flexibility and forgiveness. One method for doing so is to make the consequences progressive. For example, for the first infraction, the consequence might simply be a warning or a temporary revocation of a privilege. The following list offers a set of general rules and accompanying consequences.

Rules to Live By

Some Rules for a Happy Life

- Compliment at least three people every day.
- Be the first to say "hello."
- Never give up on anybody.
- Take responsibility for every aspect of your life.
- Learn to listen.
- Be kinder than necessary.
- Leave everything a little better than you found it.

Consequences for Infractions

- Receive a gentle reminder that you are a better person than your behavior is revealing.
- Lose one friend.
- Wonder why no one likes you.
- Feel unhappy.

Rewards for Following Rules

- Receive a smile of appreciation.
- Discover a new friend.
- Hear the word "thank you" said with feeling.
- Feel blessed.

When No Rules Apply

Occasionally, incidents occur that demand a reprimand or disciplinary action, but no rules are available to guide a teacher's decision. Just because there are no rules doesn't mean that the teacher needs to be unprepared for dealing with the situation. In cases where no applicable rule exists, yet a managerial action to retain order in the class is necessary, a three-step procedure handed down to me by my cooperating teacher, John Hichwa (1998), has worked well for me in most circumstances:

1. Identify the offending behavior by stating *what* you saw occur. (Don't argue the events or your interpretation with the offender; simply state what you saw and inform the offender that you are obligated to act on your observations. If you did not observe the event, then this procedure can't be used, and you will be forced to make decisions based on circumstantial evidence and witness accounts. If that is the case, gather as much evidence as possible, and take time to weigh your options before rendering a decision or doling out punitive actions if deemed necessary.)

2. State *why* the offending behavior was inappropriate. (In formulating this response, consider that rules are intended to regulate behavior that disrupts learning, endangers safety, or damages equipment. In most cases, the action caused or was likely to cause one or more of these outcomes and is, therefore, inappropriate in a learning environment.)

3. State the *consequence* for reoccurrence. (In most cases, the offending action will not be so severe that a penalty needs to be imposed. Identifying the action, the reason for its inappropriateness, and the consequence for reoccurrence will usually allow the lesson to proceed. However, if a penalty is necessary, don't get carried away in the emotions of the moment, but rather make the punishment fit

the crime. Recall the consequences normally relied on for rules infractions, and impose the appropriate one for the level of severity of the offending behavior.)

Following this three-step procedure gives the teacher a plan of action for unanticipated situations. It also helps the teacher remain in control of the situation by not allowing the tensions of the moment to reduce what should be a reasoned response to an emotional reaction. The teacher must, in all situations, appear calm, reasoned, and rational if the class is to retain a sense of order. This isn't always easy to do, but having a plan of action for emergency situations goes a long way in helping the teacher manage potentially unmanageable situations.

Establishing Procedures

Procedures are the operational codes of conduct that guide group behavior. They provide accepted ways of entering and leaving the class, securing equipment, and forming groups for instruction, practice, and activity. Skillful teachers most often develop and use routines to avoid repeated explanations of common tasks such as warm-ups, drills, and transitions from one activity to another (Siedentop and Tannehill 2000). Using start and stop signals, whether it be a whistle, voice command, or musical instrument, is one procedure that needs to be developed early in the class meetings. If a teacher can't get students started or can't stop them once they've begun, he has little chance of maintaining order in the class.

Skillful teachers also have well-established procedures for opening and closing a class (Lavay, French, and Henderson 1997). For example, students should know where to go and what to do upon entering the learning environment. Some teachers use the opening procedures for students to complete warm-up routines, secure equipment, or practice previously learned activities. During these times, teachers may informally talk with students to gauge their level of energy, motivation, and understanding of class material or simply to learn more about the students. Procedures for closing the lesson normally involve putting equipment away, cooling down, and summarizing the key information learned in the lesson. Because of the importance of opening and closing procedures to the success of any lesson or practice, more attention is given to these topics in chapter 9.

Maintaining Order

Once established, the order of the learning environment must be maintained for learning to proceed progressively and smoothly. Disruptions to the order of the lesson bring an immediate halt to the task at hand, and the teacher must then focus attention away from learning and onto reestablishing order. It is better for all concerned that order be maintained.

Maintaining Appropriate Behavior

Maintaining order begins by establishing acceptable behavioral practices of both teachers and students. In doing so, each knows the expectations for the other and for themselves in the learning environment. Effective managers have several strategies for establishing and maintaining appropriate behavior.

Communicate Behavioral Expectations and Work Standards

Reinforcing and restating expectations for conduct and work is necessary for maintaining order. Rules and expectations need to be stated to establish behavior, but they need to be restated for those behaviors to continue (Lavay, French, and Henderson 1997). Gentle reminders, posted slogans, or simple rewards for "best effort" are all ways that effective managers remind students of the class performance standards.

Monitor Student Behavior Closely

Effective class managers constantly observe and monitor their students. Research has revealed several monitoring practices and characteristics of effective class managers (Kounin 1970). First among these characteristics is *withitness*, or being so closely attuned to events and student actions that the teacher can anticipate and prevent problems before they occur or become serious. Because beginning teachers tend to focus strongly on what they have to do, they often miss what the students are doing. More experienced teachers have developed techniques to survey the class and monitor potential problems. For example, in most classes, a minority of students account for the majority of off-task and disruptive behavior. An experienced teacher knows to observe these students at regular intervals to check on their activities.

Being able to undertake and overlap multiple tasks at once is another characteristic of an effective manager. Teachers and coaches are often asked to respond to a student request, repair equipment, or stop a student argument—all while continuing to teach the class. Experienced teachers are able to prioritize these tasks so that learning for the majority of students continues while they deal with extraneous demands. For example, a student may come to class with an extensive medical excuse that needs to be reviewed by the teacher. An experienced teacher would ask this student to wait for a minute while she got the rest of the students involved in their learning activities. Once the majority of the class was appropriately active, the teacher would then turn attention to the waiting student. Keeping first things first is an important principle for all effective managers (Covey 1989).

The ability to maintain the momentum of the lesson through the use of signals and well-timed activities is a third characteristic of an effective manager. Well-planned lessons and lively pacing of the class help teachers maintain the continual flow of activities that keeps the momentum moving in ways the teacher intends. Clear, consistent signals speed along transitions and also contribute to the momentum of the learning. Establishing and maintaining instructional momentum will be given more attention in the next chapter.

A fourth characteristic of an effectively managed class is variety and challenge in the lesson activities. Students who are actively engaged in meaningful, interesting, and challenging teacher-planned activities are focused on the task at hand, which leaves them little time or motivation to pursue off-task endeavors. A well-planned lesson is a key factor for establishing a learning environment with interesting activities and appropriate levels of student challenge.

Finally, effective managers reward appropriate and exemplary behavior. Often teachers are quick to punish the inappropriate and ignore the appropriate. "Catch a kid being good" is one way an outstanding teacher once described a most effective management strategy (Hichwa 1998). Cataloging a list of "don'ts" has limited effect. It must be balanced by the "dos" so that when a student is or has been consistently contributing to the effective order of the class, he should, in some way, be recognized for that contribution.

Correcting Inappropriate Behavior

Despite the best-laid plans, well-formulated rules, and practiced procedures, inappropriate and disruptive behavior will occasionally occur. From time to time, hopefully not more than that, a teacher is called on to intervene in a student's actions and correct inappropriate behavior. Most often, these interventions are minor, but once in a while, major interventions are required.

Minor Interventions

Minor interventions are required when the rule infraction has not caused a serious disruption to learning, endangered anyone's safety, or damaged equipment. Types of behavior requiring minor interventions include tardiness, talking out, inattentiveness, mild forms of verbal or physical abuse, or misuse of equipment.

The key to disciplining disruptive behavior is to view what students do in the context of the class (Siedentop and Tannehill 2000). For example, talking out may not be disruptive if it advances the knowledge of the class in an appropriate manner. Effective managers ask themselves two questions when assessing whether disruptive behavior needs to be dealt with quickly: Is the behavior public? Is it contagious? If the student misbehavior is visible to other people in the class (i.e., it's public) and it is potentially contagious (i.e., it will pull others away from the task at hand), then the effective manager responds in a way that terminates the chance of reoccurrence—usually by reinforcing the rules.

A teacher has several options to terminate the inappropriate activity or reduce the chance of reoccurrence (Evertson and Harris 1992). Simply ignoring the behavior is one option. This should be chosen only if the teacher believes the action was a one-time occurrence that isn't likely to happen again or gather the attention of the class. Sometimes, however, a teacher will need to overlook the behavior to understand the motives behind it. The story told by John Hichwa (see sidebar) proves the wisdom in this action. However, you must be careful not to ignore behavior simply because you don't know what to do. Again, a well-formulated and practiced set of rules will help here.

Advice From a Colleague: Handle It With Care and Don't Get Upset!

John Hichwa (left) and Paul Schempp

It was in the middle of October, on a beautiful fall afternoon in New England, just before lunch. My sixth-grade class was to run the mile for time, and it would be recorded as part of their physical fitness test. In the previous five weeks, the coed class participated in a series of small-sided keep-away games, building their cardiovascular endurance as they played. It was my goal to have the class exercise vigorously, push themselves physically, but also have fun. The class also practiced and was timed for the quarter, half, and mile run before their official time was to be recorded. They were given cues for pacing themselves and were told that one of the goals for running a distance event was to set a benchmark for their best time and then try to better that time in the future.

After a warm-up period and a pep talk on doing their best, I arranged the students in order of their practice mile times. Then I gave them their cue: "On your mark, get set, go!" To my amazement, the entire class started walking! I could not believe my eyes! I shouted, "Go, go, go!" but to no avail. The class continued at the pace of a Sunday afternoon stroll and watched to see what I would do.

I was perplexed and really didn't know what to do. I forced myself to stay calm, and for the next 20-plus minutes, I watched them walk the mile and I recorded their scores. Then, I gathered them around me and asked the infamous question: "What happened?" No one volunteered anything. The period was about to end and I had to have closure, so I told them that we would continue the discussion in the next class. Physical education was scheduled every other day, so I had a day to think about how I would handle this situation.

I reflected on the behavior of previous classes, but there was nothing I could recall that gave me any clue to why the class behaved the way it did. There were three or four students that had been belligerent at times, but that's not so unusual in a middle school. I explained to my colleague what had happened, and we tried to brainstorm a plan for my next class with those students. We realized that my reaction would influence the success or failure of that class to some degree throughout the year. It would affect the relationship I could develop with them and might even influence how students interacted with adults in other environments. My colleague wisely advised me to handle it with care and not get upset.

If you're reading this as an undergraduate student or a physical education teacher, don't read any further. Attempt to use your own experiences to come up with ideas on how you would have handled the situation and how you would plan to address the next class.

As I reflected on what the students did, I experienced a variety of feelings—anger, frustration, confusion, self-questioning. I wondered whether any of those students were problems in other classes. I explained what had occurred to their classroom teachers in hope that they could shed some light on the matter. Our school was a grade six to eight setup, so these students were new to me and new to the school. Five weeks is a short time to be judgmental, but the teachers did agree that they, too, were having problems with a few of those students, especially one. Since I had sixth-grade lunch duty, I had the opportunity to observe the entire grade in an unstructured situation.

To my amazement, I discovered that the one child the teachers had mentioned was one of the most popular students in the grade, and the kids congregated around him like a magnet. They followed his every lead, whether it was just talking or playing a four-square game. I only had two lunch periods to do my "research," but by zeroing in on his relationships with the other kids, I got the feeling that it was possible that he could have had enough influence and control over his classmates to get them to go along with him and to walk the mile instead of running it.

(continued)

(continued)

Although I had my suspicions about what went on, I didn't know for sure what had happened. I was unsure of just what I should do, but I knew what I must *not* do! I had to control my anger and frustration, keep from pointing a finger at anyone, and keep from scolding the entire class. I knew it was important to stay calm and to try to make it a positive learning experience for us all.

Class time arrived, and I again asked the class what happened. As before, no one was willing to own up to what caused the class to walk in unison. Some shared that they did not like the mile run, others said that it was boring, and others questioned why we did it in the first place. I had heard all these before, and they were the typical middle school translations of "I really don't want to work!" But it was my job as a teacher to instill the values of a healthy lifestyle, to help the students assess their own fitness profile, and to encourage them to make adjustments and improvements where necessary. I was also very aware that I had another two-plus years with them, and it was important for me to establish a good relationship based on trust and respect. I wanted them to know that I cared for them as individuals and that what score they could get in the mile run was not my major concern. It was our relationship, our mutual respect, that mattered most.

After a five-minute discussion that revealed nothing, I continued with my keep-away unit and kept their mile run scores. I concluded that actions speak louder than words, and I hoped my behavior in the coming weeks would show them how much I cared for them and how important it was for us to work together.

In conclusion, I learned from some of the students that the one boy in question was the ringleader who got the class to walk. I never mentioned it to him, and I don't think he was aware that I knew. I continued to work with him and the class as if nothing had happened, and we eventually established a good relationship and had a good year. Sometimes doing nothing is the best approach. My patience, understanding, and acceptance helped me gain their confidence, trust, and cooperation.

—*John Hichwa, John Read Middle School, Redding, Connecticut*
1990 National Middle School PE Teacher of the Year

If a teacher decides a form of action is necessary, she should take that action quickly to terminate the inappropriate behavior while it still requires only a minor intervention. Waiting for the problem to become larger or hoping it will simply go away are often not options that effective managers take seriously. If action is called for, they initiate it quickly to stop small problems from becoming larger ones.

Changing the pace of the class or changing the activity is another alternative. This action has the effect of turning the attention of the class to the task at hand and away from the inappropriate activity. For example, students tend to be disruptive when bored. If you notice students talking among themselves, playing with equipment in inappropriate ways, or showing other signs of boredom, it may be a signal to change the activity.

Proximity is another strategy that serves as a minor intervention. Moving closer to the student will often cause the offending behavior to cease. Similarly, redirecting the student's behavior toward the task at hand is yet another effective technique. The teacher might call the student by name and ask if she needs some assistance, use the student in a demonstration, or use the student's name in a description of an activity that shows application of the concept or skill being learned. I have found this to be one of the most effective ways to maintain order because it ceases the inappropriate behavior and gets everyone's attention back on the learning task. The misbehaving student usually feels like she either dodged a bullet or was granted a reprieve for wrongdoing and willingly slips back into the learning activity.

Realizing that misbehavior often occurs when students are unsure of what to do or when they're waiting or bored, the teacher may provide additional information. Clarifying instructions and directions ensures that learning tasks and responsibilities are explicit. Leaving no doubt as to the teacher's expectations for student behavior often serves to bring students back on-task. When clarifying or reexplaining an activity, attempt to control any annoyance you may feel (no matter how justified). Keeping a cool, professional demeanor will reinforce to the students that you're serious about their learning and not easily distracted from that mission. An important consideration in class management is to keep the momentum of the class moving in directions that promote learning. Minor interventions are intended to maintain that momentum.

Moderate Interventions

If a student threatens the learning environment by disrupting learning, causing minor injury, or damaging property, then more rigorous measures are required. It is particularly important to closely adhere to the established rules and consequences at these times. Effective managers use rules and procedures for handling class disturbances more often than less effective teachers. Of note, the fairness of a teacher is often measured by willingness and ability to treat misbehavior in a consistent fashion—regardless of which student commits the offending act.

A warning is often the first response to disruptive behavior. The teacher should advise the student to stop the inappropriate behavior and make the student aware of the consequence of its reoccurrence. If the behavior occurs again, the consequence must be administered without hesitation (Lavay, French, and Henderson 1997). To fail in this duty is to lose credibility as a class manager. Students must know why the punishment is being given, and the full duration of the punishment should be served. The teacher should also convey that the action has caused the need for the consequence, and it doesn't reflect personal feelings of the teacher toward the student.

In most instructional situations, a time-out, or time away from the group, is an effective deterrent. No one likes to be excluded from a group, and physical removal for short periods of time can reinforce the point that participation in a group—any group—requires that accepted rules be followed. If a time-out fails to deter inappropriate behavior, the teacher needs to consider a fine or penalty. The precise nature of the fine or penalty depends on the circumstances involved. In a high school class, an appropriate penalty may include a detention or an after-class conference. Learning activities should never be used as punishment. Writing essays or running laps may be important learning activities and should not, therefore, be considered punishment.

Major Interventions

Fortunately, severely disruptive behavior is a rare occurrence in classes and schools. Unfortunately, it's becoming more common. Because vandalism, robbery, theft, and assault do occur in sport and school settings, a teacher must be prepared to handle such situations.

When a serious disruption occurs, the teacher must find a way to remove the student from the class. The student is posing a serious threat to the other students, and it's unlikely the class can proceed in this student's presence. Keep in mind that when removing a student from class, a teacher is still responsible for the welfare of the remaining students; you can't leave the class unless another adult is present to supervise. You may send a student to the office or to retrieve another adult while you stay with the class. Once another adult arrives, then you can leave the class with the offending student.

If a student poses a threat to the safety of classmates and it's not possible to remove this student from the class, then the next best course of action is to remove the other students from the immediate vicinity. Again, they need adequate supervision. At no time should teachers place the students or themselves in danger. In a school setting, an administrator should be made aware of the situation and appropriate policy followed. If the student's actions constitute a crime, the police must be contacted. Because of the importance of getting another adult into the class and given the remote locations in which sport and physical education instruction often takes place, it would be wise for a teacher to have a plan of action for evacuating students and for securing appropriate adult aid in an emergency.

Before the student returns to class, it's suggested that the teacher meet with parents, administrators, and other teachers so that the offending student's future actions in class can be carefully monitored and the rules of the class can be made explicit to all involved parties. The teacher should also meet with the student before reentry in the class so that an understanding and agreement regarding the expectations and rules can be reached. In some cases, it may be best to write a student behavioral contract that clearly identifies the appropriate and inappropriate in-class behavior, as well as the rewards and consequences for complying with or breaking the contract.

Characteristics of an Effective Classroom Manager

- Provides clear instructions and directions
- States desired behaviors, attitudes, and work standards frequently
- Stops disruptive behavior quickly
- Uses rules and procedures to deal with disruptive behavior
- Focuses on the task at hand and the curriculum rather than misbehavior
- Provides signals to start and stop activity
- Rehearses and consistently enforces procedures

Summary

Effective management encompasses the actions and strategies teachers use to solve problems of order in the classroom so that learning can proceed in the most efficient and effective way possible (Doyle 1986). Because of their importance to good teaching, it would serve a teacher well to review the characteristics of effective managers from time to time and try to incorporate these practices into his or her teaching.

Effective managers make clear their expectations for in-class behavior—the students' as well as their own. They identify these standards frequently and ensure that they represent the informal codes of conduct in the learning environment. To make sure that these codes of behavior form the patterns of interaction in the class, effective managers establish concrete, clear, and functional rules and class procedures. These rules and procedures are established and practiced within the first several class meetings to make sure the class begins and remains in accordance with the standards and procedures desired by the teacher. Effective class managers use rules and procedures consistently to deal with disruptive behavior.

Effective managers give clear, concise instructions and directions. Students don't spend a lot of time waiting and wondering what they should do or when to do it. Effective managers get the class moving rapidly and competently. And once moving, the main objective in the learning environment is promoting and sustaining learning by keeping the instructional activities moving. Effective managers focus on the task at hand, not on discipline. To stop a class to discipline a student is to arrest the learning process and defeat the purpose of the class.

Managing the learning environment requires forethought, planning, and the use of skills and techniques. A teacher must, and can, learn to manage a learning environment, for without order and clear procedures, the expectations for behavior and learning will go largely misunderstood. And misunderstanding is a fatal flaw in any learning environment.

Discussion Questions

1. Construct a set of rules and consequences to guide the actions of a class. The rules might be for a second grade physical education class, a high school basketball team, a personal training session, or any other learning environment of your choice.

2. Discuss ways in which you might communicate your standards and behavioral expectations to your students or athletes.

3. One of the most difficult tasks for a teacher is effectively correcting misbehavior without disrupting the learning process. Identify minor, moderate, and severe interventions you might use to correct inappropriate behavior in your learning environment.

4. Consider the teachers or coaches you have had and identify those you consider to be among the most effective managers of their learning environments. What did they do that helped them manage the environment so effectively?

Part IV

Discovery
Exploring the Art of Teaching

In part IV, you'll find the essential skills of a teacher. That is, the principles of teaching with focus and flow (chapter 8), conveying and communicating information (chapter 9), structuring potent practices and providing useful feedback (chapter 10), utilizing innovative and proven instructional strategies (chapter 11), and assessing student learning (chapter 12) make up this critical section on the road to excellence. Taken together, this knowledge and the accompanying skills represent the tasks of teachers and coaches during the actual practice of teaching. For beginning teachers, this section needs your full attention. For experienced teachers and coaches, you'll find ideas within these chapters to reinvigorate and improve your professional practice.

Chapter 8

Focus and Flow: The Tempo of Teaching

Timing is everything.

— Anonymous

DISCOVERY

Bored and sleeping students aren't found in the classrooms of good teachers. There is no time to be bored and no opportunity to sleep during a lesson in which the teaching is focused and the learning is flowing. Building and sustaining momentum in a class breathes life and excitement into a lesson, making it a dynamic, interesting, meaningful, and successful experience for students and teacher alike. A lesson with momentum gives the impression that the teacher purposefully selected stimulating activities and sequenced them at just the right moment to maximize both the learning and enjoyment of the students. One activity seamlessly meshes with the next as the pace and progress of the class carries to a logical and satisfying close. But learning to teach with focus and flow requires particular skills and knowledge on the part of the teacher. In this chapter, the techniques for orchestrating dynamic lessons are examined. The chapter opens with ideas for getting the lesson focused and initiating momentum. Suggestions for sustaining the flow of the lesson are then provided, and the chapter concludes with ideas for closing the lesson and preparing the students to take their newfound knowledge out of the class and into their world.

Getting Focused

Momentum results when two or more people work together toward a common goal. In the case of teaching, the teacher and students work together toward a shared purpose. Most often in sport and physical activity instruction, this shared purpose is the development of student skill or increased knowledge of an activity. The beginning point in teaching is, therefore, getting focused. This involves clearly defining the role of the teacher in the instructional environment. The students and teacher can then establish a clear path and purpose for the lesson at hand.

Define Your Role and Purpose

One difference between less effective and more effective teachers is the way they define their roles as teachers (Brophy and Good 1986). More effective teachers identify their primary function as instruction. They devote more of their time and energy toward activities that help students learn rather than tasks such as management or counseling. They don't provide recreational opportunities, play babysitter, or plan afternoon coaching responsibilities. They teach, and as a result, their students learn.

The very best teachers walk into a learning environment so students can walk out having learned something. The role of the teacher is to instruct, and the role of the student is to learn. For the lesson to flow, both the students and teacher must be sharply focused on these purposes. When these roles are clearly defined, the teacher enters the lesson ready to teach and the students come expecting to learn.

Find a Path and a Purpose

In chapter 6, a lesson or practice session was likened to a journey. To complete a successful journey, you need to know where you are going and make continuous progress toward getting there. Most good teachers, therefore, begin a lesson by identifying the instructional objectives and giving an overview of the lesson content. Identifying the objectives and content sets the pace of the lesson because students know what they will learn and how they will learn it. For example, when students know that today they will review a previously learned basketball chest pass, learn a new passing strategy called the "give and go," and practice these activities with some popular drills and a passing game, they understand both the purpose and path of the lesson. When the teacher and student both know the route and destination, they are prepared to travel together and ready to set the pace of the journey.

Grab Their Attention

Getting a lesson to flow begins with the very first words out of a teacher's mouth. A dull, uninspiring lesson introduction makes students want to leave before the lesson even starts. I knew the lessons were doomed when I heard teachers begin their classes with these statements: "I know you don't like gymnastics, but it's in the curriculum and we need to cover it," "I've never taught this before, but Ms. X is out and I was told to teach it," and "We're going to learn square dance today, and I don't want to hear any complaints."

The lesson should open in ways the students find novel, interesting, and engaging—regardless of the subject or topic to be learned. Instilling a sense of curiosity, enthusiasm, and excitement makes students look forward to the lesson and eager to begin. This enthusiastic excitement and dynamic class interaction initiates class momentum, and a teacher will want to carry that enthusiasm throughout the lesson. Two of the most critical parts of a lesson are the opening and the closing. Both need considerable attention from the teacher.

A carefully crafted opening that captures the students' imagination and sparks their interest is an essential element for getting the lesson moving forward. Displaying a new piece of equipment for students to view or try as they enter the learning environment is a good attention-getter. Beginning the class with an interesting question or fact (e.g., "If you put the populations of Philadelphia, Boston, and Detroit together, it still wouldn't equal the number of people who went snowboarding in the United States last year") is another way to stimulate interest and curiosity. Demonstrating a skill or having a videotape of a sport running when students come to the lesson is also a technique for getting students' attention and building interest in the subject. A skillful teacher will consider the students and subject to be taught and find a fascinating, potent lesson opening.

Setting the Pace: Get It Flowing

There are no magic formulas guaranteeing that a lesson will flow smoothly from one activity to the next or that student learning will build progressively and enthusiastically to a satisfying accomplishment. Orchestrating a lesson in which the momentum builds to an exciting and successful climax takes a knowledgeable and experienced teacher. This section reviews some of the secrets for setting the pace and getting the lesson to flow.

Build a Dynamic Climate

Get the students actively engaged in the subject matter and interacting with both you and each other. In other words, make the students active agents in their learning, not passive recipients. Ask questions to get them talking about the topic. Have them practice with partners and help one another in their learning. As a teacher, move around the learning environment and interact with the students often. The point is this: Get the students moving physically, mentally, and socially.

Because students are often socialized into silence during a lesson, many are reluctant to speak, even when asked a direct question by a teacher. Therefore, questions posed in the early portion of the lesson should be mostly of the yes or no variety.

Once the students begin responding, more in-depth questions requiring student thought and more complex answers can be posed. Beginning a lesson with questions also benefits the later portions of the class. As students feel comfortable speaking about the topic, they will more freely offer suggestions and insights as their learning progresses.

Similarly, students are often socialized in sport and physical activity environments into standing in lines and moving only when directed to do so by the teacher. Getting students to move independently and remain on-task may take a period of adjustment. Having them work in pairs, providing them with public and continuous feedback, and holding them accountable for their learning will help keep them on-task and allow the lesson to flow. Once students become accustomed to moving in the class and taking responsibility for their learning, research has shown that students will prefer this to standing in lines and having the teacher dominate the decision making (Mancini et al. 1983).

See and Support the Right Stuff

When students are doing the "right stuff"—what they're supposed to be doing, such as successful practice attempts—let them know it. People generally respond better when their successes are celebrated. But don't go overboard. Tell them what they are doing right, and then get on with the next goal. Sometimes negative statements are necessary, but recognizing appropriate behavior early in the lesson sets a positive tone, piques student interest, stimulates motivation, and gets the lesson flowing.

Keep It Flowing

A well-run class has a vitality that is obvious to the most casual observer. But how that energy is infused or maintained in the lesson is less obvious. This section presents techniques teachers use to sustain the momentum as a lesson unfolds.

Active Teachers and Dynamic Learners

Teachers who remain active in students' learning activities rather than passively observing students as they practice are best able to maintain lesson momentum. Students achieve more in classes where they spend most of their time being taught or supervised by their teachers rather than working independently (Brophy and Good 1986). Therefore, effective teachers are constantly in action: giving information, offering support, and nursing along the learning process. For a lesson to flow, a teacher must persistently infuse energy into the students' learning.

It isn't just the teachers who are active in a dynamic learning environment. Students must move if they are to learn sport and physical activity. Teachers can promote greater student participation in the learning process with a few techniques. Asking questions about the material being learned or its application to a game or activity engages the students' brains as well as their bodies. For example, asking students practicing basketball lay-ups when they might use that shot in a game gets them thinking about how the skill might actually be used. Now you have students who are both moving and thinking—dynamic learners.

Use a Brisk Pace Along the Road to Success

Pacing students briskly through activities, ensuring that they make continuous progress with high rates of success, is another hallmark of a lesson with flow. Moving students rapidly through a series of activities not only keeps the momentum of the class moving but also allows more content to be covered in less time. Students don't get bogged down in endless and mindless repetitive activities. The effective teacher also seizes the "teachable moment" and propels the class forward. A teachable moment might arise when a student asks an unexpected, but insightful, question about the activity. A good teacher will go with the question and seize the opportunity to teach additional information.

Another technique to consider for infusing the lesson with flow is to divide the activities into modified tasks, with each activity containing a subgoal of the larger goal of the lesson. Students can experience more success, and one successful activity may lead to the next, which not only builds the student's confidence but also makes the lesson a progressive series of successful learning experiences. For example, students learning soccer passing may start their practice individually by rebounding the ball off a wall with alternating feet. Next, they may find a partner and pass between them. Then, the partners may begin to move around the field as they pass. A fourth activity may have two sets of partners join together in passing two balls amongst the four. Finally, two groups of four might join for a game of keep-away. The activities are progressive and build toward an activity that is much like a soccer game. A further advantage of this method is that it minimizes the amount of time spent on one activity. Dwelling on one activity for too long makes the lesson grow stale, whereas moving from one successful experience to the next keeps the lesson fresh. People learn best when they are both nurtured and challenged. Success provides the motivation and security to reach for new heights, and new activities provide the challenge to discover more success.

Variety Is the Spice of Life

In teaching, as in any human endeavor, it's easy to follow comfortable instructional routines until they wear into deep, dull ruts. Routines can be valuable time-saving devices for teachers, but too many routines or too much routine can crush the spontaneity that brings life to a lesson. Research has shown that variety can permeate virtually every aspect of a lesson (Rosenshine and Furst 1971).

It takes a bit of imagination and some knowledge on the part of the teacher to discover new and varied ways of conducting a class (figure 8.1). Some ideas for spicing up a lesson and keeping it flowing include relying more on nonverbal behavior, using new instructional strategies, devising novel learning/practice activities, incorporating technology or learning aids, reorganizing class formations or stations, putting up posters or playing motivating music, employing different assessment techniques,

Figure 8.1 Challenging, innovative activities can keep students interested and on task.

or inviting visitors to participate in class as students or guest teachers. Searching for new ways to perform old tasks has the added benefit of not only keeping flow in the lesson but possibly refreshing and rejuvenating the teacher as well.

Timing Is Everything

Knowing when to make a change in a lesson is an important yet difficult skill that normally takes time to develop. After years of working through instructional scenarios, experienced teachers learn to anticipate situations, predict events, and generate alternatives to meet the demands of these developing situations. Inexperienced teachers have difficulty anticipating events and are often surprised and unprepared for particular situations as they occur during the lesson.

Research has, however, provided some clues to the timing of activity change and class pacing by experienced teachers (Griffey and Housner 1991; Housner and Griffey 1985). While inexperienced teachers focus on student interest in the instructional activities, experienced teachers monitor student performance more closely and attempt to maintain an appropriate level of challenge. Experienced teachers adjust the lesson based on student performance cues, whereas inexperienced teachers struggle to maintain student interest. Experienced teachers are concerned about the students' skill performance and understanding of the information being taught—which is easier to judge than someone's interest or enjoyment.

Experienced teachers are willing to make changes both quicker and more often than inexperienced teachers (Byra and Sherman 1993; Jones, Housner, and Kornspan 1997). Inexperienced teachers often make changes after dramatic, negative occurrences in class, but experienced teachers are able to monitor the nuances that signal a need for an alteration before a crisis occurs. And because they are better planners, experienced teachers are better prepared to make the changes once change is deemed necessary.

Make Transitions Smooth

Once a decision is made to change the activity, it now becomes important to make the change without interrupting the lesson flow. Momentum can often be lost when changing learning activities or when moving from one location to another. Therefore, transitions between lesson parts and activities should be signaled clearly and made quickly. Clear signals between lesson parts allow the students to better follow the flow of the lesson. Having been briefed in the lesson opening about the upcoming activities, students better understand what is expected of them with each transition signal and can restart quickly after changing activities or locations. Moving quickly from one activity to the next maintains the momentum, freshness, and focus of the lesson. It also reduces confusion and wait time, which leaves more time for learning.

Expect Success

When Tiger Woods strokes a putt, he expects the ball to fall into the hole. He expects results. Similarly, outstanding teachers get results because they expect them. Good teachers expect that students will master the skills and concepts being taught. These teachers realize that sometimes learning will occur quickly, but sometimes it may take a while before the students are able to grasp the material and show mastery. Martinek's (1996) research has demonstrated that higher expectations are correlated with high achievement. Students seem to have a remarkable ability to rise to high levels of expectations. If a

teacher is giving her best effort, it is not unreasonable to expect the same from the students.

In conveying expectations to students, teachers need to focus on individual student mastery and personal improvement rather than comparisons to others or established standards. People learn sport and physical activity skills at varying rates and levels as well as in different ways. A practice activity or piece of information that helps one person achieve a higher standard of performance will not necessarily have the same effect on everyone. Similarly, one person may see a demonstration that clearly depicts the skill to be learned, while another student standing nearby sees only a confusing commotion. But expecting each student to master the skill sets the goal of the lesson clearly as well as reveals to both the teacher and student that they need to keep working to achieve mastery.

Classes in which students constantly strive to master a skill or concept flow from one activity to the next because the teacher and students both know what they are attempting to do, and both recognize the need to keep moving toward the goal. Classes in which students are only expected to "try" or "participate" often degenerate into meaningless robotic rituals for both the teacher and students.

In setting high standards and expecting high levels of performance improvement, it is imperative that teachers attribute success to student effort and ability. Students who see their success measured in effort and see themselves as able to achieve are willing to commit to their learning. Students who believe that they lack the ability or are led to believe they are lazy will soon fulfill the prophecy of failure. Teachers, being human, often have the tendency to treat high and low achievers differently. High achievers better reflect a teacher's efforts, and the natural tendency is to expect more from them and provide them with more tangible, meaningful rewards— such as respect or admiration. Low achievers often attract either scorn or sympathy from a teacher. Low achievers will, therefore, be given unnecessary help, praised for success on simple tasks, or given acceptance for failure. Consequently, a teacher who holds high expectations for every student will enhance the learning experience for everyone.

When a teacher expects great things from students, it doesn't take long before the students begin to believe they are capable of such achievement, and they start expecting success and achievement as well. They believe they can learn the skill or concepts being taught. Students who believe themselves incapable of learning are not likely to learn, nor even try. In contrast, students who believe they have the ability to achieve are far more likely to put forth the effort to fulfill their self-imposed expectations.

A student's perception of competence is instrumental for getting a lesson to progress in ways that promote student learning. A student learning a free throw shot is far more motivated when a teacher, convinced the student is going to make a basket or two with enough practice in the proper technique, persists in teaching and encouraging. If the teacher persists in teaching, students will put forth greater effort, willingly approach learning activities, persist even in the face of initial failure, seek help, and take pride when success is finally gained. Success may come in the form of a single free throw or 10 free throws or a new world record. But success will come. If a teacher wholeheartedly believes that, so will the student.

To facilitate success, teachers need to develop solid communication skills and dependable methods of conveying appropriate information. They must also be able to structure a learning environment in which students can grasp that information and turn it into useful knowledge and improved performance. Expecting success will not, however, guarantee success. But without a teacher being firmly convinced that the final outcome will be student mastery of the subject, there is little chance for mastery to occur. Expect success and you give it a far greater chance of happening.

Goals: From Process to Outcome

Pia Nilsson (right) takes a break during a coaching seminar with other Swedish coaches, who performed a Swedish holiday celebration for other international coaches.

After the final hole of the 72-hole European championship in Italy, a Swedish Golf Federation official approached me. "Pia," he said, "it's amazing that so many of the Swedes finished in the top 10 when you don't even believe in goal setting."

That really got me thinking. What was he trying to say? Of course I believe in goal setting. Then I realized where his interpretation came from. At a team meeting a couple of days before the event, we talked about our dream outcome goals for the championship. The players spontaneously said, "We feel so good that we think it's possible for all 10 of us to finish in the top 10." Their performance ambitions were clearly high. From that vision, I wanted each one of the players to decide on their process goals for the championship. What is each one of them going to focus on while performing that he or she has influence over? It was different for each player. If they commit to their own unique process goal and follow through, it will make the outcome goal more likely to happen.

For one player it could be "I will follow through with every decision I make." For another it could be "I will finish every swing in perfect balance and hold my finish for three seconds." That was my plan for the championship goal setting. Over the years I have found it to be very successful. When our official asked me what each player's scoring goal (outcome goal) was, I didn't have an answer. That was his way of working with goals, but it wasn't ours.

—*Pia Nilsson, cofounder of Coaching for the Future and European captain of the Solheim Cup squad*

Monitor for Movement

As the lesson unfolds, a skillful teacher will monitor the lesson to ensure that progress is being made toward the instructional goal. Much of a teacher's thinking during class centers on the learners and the learning process. Monitoring the in-class activities and continually assessing the effectiveness of the activities in terms of meeting the lesson goals are vital for keeping the lesson flowing (Calderhead 1996). For example, a soccer game gives the appearance of 22 active bodies scurrying around a field. On closer look, only one or two players are actually using any skill at any given time. The rest are either waiting for the ball to come to them, or they are attempting to get the ball. Effective teachers might use smaller teams or add more equipment to get more students using the skills of soccer. Attempting to engage all learners, regardless of the size of the class, in motor activity most of the time takes careful and continual analysis. Ensuring that students have ample time to practice and demonstrate the skills being learned transforms passive observers into active learners.

Experienced teachers constantly consider alternatives in a never-ending search for the best possible set of learning activities for these students, at this time, in this environment. They spend considerable in-class time monitoring the class, looking for alternatives to keep the class focused and flowing (Swanson, O'Connor, and Cooney 1990). In a recent study, it was found that more skillful teachers differed from less skillful teachers in two important areas: first, being able to provide more activities and tasks to help students improve and learn and, second, monitoring student and class activity with a clear eye on the quality of a student's performance (Hastie and Vlaisavljevic 1999).

Avoid Momentum Blockers

It takes skill to get a lesson flowing and to keep it flowing, but it also takes some knowledge and skill to recognize and avoid events that will derail and arrest the flow of a lesson or practice. Avoiding disruptions, distractions, and delays is one secret of keeping students' attention and subsequently keeping the lesson flowing. One of the surest ways of interrupting or halting the flow of a lesson is to deflect attention away from student learning and onto other matters. For example, students coming in late, not having enough or the proper equipment to undertake the activities, or misbehaving students all stand to distract attention. Having to retrieve or set up equipment, review rules or schedules, change locations, or leave students waiting in long lines will also quickly kill the momentum of a lesson (figure 8.2). In many cases, the need to interrupt a lesson is the result of poor preparation. Therefore, time needs to be invested before class to consider not only the instructional portions of the lesson but the administration of the lesson as well.

Giving consideration to factors that are known to block the lesson flow will often lead to strategies for maintaining lesson momentum. Placing equipment in convenient locations, ensuring that it's in good working order, and working out an efficient, economical method of distribution will reduce this sometimes necessary delay. In addition, covering administrative necessities before or immediately after instruction keeps the lesson focused on learning during the most critical phases of the lesson. Reviewing class rules and expectations can also help sidestep momentum blockers. For example, let students know that you expect them not only to work hard to master the skills of the lesson but to help their peers learn as well. Learn to recognize potential misbehavior and other momentum blockers and deal with them quickly. The longer it takes for a teacher to address a potential problem, the more time the problem has to negatively affect the lesson.

Figure 8.2 Full participation ensures that students don't waste time standing in lines.

Idle time is a sure way to kill the flow of a lesson. Monitor the waiting time for students, and if they appear to be distracted or bored, find ways to reduce the wait time and increase active learning time. Planning easy, efficient routines and pathways when a change in the instructional location is called for keeps the lesson flowing. Perhaps some useful activity can take place during the transition. For example, a conversation on the topic at hand or a related game-like activity that can be initiated during transitions can keep the learning moving forward.

Drawing to a Close

As the end of the lesson draws near, you must carefully consider how you would like the lesson to end. If you are teaching children, you will need to calm them down before they move on to their next activity. If you are teaching adults, you will want to find a way for them to carry the enthusiasm, good feelings, and valuable ideas gained in the lesson into their world. Like a good piece of music, a well-orchestrated lesson comes to a memorable and purposeful conclusion. Here are some ideas that may help your lessons end on a good note.

Final Remembrances

Students will most often remember best what they did last in the lesson. Therefore, the final activity needs to be selected so that the most important aspects of a lesson are highlighted. Inexperienced teachers simply end the lesson when time is up or with a game. Giving little thought to what a student leaves the lesson with is simply not smart teaching. Good golf instructors, for example, intentionally end the lesson with a student hitting a successful shot so that the student leaves the lesson tee with a positive image of herself as a golfer. A discussion at the end of class is a technique teachers sometimes use to highlight the major concepts learned. Don Hellison (1995) often has his students record their lesson experiences in a journal at the conclusion of class and then holds a discussion regarding what was learned in the lesson. Although there is no single right way to close a lesson, a skillful teacher builds the lesson to a deliberate, memorable close.

Trailers and Teasers

One way movie promoters attempt to attract an audience to a movie is by showing trailers, or "teasers." That is, they show small, but meaningful, segments of the movie to seize your attention and to make you think about coming to see the full feature. Teachers can do the same thing. Let students know that what they just learned is part of a "bigger picture." The new skill learned in class can be used in a game they might play outside of class, or the new skill will be built on in the next lesson, or the newly learned concepts need to be practiced so that they can develop further and lead to permanent improvement. In short, attempt to make the students look forward to coming back to the next lesson. Learning is progressive. It shouldn't end with the lesson that is closing; rather, the lesson you are now closing should open a door to future learning and more rewarding experiences in sport and physical activity.

Summary

Meaningful and interesting learning experiences are strongly dependent on a teacher's ability to give a lesson purpose and to keep the learning fresh and invigorating. In other words, a skillful teacher teaches with focus and flow. Identifying a specific purpose for the lesson and reminding the class participants why they're doing what they're doing keeps both teacher's and learners' attention on a meaningful outcome to the lesson. Undertaking instructional practices that get students actively involved in the lesson, their attention centered on the task at hand, with quick changes between briskly paced lesson activities allows the lesson to build momentum to a successful and satisfying close for both the teacher and learners.

A lesson that takes on the appearance of a dull dance by unwilling participants is not a pleasant experience for anyone. The lessons of good teachers are dynamic events in which successful experiences lead to long remembered and valued lessons. Successful lessons are, therefore, dependent on a teacher adopting and developing strategies that allow the lesson to unfold with focus and flow. Good teachers use strategies to get the lesson moving, maintain momentum, and then close the lesson with a purposeful, memorable experience.

Discussion Questions

1. Can you recall a lesson or practice session that you participated in as either a student or teacher that seemed to really flow well? What were some of the characteristics of that lesson that made it an extraordinary learning experience? How did you feel during the lesson?

2. What are some "attention grabbers" that you might use to open one of your lessons?

3. Select a skill or activity you might teach and identify multiple activities that you could use to pace your lesson briskly and achieve high levels of student success.

4. What are some characteristics or events that you would look for that would signal a need to change learning activities to maintain a lesson's momentum?

5. Identify specific activities to close a lesson that would allow your students to leave the lesson (a) with a clear idea of what they learned and (b) feeling successful for having participated in the lesson.

Chapter 9

Communicating

Good communication is as stimulating as black coffee, and just as hard to sleep after.

— Anne Morrow Lindbergh

Students seek from teachers the knowledge that leads to increased understanding, improved performance, and a deeper sense of satisfaction brought by skillful participation. Although teachers are often quite knowledgeable in a sport or activity, simply knowing something doesn't mean they can teach it. A primary responsibility of teachers, therefore, is to communicate their knowledge in such a way that a learner can comprehend it, find value in it, and apply it. When teachers communicate clearly, purposefully, and effectively, learners have a greater chance of converting the information of a lesson into knowledge for a lifetime. In this chapter, three ways that sport and physical activity teachers effectively communicate will be presented: organized information, powerful presentations, and dynamic demonstrations.

Organized Information

Carefully arranging the order and pattern of information is often as important as the method used to convey that information. The amount, form, and order of the presented material significantly affect how much of that information is carried out of the lesson and later used by the learner. A teacher can take several steps when organizing the manner and timing of the information covered in a class. The information organization strategies discussed in this section include giving lesson overviews, identifying the main points of a lesson, signaling transitions in the lesson activities, and providing lesson reviews.

Start With an Overview

Beginning an instructional presentation by identifying the topics to be covered and the purpose of the lesson tells students what they will learn and why. Going over the information to be learned and the goal to be attained sets the tone of the lesson because students know what to expect and can better organize and assimilate information as the lesson unfolds. Knowing what will happen and why makes the lesson more meaningful for students and allows them to identify and learn the essential messages of the lesson as the lesson proceeds. Starting with a strong purpose and a clear path makes it easier for the teacher to stay the course and guide the lesson along a decisive direction. An overview also ensures that the teacher and learner are striving toward the same end.

Make the Main Points Clear

Renowned educational philosopher Alfred North Whitehead wrote, "Let the main ideas which are introduced be few and important, and let them be thrown into every combination possible" (1929, p. 14). In lessons taught by effective teachers, the main points of the lesson can't be missed. The key concepts are presented boldly, clearly, and with a degree of redundancy. The main points in the presentation are also logically presented so that they have a cumulative and collective effect. Taken together, the main points form a potent body of knowledge for the learner.

The main points need to be restricted to only those few ideas that are absolutely fundamental for improving the learner's performance (figure 9.1). In other words, these points must be directly related to the purpose of the lesson and aimed at improving the student's performance. Sometimes all that is necessary is a single piece of information. An expert will present a single point from a multitude of perspectives, use different forms of presentation (e.g., explanation, demonstration, analysis of student performance), and have the student

Figure 9.1 A teacher needs to be careful not to inundate students with too many instructions at once.

practice the concept using different drills and activities all focused on developing the main idea being stressed in the lesson (Baker, Schempp, and Hardin 1998). At the end of a presentation, ask your listeners to identify the two or three most important things they learned, and if they directly correspond with the major concepts you are attempting to teach, you know you've had a successful lesson.

Keep Them With You

If the activity changes during a lesson or a new concept is introduced, the learners need to know in no uncertain terms that a change is taking place. In the lessons of effective teachers, transitions are signaled clearly and made quickly. In the previous chapter, smooth transitions were identified as necessary for keeping the lesson flowing. Good transitions are also necessary for effective communication. Clear signals allow the students to better follow the information stream of the lesson. For example, if you are providing information on shooting a basketball jump shot but would like to provide additional information on defending the jump shot, make sure you tell your players that you are shifting to a different topic. If you decide to shift back to the original topic, let them know that as well. In other words, keep them with you whether you are making a physical transition by moving from one area of the learning space to another or making a conceptual transition by moving from one topic to another. By having been briefed in the overview as to the content of the lesson, students better understand what information is coming and why.

Make a First and Last Impression

Because of their importance to student learning, the opening and closing of an instructional period need particular attention. An effective class opening stimulates interest, sparks curiosity, and prepares the student to undertake the demands of the class or practice. Making the first element an interesting fact, a pertinent question, or an engaging demonstration can all be effective openers. A carefully selected opening should be followed by an overview of the lesson, then immediately followed by the learning activities. Although the opening should be brief to allow maximum time for teaching and learning, the opening sets the stage for all that will follow. The story "A Cup of Tea" illustrates this point beautifully.

A Cup of Tea

Nan-in, a Japanese master during the Meiji era (1868-1912), received a university professor who came to inquire about Zen. Nan-in served tea. He poured his visitor's cup full, and then kept on pouring. The professor watched until he could restrain himself no longer. "It is overfull. No more will go in!"

"Like this cup," said Nan-in, "you are full of your own opinions and speculations. How can I show you Zen unless you first empty your cup?"

A short time ago, I visited a high school teacher who was going to teach his students the high jump. As we walked down to the track, the students and I noticed a high jump bar set at a ridiculously high height. The teacher slowly walked under the bar, turned to the group, and stood silent for a few seconds with the bar towering over his head. All eyes focused on him and everyone wondered, *What next?* The teacher then said, "In the last Olympics, Charles Austin of the USA cleared a bar set at this height, 7 feet 10 inches, to win the gold medal. Today, I'm going to show you the technique he used to do that." It was a very effective opening to a wonderful lesson.

When it's time to close the lesson, remind your students of what they have learned. Effective teachers review and summarize the main ideas at the conclusion of the lesson. Achievement is higher when information is presented with a degree of redundancy (Smith and Sanders 1981). As stated in previous chapters, students tend to remember the end of the lesson more clearly than the beginning. Therefore, make a strong finish to the lesson by reviewing the main ideas. This reinforces the importance of the concepts and leads to greater retention of the lesson content.

Finally, let students know that the lesson is only part of the learning process. They must now move forward and practice what they learned that day. The road to improved performance in any skill or activity is paved with practice, and the only way students will find consistent improvement is if they link their learning today with practice tomorrow. Because practice is so important to learning, it will be discussed in depth in chapter 10. Finally, a good closing should contain a sincere compliment to the learners for their efforts and achievements that day. If you enjoyed the lesson, thank the students for their part in your enjoyment. If they learned something in your lesson, congratulate them on their newfound knowledge.

Organizing Information

- Start with an overview of the lesson.
- Make the main points clear.
- Keep them with you.
- Make a first and last impression.

Powerful Presentations

The most common way sport and physical activity instructors deliver information to students is through a presentation or an explanation. Presentations and explanations can take a variety of forms. A high school coach may be called on to give a presentation to a local civic organization on the prospects for the coming season, teachers are often required to present a curriculum innovation to a committee, and a sport instructor may need to effectively describe the intricacies of game strategy to a group of students. In all cases, these teachers must possess the tools to effectively present a body of knowledge—whether it is skills, rules, training procedures, etiquette, or game tactics. If teachers can't communicate, students can't learn. The heart of a teacher's professional practice resides in communication skills (figure 9.2).

Effective speakers possess qualities that make them both interesting and individualistic. There is much art in a good presentation. A good presentation entertains, informs, and moves the audience to action (Carnegie 1990). But as memorable as an effective speaker might be, there are skills common to all good speakers. This section describes techniques for

Figure 9.2 Many of the traits of good public speaking that teachers use in presentations for their colleagues can be transferred to crafting dynamic presentations for their students.

preparing powerful presentations, making dynamic deliveries, and ensuring effective explanations.

Crafting Powerful Presentations

Crafting a powerful presentation requires four essential traits. All four characteristics are necessary for a presentation to succeed.

Be Passionate

A powerful presentation begins with strong and persistent passion by the speaker. The teacher must firmly believe that he's presenting essential information for the learner's well-being and long-term development. If the teacher isn't convinced that what he's saying is important to the learner, the learner won't be, either. A strong and persistent passion to convey a body of knowledge provides the speaker with the focus and desire critical for a good presentation.

Know the Topic

A good speaker knows thoroughly what she will say. She has rehearsed the main ideas of the presentation, carefully sequenced the order of the ideas, and organized supporting materials, stories, or anecdotes to deliver at just the right moment. If the listeners show interest in a particular point in the presentation, she's prepared to supply additional information and secondary sources. One of the distinguishing characteristics of expert teachers is their extensive knowledge base. They know their subject thoroughly, and this comes across in their presenta-

tions. The ammunition in a powerful presentation is the knowledge conveyed, and a good speaker has plenty of reserves.

Project Confidence

Most people, regardless of their experience, feel nervous when addressing a new audience. Nervousness is a natural reaction to public speaking. Although it is often difficult, if not impossible, to control emotions, you can control behavior, at least to a degree. If you can't feel confident, you can at least learn to act confident. The first step toward confidence comes from being prepared. The second step is to stop thinking about yourself (e.g., your appearance, your notes, your equipment), and start thinking about your audience—which is, after all, the reason you're there. The people in the audience believe they can benefit from what you are about to tell them. Therefore, concentrate on them and what you can say that will be of most benefit. Look into someone's eyes, and speak to that person as if he were the only person in the room. And then search for another set of eyes, and speak to that person. The audience, whether it is one or one thousand, did not come to criticize or find fault with the speaker but rather to learn. Good teachers direct their thoughts toward student learning and success. As a teacher focuses more on the students' needs and interests, he will find nervousness dissipating and confidence growing.

We're often fooled by great speakers, not by what they say but rather by how they act. A talented speaker appears calm, relaxed, and natural—so much so that her entire address appears to be impromptu. The words seem to fall from her lips with such a natural cascade that the audience believes she is simply telling us whatever happens to be on her mind. Despite the appearance, nothing could be further from the truth. Mark Twain, one of America's premiere lecturers, described his secret for public speaking as "counterfeit impromptu" and once confessed "it usually takes me three weeks to prepare an impromptu speech" (Ayres 1990, 218).

Rehearse the Essentials

An essential part of Twain's preparation was practice. The delivery of important points of information needs to be carefully and continually rehearsed. Explore alternative ways of conveying the information. If nothing else, rehearse the first and last statements, as well as the main points, into a smooth, purposeful, and comfortable delivery. Practicing the essential presentation components allows you to carefully choose the appropriate words, plan proper pauses, and deliver the critical points with confidence and authority. You can practice a presentation, either in whole or in part, virtually anywhere—driving a car, looking into a mirror, sitting at a desk, or standing in your living room. However, it's important that the practice be verbal. Actually speak the words out loud so you can rehearse the cadence, flow, and feel of the words as they leave your lips. Any performance benefits from practice; presentations are no exception.

Crafting Powerful Presentations

- Care passionately about your topic.
- Know your subject thoroughly.
- Act confident.
- Rehearse the first and last statements and the main points.

Delivering Potent Presentations

We've already established that impressive presentations more effectively reach learners. Here are some ways to make your deliveries dynamic.

Be Prepared

Preparation is the first step in delivering a potent presentation. Take time to assemble thoughts, convictions, and ideas, particularly if you're making an important presentation to a large audience. Research the topic to make sure the information is accurate, current, and complete. Consult with experts on the topic(s) you teach. How and what do they teach? Reflecting on personal experiences as a learner is often helpful to a teacher preparing instructional material. Dynamic speakers are always looking for new approaches and fresh ideas, polishing and refining old ideas, and using every source possible to improve their presentations. President John F. Kennedy, a renowned speaker, kept a file of quotes and anecdotes that he referred to when drafting a speech. The importance of planning and preparing a lecture or presentation cannot be overstated.

Strive for Clarity

A teacher's clarity is consistently correlated with student achievement (Land and Smith 1979). Knowing what to say and how to say it comes easier with forethought and planning. In preparing a topic for teaching, consider the main points you wish to stress. It's far easier to be clear in a message if you clearly know the message you intend to deliver.

The key to transmitting clear meaning, according to Chapman (1999), is selecting each word carefully and using delivery devices that will trigger the desired response in the student. A clear speaker selects precise and accurate words when communicating information and articulates them with a degree of eloquence. To increase specificity and improve clarity, clear speakers avoid vague or ambiguous words such as *some, almost, things, probably,* and *maybe*. Would John F. Kennedy's message have been as clear or convincing if he had said, "I believe that this nation should *probably* commit itself to achieving the goal, before this decade is out, of landing a man on the moon and *maybe* returning him safely to the earth"?

Clarity and simplicity often go hand in hand. Many of the skills taught by sports instructors can be complex and multifaceted, but good teachers strive to simplify the complicated. They use a few well-chosen words over a complex compendium of verbiage. A story or metaphor is often an effective, interesting way to make a point. Although a biomechanist might explain the stance for a golf swing in terms of the angles and levers created by the relationships of the feet, knees, hips, spine, shoulders, and head, legendary golf instructor Harvey Penick simply told his students to "Face the ball plain, as if you are about to shake hands with someone on the other side of it" (Penick and Shrake 1992, 110). His point was both simple and clear.

Be Enthusiastic

People reveal their enthusiasm in different ways, and an instructor must determine how students act when enthusiastic and then promote those behaviors through their teaching. For most teachers, enthusiasm begins with a love of two things: their subjects and their students (Locke and Woods 1982). Affection for an activity and those learning it are keys for motivating students to improve their performance. Enthusiasm, one of the most contagious of all human characteristics, will soon pass to students. Research has found that enthusiastic teachers inspire greater intrinsic motivation and vitality in their students (Patrick, Hisley, and Kempler 2000).

Teachers convey their enthusiasm in many ways, such as revealing a passion for the activity, smiling, using descriptive or animated explanations, and investing time in planning and reflecting on the lesson. Getting students to be active, both physically and verbally, also promotes enthusiasm in a lesson or practice. An active teacher shows more enthusiasm for the lesson and the subject than a teacher who merely observes the students going through the practice motions. Great teachers love what they do and find ways to show it.

Control Your Voice

All good speakers are masters of voice control. Like a conductor with a symphony, a good speaker adjusts his voice to best effect. When making a forceful point, he projects a strong, powerful voice. When making a sensitive point, he uses a soft, assured voice. Projecting your voice is essential for the audience—particularly in sport and activity environments that are normally large, loud places. Voice projection is not screaming; it is throwing your voice so the listener receives a clear, confident, natural sounding message.

Good voice projection begins with good posture: chest up and stomach in, weight evenly distributed on the balls of the feet, shoulders square to the learners, and head up for good eye contact. Using the diaphragm to take a deep breath before speaking and breathing normally while speaking provide the fuel for a well-projected voice. The vocal cords need a good amount of air to be exercised fully. Good speakers don't strain the voice or scream but speak naturally as they would in a normal conversation. Their voices carry because of posture and breath control. Fill your lungs with air and stand tall, and you'll notice a difference in your voice.

Changing the pitch of your voice and the rate of speaking go a long way toward making your presentation interesting. A boring monotone interests no one, and without interest, your audience isn't likely to get the message. A little practice and attention to pitch and pace can pay big dividends. Voice modulation can make a speaker far more interesting and engaging. For example, a word spoken slowly and softly can often have a large effect. Read the following sentence aloud and say the first word softly and slowly, then read the remaining words at normal pace and pitch: *Relax* your grip.

Stress the Important

Emphasizing the important words in a sentence and downplaying the less important ones is a technique common to good speakers (Carnegie 1990). Again, preparation and practice will help you identify the important words in your message. Read the following two sentences aloud:

> When making contact, focus on the center of the ball.

> When making contact, focus on the *center* of the ball.

Clearly, the second sentence would draw the students' attention to the main point. You can also effectively make an important point with a pause. Pausing before and after an important idea sets it apart from the rest. A second of silence before the main idea alerts the listener's ear. A second of silence after the main idea gives the listener a moment to digest the information. For example, "What makes Mia Hamm a great soccer player? (pause) Confidence. (pause) What will make you a better soccer player? (pause) Confidence. (pause)" Communicating in this way clearly conveys the important concept.

Delivering Potent Presentations

- Plan and prepare.
- Deliver your message clearly.
- Be enthusiastic.
- Project and control your voice.
- Vary the pitch of your voice.
- Stress important words.
- Pause before and after important points.

Effective Explanations

There is no single correct way to explain a skill or concept. Put 100 great teachers in a room and ask them all to explain a particular skill, and you'll likely hear 100 different explanations. Unlike presentations (which tend to be lengthy, in-depth narrations of a subject), explanations are brief, pointed descriptions of a particular topic. Presentations need to be developed and orchestrated, whereas an explanation needs to be compact and efficient for it to be effective. The best explanations communicate the most information in the fewest words. Good explanations help students remember the most important bits of information for improving performance. Therefore, the teacher must first know the essential information for her students and then convey this information in the shortest, clearest way possible.

Two instructional devices that help increase learning but decrease listening are metaphors and mnemonics. Metaphors are ways of representing knowledge in nonliteral terms. It's sometimes difficult to succinctly explain a sport skill using literal language. For example, how do you explain the feeling of contacting the "sweet spot" or catching with "soft hands"? Accomplished teachers discover knowledge the learner already has and then select a metaphor that draws a direct association between that previously learned skill and the skill being learned (Schempp and St. Pierre 2000a). When teaching a tennis serve to a baseball pitcher, a teacher might say, "Think about delivering a fastball right into the service court." Metaphors drawing on previously learned skills not only make for economical and vivid explanations, but they also preprogram the learner for success. The baseball pitcher thinks *If a tennis serve is like pitching, I can do it.*

Mnemonic devices are memory cues that use rhymes or letter combinations to place a large body of knowledge into a grouping the learner can remember. Identifying the number of concepts in a particular skill performance helps the learner remember those concepts. For example, a teacher might say, "When shooting a free throw, remember three things: (1) *Balance* with knees flexed, (2) *focus* on the target, and (3) *release* the ball with the fingers pushing toward the basket."

Sometimes, making up a name or using a common word or sound helps a student remember the information. When teaching rhythm in baseball batting, remembering SSSH can help: See the ball; Step toward the pitcher; Swing the bat; Hit the ball. Often a rhyme or story makes it easier to remember the important points. When playing golf on windy days, a little rhyme my friend Charlie Sorrell taught me never fails to come to mind: "Into the breeze, swing with ease."

A creative teacher always searches for ways to help students remember the key points of a lesson. Novice teachers tend to focus simply on getting the information out of their mouths. Expert teachers focus on getting information permanently into a student's head.

Dynamic Demonstrations

Although oral presentations and explanations are important modes of instruction, demonstrations are often critical for physical education instructors to use when presenting sport and physical activity information (Magill 2001). For many people, seeing is preferred over hearing when attempting to learn. In observational learning, the learner acquires information about a new physical activity by watching another perform the movement. When teachers provide a model or demonstration, two actions are necessary: observation and imitation. In other words, students must first observe the activity to be performed, then attempt to imitate the performance as closely as possible. Students learn a great deal through the process of observation and imitation, and this learning isn't confined to just sport or physical activity skills. In this section, the concepts of modeling and demonstrating will be addressed separately.

Modeling

If a picture is worth a thousand words, a clear and accurate model is invaluable to a learner. Teachers traditionally serve as models in three capacities: physical skills, attitudes, and social behaviors. Teachers are not the only models found in a learning environment. Other students or participants serve as models (figure 9.3), as do support staff, assistants, parents, and anyone else who may be intimately associated with the learning or performance environment.

Figure 9.3 Teachers can have success when they ask students to be involved with demonstrations.

Modeling occurs all the time, whether the instructor is aware of it or not. Students learn social skills, attitudes, thinking patterns, moral values, manners, traditions, dress, cultural values, and a host of related activities that are associated with the learning environment. A teacher's credibility is placed in peril if he enforces one set of rules for the students yet appears to abide by another. For example, it's difficult to convince students that conditioning and fitness are important when the teacher is sadly out of shape. If the teacher believes in social equity, she should strongly and consistently model this. Teachers are significant role models in all respects by the nature of their importance to students. Many teachers fail to realize just how influential they may be.

Demonstrations

A demonstration is a performance that conveys information about how a skill is executed (Magill 2001). A form of modeling, demonstrations are restricted to a specific purpose and focus on a particular concept or skill component. They are most often used to provide visual information on a skill performance, but strategies, rules, and plays can also be demonstrated.

The teacher can either provide the demonstration himself or select another student or assistant to perform the demonstration. An entire skill can be demonstrated or just selected portions of the skill depending on the learner and the learning goal. If the teacher is not highly skilled but is working with a skilled athlete, he may choose to demonstrate only selected portions of the skill so he doesn't provide a poor model. If the teacher is a highly skilled performer and the learner is a shy beginner, demonstrating a perfect skill may do more to intimidate the learner than to inform her. Research reveals that beginners can learn much about a skill and improve their performance by watching other beginners practice the skill (Hebert and Landin 1994).

Demonstrations can be particularly helpful when language is a barrier to effective communication, as might be the case with small children, with students whose primary language is different from the teacher's, or when a skill is difficult to describe verbally. Time is another reason for using a demonstration when teaching. In the same amount of time, far more information can be conveyed in a single visual demonstration than through a verbal explanation. Finally, a demonstration reassures the student that the skill being described can actually be done. Seeing is believing.

Unfortunately for both the teacher and the learner, merely watching a skill performance doesn't guarantee the observer can then repeat the performance. However, several factors will help the learner get the most from a demonstration. First, the teacher must be reasonably certain the skill being demonstrated is appropriate for the abilities, condition, interests, motivation, and attitude of the learner. If the learner is convinced that there is no way she can perform the skill, she will be telling herself *I can't do that* while watching the demonstration. It doesn't matter how good the demonstration is if the learner believes she can't learn the skill. Learners sometimes need to be convinced that the skill they are about to see is well within their capabilities. With knowledge and practice, they too can perform the skill.

Paying close attention is a critical prerequisite for the learner to extract maximum information from the demonstration. If the learner can't remember the demonstration, he has little hope of performing the skill with any degree of accuracy. By observing closely, however, the learner can identify and differentiate the important features of the skill. With key features highlighted and the entire performance pictured in his mind, the learner can then attempt a reasonable repetition of what he just saw. A skillful teacher ensures that all eyes are on her before beginning and that the learners can see the key features of the skill being demonstrated. Good demonstrators do not talk during the demonstration, so the learner can completely concentrate on watching the skill. It's better to give verbal cues before or after the demonstration, not during (Wiese-Bjornstal and Weiss 1992).

There are several potential problems with demonstrations. Among the more common is that they may present too much information for learners to absorb in one viewing. To offset this, a teacher should demonstrate the skill several times. Repeated performances offer a redundancy of information that promotes learning. For most sport skills, two demonstrations are minimum, while three or four repetitions are even better.

Because it's important for the learner to revisit the information source while learning, a teacher should space demonstrations out over the course of the class. In this way, the learner can watch the skill, practice it, observe again, and practice some more. Students can then recheck the accuracy of the cues they are using. They will usually see things they missed the first time and gain additional insights after the initial information has been mastered.

Teachers must be confident that they are demonstrating the skills correctly. Learners can only reproduce what they see. Incorrect demonstrations impair learning by conveying errors and irrelevant information. The teacher should rehearse and practice the skills to be modeled before class to ensure correct technique. If the teacher feels that a student can perform the skill with greater accuracy, it might be better to ask the student to demonstrate. If this strategy is used, it's a good idea to let the student rehearse the skill under the teacher's supervision before it is demonstrated to the class or team. Videotapes or pictorial displays of the skill can also serve as effective demonstration devices. It doesn't really matter who demonstrates the movement as long as it's demonstrated correctly and skillfully.

Verbally identifying the important parts of the skill focuses the learners' attention on specific, critical components of the skill being demonstrated (McCullagh 1993). Before demonstrating a swimming stroke, for example, you may cue the students by saying, "Pay particular attention to how my hand enters the water—palm out—and how I extract it from the water—elbow leading." The students can then use these cues to recall the portions of the demonstration that need emphasis during skill practice.

Encouraging learners to verbally rehearse the information they receive is also effective for promoting retention and subsequent performance. Some motor skills have a particular sequence that can be verbally rehearsed, and learners should be encouraged to use this rehearsal strategy. For example, when teaching students to execute a proper groundstroke in tennis from a "set" position, the instructor may have the students say to themselves "pivot, step, swing" as they execute the skill. This verbal rehearsal is useful not only for rehearsing the proper mechanics but also for learning to smoothly sequence the skill performance.

Through careful planning, teachers can significantly enhance the benefits their students derive from in-class demonstrations and modeling. It will take some experimenting for teachers to find the right formula for their demonstrations. But the time invested in improving this important aspect of teaching sport and physical activity will make the learning experience more effective and rewarding.

Keys to Good Skill Demonstrations

- The learner must pay close attention.
- Perform multiple demonstrations of the skill.
- Perform demonstrations periodically during practice.

- Demonstrations must be technically correct and skillfully performed.
- Learners should be cued to important components of the skill.
- Verbal rehearsals should be used when appropriate.

Make Use of Props

Using props often makes a good demonstration great (figure 9.4). Props are helpful for keying on the critical element or elements of the skill being demonstrated and can often exaggerate the portion of the skill being emphasized. For example, sports that use a striking instrument often have a modified bat, club, or racket that emphasizes the correct grip or contact point. A learner observing or using this prop begins to understand the concept faster and better than if no prop is used. When demonstrating basketball shooting skills (a skill that I have modest success with most of the time), I use a junior basketball. It's much easier to put a smaller ball through the hoop than a larger one. Students never seem to notice that I've switched the ball, and the fact that the shot is successful proves that the demonstrated technique is sound.

Experienced teachers often have a closet full of props that they have either purchased or made. A

Figure 9.4 Props can help get students' attention during demonstrations.

little ingenuity on the part of the teacher can produce a remarkable learning device with little expense. The keys to using props effectively are knowing which element of the skill is most important for the learner using the prop, designing or selecting a prop that requires the learner to correctly repeat that skill element, and providing a prop that is both easy and fun for the student to use.

sport and activity skills. Being prepared, enthusiastic, and clear are hallmarks of effective communication, while useful demonstrations must be performed in a technically sound fashion and repeated often for a learner to find them useful. Teachers who carefully arrange and deliver information will see their efforts result in improved performances and greater satisfaction in their students.

Summary

Communication is a critical skill for good teaching. A teacher must communicate in ways that make it easy for the learner to understand, value, remember, and use the information presented. This chapter described three elements necessary for skillfully presenting information: organized information, verbal presentations, and modeling and demonstrating.

The amount, form, and order of the information students receive in a lesson significantly affects how much will be remembered and used by the learner. Providing lesson overviews, identifying the main points of a lesson, signaling transitions in the lesson activities, and closing the lesson with a review all help insure that the student leaves the lesson with the information the teacher intended to convey. In sport and physical activity instruction, teachers must not only be clear with their verbal explanations, but also find effective ways of demonstrating important

Discussion Questions

1. What makes for a great demonstration? As a teacher or coach, what are some techniques you might use to provide effective demonstrations?

2. Preparation is an important element in delivering a potent presentation. If you had to justify your instructional program, identify some strategies you might use to assemble information and prepare yourself to deliver a convincing presentation to a school board or board of directors.

3. As a learner, how does a teacher's enthusiasm influence you? As a teacher or coach, how will your enthusiasm for the subject, your students, and your students' learning be conveyed to them?

4. In your opinion, what makes a teacher or coach an effective communicator? How do you recognize one? How can you become one?

Chapter 10

Importance of Practice and Feedback

Practice, practice, practice—win!

— Babe Didrikson Zaharias

DISCOVERY

Sport and physical skills are learned through practice. No one learns to throw, catch, shoot, hit, or dribble a ball simply by listening to a lecture or watching a performance. Although listening and observing help someone understand how a skill is performed, it is in the hours and hours of practice that the skill becomes refined and mastered. With sufficient practice, a person can perform the skill effortlessly, efficiently, and automatically on demand and under pressure in a game or activity.

However, beginning teachers commonly believe that if they aren't talking or demonstrating and the students aren't watching and listening, they aren't doing their job and the students aren't learning. Beginning teachers feel obligated to tell the student all they know about the skill and the student's problem with that skill. The problem is then compounded if the student is put in a practice session that amounts to a single turn after waiting in an endless line or immersed in a large-sided game where only a few touch the ball while the rest watch. This sort of teaching actually interferes with and stunts learning.

In contrast, experienced teachers tell the student only what they feel the student can remember and what the student most needs to hear. They then get the student to practice, and they modify the practice activity as the student shows learning progress (Baker, Schempp, and Hardin 1998; Housner and Griffey 1985). Students learn more and learn more quickly when teachers keep information concise and let students practice right away. The teacher then provides performance feedback during and after practice. In this way, the teacher is teaching while the student is learning because feedback becomes instruction during practice. Good teachers promote learning and maximize student practice by giving feedback that stimulates achievement. In this chapter, the principles of good practice and effective feedback are presented.

Practice: The Road to Learning

Learning requires deliberate and focused practice. This is particularly true of sport and physical activity skills. Students must engage in activities that are appropriate for their skill and motivation levels. Appropriate practice of a great many correctly performed repetitions of the skill is the only road to competence and mastery (Siedentop and Tannehill 2000). There is no substitute for practice in the learning equation.

Time On Task

One important dimension of practice is time on task, the amount of time someone spends practicing a skill. Research has shown that the more time someone engages in a skill, the higher the rate of learning (Driskell, Willis, and Copper 1992). The critical variable in practice time is repetition rather than the actual number of minutes or hours devoted to practice (Siedentop and Tannehill 2000). However, it normally takes about 10,000 practice hours to develop true mastery of a skill (Ericsson, Krampe, and Tesch-Romer 1993).

When organizing practice time, teachers must control two practice killers: waiting and fatigue. In classes with multiple students, selecting and organizing practice activities that minimize students' waiting will increase the number of chances to perform the skill. Long lines in which one or two students perform the skill while six or more wait for their turns is a common practice killer. If lines are necessary, use more lines with fewer students. Better yet, strive to eliminate any wait time by using no lines. When practicing skills such as soccer or basketball dribbling; rolling, throwing, striking, or catching balls; or most any other skill, a clever teacher devises ways so that all students practice the activity at the same time. To the untrained eye, so much activity at one time may look chaotic, but there's a great deal of learning taking place in a room full of people practicing purposeful skills. Safety, however, needs to be considered. Having 25 students simultaneously practicing their javelin throws will provide the wrong kind of excitement in a class.

Student fatigue should be monitored closely because it often leads to poor form. It's better to rest and come back to the task refreshed than to accumulate hours of poorly performed practice. Boredom can also lead to ineffective practice, with the learner simply "going through the motions." And if, as the saying goes, "you play like you practice," ineffective practice will result in ineffective performances.

To combat this negative practice pest, students should practice frequently for short time periods, keeping both the challenge and the success high. Shorter, more frequent practice sessions are more effective for promoting learning than fewer longer sessions (Magill 2001). Making practice fun, stimulating, and successful not only offers a more enjoyable experience for the learner, but also allows her to practice with a maximum positive effect on performance.

A single lesson seldom provides ample practice opportunity for any skill or activity. Students must practice the newly learned skills outside of class and independent of the teacher if significant progress is going to be made in the quality of performance. It is therefore imperative that the teacher supply the students with adequate practice activities that can be completed at home or at a practice facility available to the learner. This is a common situation for physical education teachers. Given the limited amount of in-class time available for physical education students, devising and offering practice opportunities outside of class is a valuable way to extend the students' learning beyond the class time.

Some teachers find that journals or practice diaries let students log their practice time, identify practice goals, and monitor their progress in learning (figure 10.1). Appendix D provides an example of a take-home practice diary for basketball shooting. When suggesting drills and practice activities, select activities that

- can be done with the equipment and space available outside class,
- can be correctly completed with little supervision or teacher-directed feedback,
- specifically work on the concepts and ideas from the lesson, and
- are fun and challenging so that the motivation level remains high.

Figure 10.1 Teachers are effective when they make a record of practice activities, goals, and key points to address with their students.

Practice Correctly With Purpose

Another practice fundamental is performing the skill correctly. As basketball legend Larry Bird put it, "When I was young, I never wanted to leave the court until I got things exactly correct. I wanted to be a pro." Spending hours practicing a skill incorrectly will ingrain poor habits and ineffective technique. Therefore, monitor practice performances carefully to ensure that the skill is being performed correctly.

Simply repeating a skill performance time and again does not guarantee that the performance will improve. For example, most people spend years handwriting, but their writing doesn't get better. In many cases, it even deteriorates. The point is this: To merely repeat a performance is *not* practice. To perfect a skill performance, the student must practice with a purpose, or goal, with an eye toward improvement.

The teacher must identify the skill to be improved, as well as the specific components that need refining, and then structure the practice time to meet the goal. If this is a new skill or series of skills, the teacher can determine the important components to be practiced. If the student performs the skill regularly, it's best to analyze the performance to determine which skills or skill components need to be practiced (figure 10.2). This is an essential principle for competitive coaches. For example, a basketball coach can chart the shots taken in a game to determine which shots need the most practice. If the intention of practice is to improve game performance, practice and performance must be linked in meaningful ways. Too often, practices are structured based on traditions or the coach's beliefs of what athletes need rather than actual data from game performances. But according to legendary football coach George Halas, "Don't do anything in practice that you wouldn't do in the game."

Finally, establish ways to check whether the skill is indeed improving. Videotape pre- and post-practice sessions, set realistic practice goals to signal the successful end of a practice session (e.g., hit the target 4 out of 5 attempts and then stop), provide a task sheet for students to complete that identifies performance

© Mary Langenfeld Photo

Figure 10.2 Practice is a time to earnestly address concerns that coaches have after analyzing performance.

goals (e.g., make 5, 8, or 10 out of 10 and then move on to the next skill), tie practice achievement with a physical education grade, or monitor the skill performance quality during a performance or game. Without this feedback, students can't be sure they are actually improving, and they begin practicing as a matter of routine rather than with a purpose.

Variety Is the Spice of Life

Because motor skills are seldom performed under the same conditions every time, variation in practice conditions helps the learner adjust to performance conditions (Schmidt 1987). When practice conditions vary, students retain more of the information being learned because they see the same concepts applied in different situations. Variation in practice also prepares the learner for variation in the performance environment. For example, sport skills are most often performed under competitive circumstances. There is a big difference between casually practicing soccer dribbling alone on a field and moving the ball downfield with minutes left in a championship game against talented opponents and the stands filled with fans rooting against you. A player who has practiced dribbling under competitive and noisy conditions is better prepared to handle the ball when it most counts.

When planning a practice schedule, consider providing several activities that let the learner practice the skill correctly under a variety of performance-like conditions. This not only provides a better learning environment, but it can also make the practice more enjoyable. The story "Swedish Candy" gives an example of such a practice environment. For physical education teachers introducing new skills to their students, a variety of practice activities makes it more likely that the students will learn and find an activity they enjoy. If students or players enjoy what they are doing, not only will they practice with greater intensity, but they are also inclined to practice more often. When once asked about the boredom of swimming lap after lap, Olympic champion Tracy Caulkins replied "I know a lot of people think it's monotonous, down the black lines over and over, but it's not if you're enjoying what you're doing. I love to swim and I love to train."

If there are certain constants (i.e., things that don't change) in the performance environment, then they shouldn't vary in the practice environment, either. In the previous soccer dribbling example, there would be little value in practicing dribbling barefoot or with different sized soccer balls. Those are condition variations that the player would never see in a game.

Swedish Candy

Peter Mattsson

When Peter Mattsson, the head coach of the Swedish National Golf team, organizes his annual training camp, one of the most important items on the equipment list is a large supply of candy. Most coaches are not inclined to make candy an indispensable part of a training camp, but for his athletes, it provides a motivation that rivals most any trophy or championship. Several team members are on college golf scholarships in the United States. Every November, when campuses across the United States close for the Thanksgiving holiday, Peter uses this opportunity to convene the team for an intensive four-day training session. The annual "Turkey Camp," as it's now called, has become an opportunity for the players to work on specific skills related to their golf performance.

To better link practice with performance, the camp's activities are all set in a competitive environment, and the reward for the player doing the best in each practice activity is a package of Swedish candy. Regardless of whether the players are working on improving their putting technique, trajectory control, pitching skills, or even knowledge of rules, those having the best results are rewarded with candy that Peter and his coaches bring from Sweden for the occasion.

The dozen or so players in camp compete intensely for this valued (but inexpensive) prize. As they practice, they tease and taunt one another about who will win the candy and how good "their" candy

(continued)

(continued)

is going to taste. At times, these longtime friends and highly competitive athletes seem bent on beating each other's brains out. Gamesmanship and earnest effort go hand in hand as each athlete aspires to turn in the best practice performance. It would be unusual to see players practicing harder than these talented individuals, many of whom are college tournament champions and all of whom are international-caliber players. Regardless of how intense the competition becomes, however, after the practice activity ends and the winner claims the prize, he or she immediately shares the candy with the other team members so that everyone enjoys a taste of "home."

—Peter Mattsson, head coach, Swedish National Golf team

Amount of Practice

An often asked question is how much practice is needed to learn a skill. Unfortunately, there are no absolute answers to this question, but there are several ways to determine the length of practice. One of the easiest and most efficient is goal setting. In goal setting, some predetermined criterion is selected, and the learner practices until the goal is achieved. Ability, motivation, and current skill level must all be considered. For example, when learning a badminton serve, a student may practice the skill until he places 10 out of 10 serves in the service court. If the student is an advanced player, the goal might be to hit a small target placed within the service court 10 out of 10 times.

It's important for the practice criteria to be set appropriately so that the learners are challenged but can find success for their efforts. Expectations that are too high discourage learners from continuing and may even promote inappropriate performance mechanics as the learner strives for almost unobtainable results. As practice and learning continue, the instructor and student should review practice goals and set new goals when previous ones are easily attained. Reviewing practice goals also helps determine when it's time to move on to new skills.

Length of Practice

A second question to be addressed by the student and teacher is how long a practice session should last. Once again, no clear evidence identifies the precise length or number of practice sessions. The skill level, motivation, and physical ability of the learner must again be considered, as well as the complexity of the skill. One factor that may help determine a practice schedule is fatigue. With many physical skills, repeated performance leads to the learner becoming tired. As the learner becomes increasingly fatigued, in most cases the quality of the performance begins to deteriorate. It does little good to practice a deteriorating performance.

A teacher and student may therefore want to consider distributing the practice. That is, schedule more practice sessions but for limited amounts of time. Instead of practicing the swimming breaststroke for 60 minutes one day, perhaps 20 minutes per day for three days may prove more efficient for the learner. Also, if physical conditioning is part of the practice session, the student should practice the skills first and then complete the conditioning workout so that she is fresh and not fatigued when practicing.

Mental Practice

No physical skill can be learned without actually performing the mechanics of the skill. But another form of practice can assist the learning process. Mental rehearsal has been associated with increased learning in the practice phase of motor skill acquisition and therefore should be considered by the teacher and learner. Mental rehearsal, or mental practice, involves the student imagining the actual skill performance. Research in motor learning has found this technique effective for learning, performing, and retaining motor skills (Magill 2001).

Mental practice requires students to focus completely on the correct performance and rehearse it in their minds before they practice it (figure 10.3). The student actually "sees" herself performing the skill correctly and successfully. A gymnast, for example, might picture himself performing a flawless routine and then attempt to recreate that image in practice. Imagining the correct performance immediately after practice is also effective. In addition, mental rehearsal is useful when actual physical practice isn't possible because of time constraints, inclement weather, lack of equipment, or injury. When using this technique, it is imperative that the students imagine performing the skill perfectly with highly

Figure 10.3 Sport psychologist Bob Rotella (right) works with athletes on mental imagery. He is shown here at the Masters golf tournament in Augusta, Georgia, in 1996.

desirable outcomes. Seeing themselves as successful performers is critical for becoming successful performers.

Practice Principles
- To master a skill, a student must practice.
- Set a goal for each practice session.
- To learn a skill correctly, it must be practiced correctly.
- Performance conditions change; therefore, vary practice activities and conditions.
- Fatigue reduces practice effectiveness. Instruct students to practice often in short time periods.
- Mentally rehearsing skill performances before and after practice improves performance.
- Suggest activities for your students to practice after the lesson to reinforce learning.

Providing Effective Feedback

Feedback is the response teachers give to students about the quality and correctness of their skill performances. Most often, teachers give feedback during or immediately after the practice performance. Providing feedback doesn't ensure student learning, but it can help. A learner's ability plays a big factor in acquiring a skill. Time on task and practice conditions also influence learning (Schmidt 1987). But feedback during student practice can make the learning process more effective—especially if the

teacher follows the principles of effective feedback (Magill 2001).

Although feedback holds the potential for increasing learning, it is not always necessary. Learning can occur without feedback, and feedback can even inhibit student learning if it's mistimed or inappropriate for the learner. A teacher must therefore give careful attention to the role of feedback in their students' learning and development.

Types of Feedback

Feedback comes in two forms: knowledge of technique and knowledge of results. As the names imply, knowledge of technique refers to the information the performer receives regarding performance mechanics (e.g., was the grip appropriate on that swing?), whereas knowledge of results refers to performance outcomes (e.g., did the ball go where it was supposed to?). A teacher is most helpful for providing technical knowledge because students can usually see the results for themselves. From proper technique can come improved results. Good results can sometimes come from poor technique but not with any degree of consistency. Improvement in the quality and quantity of results, therefore, requires students to gain knowledge of proper skill technique through appropriate feedback.

Purpose of Feedback

The importance of feedback during practice is threefold (Magill 2001). First, feedback gives the learner the necessary information to repeat correct portions of the performance. Understanding what was done correctly is essential reinforcement for the learner. If you tell a student what he's doing correctly, he'll likely do it again. Second, feedback provides the learner with the information needed to correct errors in the performance. Repeated errors in a performance must be corrected before they become ingrained. Third, feedback is a necessary ingredient in learner motivation (figure 10.4).

If They Got It Right, Let Them Know

People learn more quickly when they experience success (Brophy and Good 1986). Teachers of physical skills must therefore identify what their students are doing correctly in their performances. This is particularly important in the early stages of learning when the results of the performances may be inconsistent. For example, a student may be using acceptable technique in putting a golf ball but has

Figure 10.4 It takes a team. Golfer Carl Pettersson prepares for the final round of the 2002 British Open under the watchful eyes of his caddy, his coach, and his father. Feedback from supportive people can be a powerful motivator for students and athletes.

not repeated the skill often enough to develop the necessary "feel" for hitting the target consistently.

Learners may get discouraged if they continually see themselves falling short of the target or finishing last. They are likely to alter correct mechanics in the search for better results. Unless a teacher identifies and reinforces the performance aspects being done correctly, they aren't likely to be repeated by the learner (Siedentop and Tannehill 2000). This concept is often lost on beginning teachers. Catch students doing something correctly, and let them know it.

Perfecting the Performance

The verbal or visual information a learner receives after performing allows her to understand how closely her current performance matches a technically correct, or ideal, performance. The student and teacher must therefore have a clear conception of the ideal performance so the teacher can supply information specific to the desired movement pattern (Magill 2001). Random or disconnected information is difficult, if not impossible, for the student to understand and apply. For example, if you instruct a student in the proper knee lift and leg drive during a run, don't offer feedback about the arm swing. The feedback should remain focused on the topic at hand. If you detect errors, make a note of it and correct them with additional instruction later. Don't abandon the original information until the student has a firm grasp of it. Once the student masters the leg drive and knee lift, then work on the arm swing if needed.

Motivation Through Feedback

The best feedback motivates learners to do better. It's important for students to believe they can learn and to see that they are making progress. A positive, nurturing environment is more conducive to learning than a critical, negative one (figure 10.5). All too often, teachers focus on the negative aspects of performance and seldom celebrate performance successes. They get so focused on the performance that they forget the person.

For beginning learners especially, knowing that they're doing at least some portions of the performance correctly justifies their continued efforts and boosts their self-confidence. The relationship between the teacher and learner is critical here. At times, the teacher must act as a cheerleader or motivator. For teachers who see their success in the achievements of their students, this is easy. Find something your student is doing well and let him know it. Identifying only the incorrect convinces the learner, particularly the beginner, that he is largely incompetent and unable to execute the sport skills or activity being learned.

Dr. Rod Thorpe of the University of Loughborough in England once told me "After 14 years of teaching tennis, I woke up one morning and realized that I hadn't been teaching tennis at all. Rather, I had spent the last 14 years convincing people that they *couldn't* play tennis. I then realized it was time to make a change." Even when given with good intentions, negative feedback has limited value for a learner, particularly a beginner. Dr. Thorpe was insightful and honest enough to recognize this. He changed and, in doing so, has changed the way

© JimWestPhoto

Figure 10.5 Teachers should provide positive support for their students.

many people now learn sport skills (Griffin, Mitchell, and Oslin 1997).

Effective Feedback

Feedback should be directed at a specific aspect of a movement under the control of the learner. Identifying one or two aspects of a skill performance lets a learner focus on refining skills in accordance with proper technique. To focus a practice, expert teachers locate the skill components that will make the biggest difference in the learner's performance if refined or corrected. For example, tennis instructors will first look at a student's grip. Regardless of what else is or isn't being performed correctly, if a player has an improper grip, it's unlikely she'll effectively stroke the ball.

Specific feedback is the best feedback. In other words, teachers should identify the specific components accounting for the achievement, thereby reinforcing the learning. Telling a student "Your thumb was exactly where it needed to be throughout the entire swing" is far more helpful than the traditional "Good swing." In this way, students come to understand the fundamental elements of the skills and concepts they are learning. They begin to attribute mastery of the skill to proper performance of the sequential skill components. Reinforcing the particulars of the achievement helps students repeat the skill again in its proper form.

Feedback is not a time for lengthy explanations but rather for brief comments on key features of the performance. Feedback should therefore consist of short, specific comments directed at performance improvements (Magill 2001). Comments such as "Good job," "Try harder," or "Well done" pale in comparison to "Now you're using a follow-through," "Let your left foot lead the way," or "Your shoulders were square that time."

Error-Focused Versus Success-Oriented Practice

One of the most disheartening experiences I've had in sport occurred one day when I stopped to watch a youth league baseball practice. The coach, one of the boys' fathers, hit balls to the players, who were supposed to field the ball and throw it back to the coach. The little boy in right field, who looked to be all of eight years old, battled vainly to catch the fly balls hit to him. But try as he might, he could find no way to get his glove anywhere near the ball as it fell to earth. He scampered after each missed ball and returned it quickly. After several attempts, and with

dejection and embarrassment clearly on the boy's face, the coach yelled out to him "You miss one more and you run laps! Keep your eye on the ball and catch it!" The little boy doubled his efforts as his eyes went skyward, and he scurried around where he thought the ball would fall, but his final attempt was no more successful than the previous ones. "Two laps and then you sit on the bench until you can get your head into this game!" came the command from the coach. The little boy began to run the outskirts of the field. Tears were rolling down his cheeks as he went by.

Standing over a struggling learner and berating a poor performance or continually pointing out mistakes is more likely to drive the person away from the activity than inspire a better result. It's unlikely that dwelling on the negative, especially for a beginner, will promote learning. For an expert performer, someone who has to a large degree mastered a series of skills, identifying performance errors is critical for improving performance. But for beginners or intermediate participants, identifying only the errors in a performance is more likely to reinforce the belief that they cannot, and perhaps never will, learn the skill. Practice then becomes a proving ground for failure rather than an opportunity to learn and improve.

Most teachers don't intend to be critical of their students and often don't realize they are. When analyzing a student's performance, however, it's the errors that stand out to an instructor. The analysis then becomes error-focused. In an effort to be helpful, the instructor identifies the errors and offers ways to correct them. This sort of feedback is known as error-centered practice. The instructional episode for the student consists of having mistakes continually identified and made public by the teacher.

In success-oriented practice, the teacher looks for the skill components being properly performed. Because it's easier to identify mistakes in a performance, it can sometimes be challenging to see what is being done correctly—particularly when the performance is largely inadequate, as often happens with beginners. However, for an instructor who has identified a skill's key points, the search for any one of these components being properly performed should be the focal point for feedback. Although a successful performance may be a long way off, knowing that they've gotten at least one part of the skill correct may reassure learners that with practice they can master the other components.

An instructor cannot, however, ignore repeated performance errors if the student is to learn. Practicing errors only ingrains them and impedes improvement. In fact, research supports the notion that feedback based on performance errors is more beneficial and leads to better learning than feedback based on correct movements (Magill 2001). Teachers must therefore find a way to correct their students' errors. However, correcting errors doesn't necessarily mean telling students what they're doing wrong.

In success-oriented practice, teachers tell students what they're doing correctly and what they need to do correctly. Rather than identifying a student's errors, expert teachers quickly point out the properly performed movements, compliment the student on successful performance, and offer suggestions to improve the performance even more (Baker, Schempp, and Hardin 1998). This technique has been labeled "reteaching." In other words, rather than taking on the task of "fixing faults in the student," these teachers celebrated the success shown in practice and then "retaught" the skill to find the next success. One small success in the skill built to the next.

Although the suggestions for improvement are based on performance errors, students in expert teachers' classes aren't made to feel they are committing mistakes. Rather, students get a sense of refining, learning, and improving. As an example, a teacher might say "Don't worry about not getting the golf ball in the air. That will come. You held the proper grip throughout your entire swing. We're working on the grip, and you did it right! Next, let me see you touch your right elbow to your right hip to start your downswing." In this sequence, the student knows he has done something right and what he needs to do to perform even better. The emphasis is on the student's success, not on detailing his mistakes and shortcomings.

However, an error-centered practice is appropriate at times, but these times are rare. Expert or highly proficient performers sometimes feel like something "just isn't right," and they need a skilled and objective eye to identify the problem. Once identified, the athlete can often work through the problem or can solicit advice from a coach. But for most teachers and coaches, making practice success-oriented will lead to both successful learning and a learning environment characterized by success. John Wooden, whose teams won 10 NCAA basketball championships, used far more praise with his players in practice than he ever did criticism (Tharp and Gallimore 1976).

Make It Count

Effective feedback has particular qualities that distinguish it from ineffective feedback (Brophy and Good 1986). To make your feedback count, base it on these characteristics. Effective feedback is delivered selectively. It focuses on a specific achievement. It is not doled out simply because an attempt was made but rather because the student demonstrated a detectable improvement over previous performances.

A teacher doesn't have to comment after every single performance by the learner. Evidence suggests that giving feedback less than 100% of the time isn't detrimental to learning motor skills (Magill 2001). In fact, providing more meaningful feedback every couple of tries that is specific to what's being learned is more beneficial than having students hear "Good job" or "That looked good" after every attempt they make.

Effective feedback shows spontaneity, variety, and other signs of credibility (Brophy and Good 1986). Students have to believe a teacher means what she says if the teacher intends to make a difference in the life of the students. Tired clichés and 101 ways of saying "good job" do little for students. Good teachers recognize true achievement. They are sophisticated enough to know why one skill performance is better or worse than another, and they help students learn by sharing this information in the form of feedback. Good teachers do not feel compelled to comment every time a student performs a skill. Rather, they recognize real progress and reinforce it when they see it.

Finally, effective feedback provides information regarding the value of the achievement. Students need to know why they are learning what they are learning. Giving them feedback about why their achievement is valuable provides that information. This type of feedback tells the students they have learned something significant that will help them enjoy the sport or physical activity all the more. "You dribble with that much control in a game, and no one will get the ball away from you" is an example of feedback that reveals the value of a learned skill and improved performance.

Effective Feedback

- Deliver feedback selectively.
- Be specific to what is being learned.
- Be spontaneous.
- Recognize the significance of the achievement.

Training Aids

Purposeful practice intends to refine a skill performance, so it must focus on particular and specific components of a skill. For example, a track athlete might work on body position in the starting block, with a focus on back alignment, foot placement, and weight distribution. He would not attempt to also work on hip rotation, stride length, or arm swing during the run. That would be too much to remember, and the practice would be largely ineffective. Because specific skill components are targeted during practice, learners and teachers often find it useful to incorporate a learning prop, or training aid, in the practice routine.

Training aids may be as simple as a suspended tire used as a target when practicing a forward pass in football or as sophisticated as an entire computer system simulating virtual reality for a pitcher in baseball or cricket. Commercially produced training aids, such as video cameras, ball machines, or computerized devices designed to assist learning, are becoming increasingly popular for practice sessions. However, many teachers and coaches make their own. For example, clever physical education teachers make targets, striking implements, modified balls, boundary markers, swing devices, or just about anything else that will help their students learn. Wander into the equipment room of any experienced coach and you're likely to find some device she invented to help her players practice.

Props can be effective for some learners and should therefore be considered. But training aids cannot take the place of sound instruction and purposeful, sustained practice. They can only assist in learning, not produce it. Because of their potential benefits, however, training aids should be considered when developing practice activities.

Summary

Learning sport and physical activity skills is largely dependent on the quality and quantity of practice.

Clear explanations and motivated students are certainly important ingredients for learning a skill, but skills are mastered in practice. It takes hours of deliberate practice to learn a skill that can be correctly repeated in varying conditions. To learn a skill correctly, students must practice with a goal in mind and use proper form. Under most circumstances, it's difficult for a student to receive enough practice time in a single lesson to thoroughly learn the skill. It is therefore suggested that teachers recommend activities for students to practice outside of class.

Purposeful, positive feedback increases the efficiency and effectiveness of the practice session. Feedback should be seen as an opportunity to reinforce learning rather than a time to identify only performance mistakes. Feedback should be spontaneous, periodic, and given to the student with the practice goal in mind. Finally, teachers who use feedback to recognize a student's achievement and then identify the significance of that achievement are more likely to have students leaving class with newly gained knowledge and feeling good about what they have learned.

Discussion Questions

1. What, in your opinion, makes a practice successful? Recall practice experiences that have been successful for you or others. How would you structure practices to maximize the benefits for your students or players?

2. Why are practice goals so important?

3. Discuss using mental rehearsal, or imagery, with students or athletes who have problems with (a) motivation, (b) confidence, and (c) fear of failure or success.

4. Identify the characteristics of effective feedback and come up with examples of feedback statements you might use to help your students learn.

Chapter 11

Teaching Strategies

Knowing is a process, not a product.

— Jerome Bruner

DISCOVERY

Many approaches are available for creating learning environments and providing effective instruction. Different and tested patterns of instruction offer teachers and students a stimulating assortment of teaching styles. These instructional patterns are called teaching models, or instructional strategies. Metzler defines a teaching model as a distinctive set of teaching patterns that "ties together theory, planning, classroom management, teaching and learning processes and assessment" (2000, xxiv). An instructional strategy, or style, is usually preselected by the teacher, but experienced teachers often alter teaching strategies mid-class. An instructional strategy focuses on the content presentation and student involvement with that content.

Because there are many styles of "good teaching," teachers should acquire, refine, and develop several strategies to offer variety in their teaching as well as adjust to different learners, content, and teaching environments. Teachers should select strategies based on the content they intend to teach; the needs, motivations, and abilities of the learners; and their own level of skill and comfort with the teaching technique. A teacher shouldn't be afraid to experiment with different strategies or even invent new ones. Developing and trying new strategies keep a teacher challenged and fresh; it's all too easy to slip into repetitive patterns of teaching.

Many different models of teaching have been developed, and various authors and teachers have designed and described numerous strategies for teaching sport and physical activity (Mosston and Ashworth 2002; Metzler 2000). To provide you with popular instructional options, the following six teaching strategies are described in this chapter. These strategies were chosen to represent a range of instructional styles, but this list is by no means exhaustive.

Look, listen, and learn: A traditional approach

The repairman: Diagnostic/prescriptive teaching

Task cards and contracts: The learner takes responsibility

Guided discovery and problem solving: Thinking your way to success

Experiential learning: Your problem, your solution

Critical pedagogy: Learning as social change

Look, Listen, and Learn: A Traditional Approach

Your first response when attempting to learn something new is to look and listen. In the opinion of Olympic gold medalist Jean-Claude Killy, "The best and fastest way to learn a sport is to watch and imitate a champion." By watching someone else perform the skill, you get an idea of how it's done. If the performer explains his performance, you listen intently for the critical insights that will lead to a smooth, repetitive, and successful performance of your own. If Michael Jordan were to offer a shooting clinic, few eyes and ears would focus on anything but Mr. Jordan.

Many of the motor skills you currently possess were learned precisely this way. This method of instruction fits well with the phases of motor learning described in chapter 4, and is particularly effective for providing information in a quick, efficient manner. The most common of all teaching strategies can be summed up as look, listen, and learn. With a teacher providing a demonstration and explanation, the student looks and listens to learn.

Step One: Look

Using this teaching style, a teacher must focus on three critical elements in both preparation and in-struction. The first is the skill demonstrations (look). If a teacher isn't proficient at the skill to be demonstrated, she must practice until she can competently demonstrate the skill to her students. It's not critical that the teacher perform the skill with such expertise that the performance results in a successful attempt; the main goal is to let the students observe the important sequential components of the skill. For example, in demonstrating a basketball shot, it's more important that students observe the proper release so that backspin is generated. A poor technique can result in a successful shot, but the teacher is attempting to teach proper technique, so that is what needs demonstrating. Chapter 9 offers additional suggestions for effective instructional demonstrations.

If the teacher is unable to demonstrate proper technique, other alternatives are available and sometimes even preferred. Perhaps a student in the group can perform the skill at a high level and may be willing to demonstrate the skill for the benefit of the other students. Discussing the demonstration before class with this student is usually a good idea so the student knows what elements of the performance the teacher will emphasize. Videotape or photographs may also serve as a good substitute for a demonstration. Having beginning players observe the forehand of Martina Hingis, perhaps even in slow motion, is a wonderful way to show the proper movement sequences of a tennis forehand. The idea is to provide a correct model so students get a clear, accurate picture of the performance they will attempt to imitate.

Step Two: Listen

The second critical element in this teaching style is the teacher's explanation of the skill or concept to be learned. Clear and concise are the keys to successful explanations. The fewer elements of the skill explained, the more likely the student will remember the elements covered. A lengthy biomechanical analysis of a football pass emphasizing stepping in opposition, rotational torque of the trunk, and proper shoulder/target alignment will have less chance of being recalled by a beginning learner than "Grab the laces with your finger tips, and then push your fingers toward the ground as you release the ball. Try it."

The cues for successful performance should be few but important. Therefore, a teacher needs to think carefully about what she will say and the length of time needed to say it. One common mistake made by beginning teachers is overexplaining the skill to the point that learners lose interest, become convinced the skill is so complicated that they will never learn it, or become so confused they no longer know what is important and what is secondary in performing the skill. Consider carefully the words needed to make your point, and use no more than necessary.

Step Three: Learn

Looking and listening give students the information necessary to perform a skill, but they will not actually learn the skill without practice. Therefore, in the third and final element of this teaching strategy, teachers provide practice activities that best promote student learning. Most often, this refers to drills performed individually or in small groups. The best drills allow for maximum participation by each student in conditions that promote proper technique. Chapter 10 highlights some of the critical elements of effective practice.

Look, listen, and learn can follow the traditional path of an instructional episode in which a teacher introduces a skill with an explanation, follows the explanation with several demonstrations, and then allows the students to practice the skill. However, look, listen, and learn can also follow a cycle in class. For example, the teacher briefly explains the key components of the long jump before giving several demonstrations; then the students are given time to practice, with the teacher giving feedback on the main points covered in the explanation. After a few minutes of practice, the teacher gives a second demonstration of the jump, with additional information he believes will be helpful to the students, followed by more practice. In this way, the student isn't inundated with all the information at once, and seeing demonstrations repeated throughout a class is often more effective than seeing several performances in a single demonstration at the beginning of class.

The Repairman: Diagnostic/Prescriptive Teaching

An efficient, powerful tennis serve, a gracefully coordinated forward roll, and a consistently accurate basketball jump shot are all examples of skills that people want to learn and teachers attempt to teach. As learning progresses in physical skills, two teaching abilities become strategically important:

analyzing performance errors and helping students correct those errors. Put another way, teachers must be able to diagnose performance errors and provide prescriptions for remedying the deficiencies. Some teachers view their primary duties much like a repairman: find the faulty part and fix it (McCullick, Schempp, and Cumings 1999). This teaching strategy has become so common in sport and physical activity instruction that one well-known instructor even titled his book *Faults and Fixes* (Leadbetter et al. 1996).

Make the Diagnosis

A teacher must be able to adequately analyze a performed skill to reinforce the properly executed aspects and correct any deficiencies. Observation is the most common form of information gathering for diagnosis—simply watching your students perform the skill. Some skills are performed at such a rapid rate (e.g., baseball swing, springboard diving, pole vaulting) that videotape recordings using slow motion and stop action are necessary to get an accurate analysis of the performance. For instructional purposes, the teacher must focus on the skill components being taught. For example, if the teacher detailed a proper grip in an earlier instructional phase, the lesson must then concentrate on the proper execution of the grip during performance. Analyzing additional components adds more information to the learning mix before the first lessons are fully learned.

In large classes, it can be difficult, or perhaps even impossible, to adequately diagnose the performance problems of all the students. In such circumstances, experienced teachers will often scan the learning environment to determine the most prevalent problem among the students. A physical education teacher observing several dozen students practicing an overhand throw may notice that many of the students aren't stepping properly when delivering the ball. This observation may then provide the basis for identifying a problem common to a majority of the students.

Sometimes a teacher wants to observe a performance first before deciding what to teach the student or students. During the initial observation, the teacher identifies the errors consistently being made. Good teachers can identify the most significant flaws, while less experienced teachers often identify only the symptoms resulting from larger problems. Once the most critical problems have been detected, the teacher then decides which error is in greatest need of correction. Normally, this means identifying the error that, once corrected, will lead to the greatest performance improvement for the student.

After identifying the strengths and weaknesses of a student's performance, the next phase is relaying that information to the student along with recommendations for reinforcing or remediating the skill components being learned. In other words, the teacher needs to write a prescription to cure the performance ailment. Skillful teachers present the results of their diagnoses in positive rather than negative terms. For example, hearing "You'll see big improvements in your performance if we work on your ready position and follow-through" sets a more positive learning agenda for the student than hearing "Your ready position and follow-through are dreadful."

Sometimes teachers believe a student doesn't need to know all the problems with her performance, she just needs to know how to make it better. At times like these, a teacher may decide to withhold some or even all of his diagnostic conclusions. He simply gives the student the necessary prescription. For example, "If you turn your shoulder more, you'll find you can get more power behind that throw" may get the job done without a long list of all the performance deficiencies that are robbing the student of power in her throw. The important point is that the diagnosis identifies the information that will be of greatest value for improving the student's performance. The diagnostic information, therefore, becomes the basis for constructing the lesson's learning objectives.

Write the Prescription

With the lesson goals identified, the next step is providing the student with information and activities that will fix the performance faults and lead to improved performance. It's important to stay focused on the lesson goals until the performance faults are cured and new habits ingrained. One or two correct performances do not ensure that the performance fault is gone—it may have just taken a temporary vacation while the student was under a teacher's watchful eye. To make sure that a new habit is ingrained and the fault is gone for good, the teacher should present several prescriptions, or practice activities, and situations for the student. Altering the performance conditions and requirements of a sport skill helps ensure that a correct movement has become a relatively permanent change in the learner's performance pattern. Periodic evaluation of progress toward the learning objective may also prove helpful as the lesson moves along.

Drills that emphasize proper execution in a practice setting are the most common form of prescription. Teaching aids such as weighted clubs, spotting belts, smaller targets or goals at which to aim, and modified balls are also methods by which a skillful teacher can remedy or reinforce proper skill execution. Let the student leave the lesson with several activities that may be performed at home. Mastering the proper sequence and movement of a sport skill seldom occurs in the practice of a single lesson. Homework helps.

Golf instructors commonly use the diagnostic/ prescriptive teaching strategy by first observing a student hit golf balls (McCullick, Schempp, and Cumings 1999). The observation period is used to identify areas of strength and weakness in the golfer's swing. During this time, the teacher might also ask questions to assess the student's background, motivation, and goals. After collecting and analyzing this information, the teacher devises a prescription in the form of information and drills for the student to perform. The teacher might use videotape to share the diagnosis with the student or use training aids such as a weighted club, swing devices, or targets as part of the prescription. The teacher normally closes the lesson by giving the student several prescriptive activities to work on at home. This teaching style works equally well for teachers and coaches of other sports.

Task Cards and Contracts: The Learner Takes Responsibility

The more ways a learner receives information, the more likely he will retain the messages of the lesson. Task cards and contracts offer yet another method of conveying information (Mosston and Ashworth 2002). The subtle shift in these approaches lies in moving the responsibility for learning from the teacher to the student. Task cards and contracts hold the learner responsible for acquiring the pertinent information, selecting the practice activities, and completing the activities.

For both task cards and contracts, information is presented to the learner—usually in written form— and the learner chooses what she wants to read or learn and subsequently practice. The student is given information pertinent to proper skill performance or concept application, along with suggestions for practice. Most task cards and contracts also include a way for the student to record the amount of practice in the particular skills and her success rate at performing the skills.

Task Cards

Task cards provide progressive, individually paced information for the learners. They offer a degree of freedom for both the teacher and the student. The teacher is no longer required to explain the details of a skill to be learned, provide constant suggestions for practice activities, or monitor progress. Being free of these responsibilities allows the teacher to circulate in the learning environment and provide individualized feedback to students. The student selects the activities he deems appropriate for his skill level, revisits information or activities as necessary, chooses the appropriate time to increase the challenge, and monitors his own progress. Another advantage of task cards is that the student can take them home or to a practice area and continue his learning without being directly dependent on the teacher. A sample task card can be found in appendix E.

Contracts

Contracts are written agreements signed by the learner and the teacher that specify what is to be learned, how, and to what level of proficiency. In signing a learning contract, the student agrees to fulfill the specified requirements within a certain time period. A contract may be completed during a planned lesson, a series of lessons, outside of class, or any combination thereof. Planning a contract is similar to planning any other instructional activity.

The first items to be decided and incorporated into the written contract are the learning objectives. In other words, what specifically will the student have learned when this contract is fulfilled? The next items to be written into the contract are the learning activities. The clearer and more specific the objectives, the easier it is to select appropriate learning activities. These activities often include both information gathering activities (e.g., viewing videos, observing demonstrations, seeking explanations, reading) and practice activities (e.g., drills, game-like activities). At this point, the teacher needs to ensure that adequate resources are available for the student to successfully complete the contract. The final element of the contract is the terms of completion. What must the student do to demonstrate that she has met the learning objectives and mastered the identified skills or knowledge pertaining to the contract? For example, being able to make 35 out of 50 tennis serves, run a mile in less than nine minutes, or successfully compete in a citywide softball tournament may all demonstrate attainment of a contract's learning goals. To maintain motivation and make sure that timely progress is being made in fulfilling a learning contract, a timetable of periodic checks is suggested so that progress can be monitored by the student and teacher.

Learning contracts work particularly well with motivated learners or students who learn better independently. Contracts may be a primary teaching style for a class, or they may prove to be effective supplements mixed with other teaching styles. Perhaps students can use contracts to learn certain skills during a sport unit while the teacher uses other instructional styles for other skills.

The contract method of teaching has several advantages. Contracts permit a degree of flexibility for both the student and teacher in terms of learning goals, resources, time schedules, and location of instruction (contracts can be completed anywhere). Contracts also allow students to play an active role in decisions affecting their learning. Students identify activities they find particularly appealing and then take responsibility for learning them. Therefore, students assume a major role in planning their learning. A disadvantage, however, is that students with little practice in planning their instruction and learning may need assistance to successfully complete the contract. Finally, contracts provide another viable option for teaching and learning, and the more tools available for teachers and students, the greater the chance of having the right tool for promoting student learning. Appendix F, appendix G, and appendix H provide examples of, respectively, a contract, a course evaluation sheet that specifies how the contract fits into the overall course picture, and an independent skill assignment sheet that is part of the requirements necessary to meet the terms of the contract.

Guided Discovery and Problem Solving: Thinking Your Way to Success

Students learning through guided discovery and problem solving hold not only part of the responsibility for learning but also part of the responsibility for instruction. In these techniques, students are presented with a series of problems for which they either discover a predetermined solution (guided discovery) or devise an appropriate solution to the problem at hand (problem solving). In both guided discovery and problem solving instructional strategies, the teacher selects the content and skills to be learned and designs a series of tasks or experiences to lead learners in acquiring, improving, or applying the selected skills and concepts. The teacher relies heavily on the use of questions to present the problems and challenge the students in this approach.

The difference between the two styles is that in guided discovery, the teacher has a predetermined solution or performance conception in mind, whereas in the problem solving approach, the students determine the appropriateness of the final outcome. If the solution solves the problem to the students' satisfaction, then learning has occurred. The advantage of both models resides in the dependence of the teacher on the students and the students on themselves. Requiring students to take responsibility for and direct their learning takes learning out of the repetition and memorization mode and into an approach that requires thinking and decision making on the part of the students. Students schooled in these approaches are thus able to figure out learning problems without the aid of a teacher and become more self-sufficient learners.

Guided Discovery

When using this approach, the teacher first determines the knowledge she intends the students to learn. Second, a problem or series of problems is structured and posed to the students so that in solving these problems, they make the intended discovery. The closer to "real world" situations that the teacher can bring the problem set, the more relevance and meaning the learning will have for the students. Third, the teacher must assemble the resources necessary for the students to successfully solve the problems. The final step requires the students and teacher to discuss both the process leading to the discovery and the discovered knowledge itself.

As an example, a physical education teacher wants her students to learn that a healthy lifestyle requires a balance of diet and exercise. First, the teacher poses a series of nutritional and exercise problems. She then ensures that the students have the necessary resources to solve these problems. One problem may be to design a practical daily diet of no more than 2,500 calories, with the calories coming from the necessary nutritional sources. Students will need access to caloric and nutritional guides so appropriate foods and serving sizes can be selected. A second problem might require the students to structure their daily physical activities so that they consume 2,500 calories. Again, appro-

priate information and even perhaps exercise equipment must be supplied. Whether the teacher will require the students to test their potential solutions is another matter. When students have finished the activity, a discussion is held about the problem solving process as well as the "discovery" of the need for a balance of diet and exercise in daily life. This discussion is an important component of guided discovery because students need to articulate and share their discoveries. At the same time, teachers should reinforce and supplement the discovered knowledge as well as comment on the process used in discovery.

Problem Solving

Learning is much more than the memorization of facts or repetitive practice of isolated skills. Learning, particularly for advanced students, often involves transferring and applying previously learned knowledge to new and unfamiliar situations. In sport and physical activity, new or unfamiliar situations occur regularly; there is constant change in equipment, facilities, opponents, teammates, and even the weather. The new and unfamiliar often brings with it a set of challenges for which the performer must transfer and apply knowledge from previous experience.

Perhaps better thought of as a learning strategy than a teaching style, problem solving requires the learner to define the problem, determine the desired resolution, identify possible solutions, test and evaluate the potential solutions, and select the solution that best achieves the desired resolution (Mosston and Ashworth 2002). For example, in a basketball game, one problem might be an opponent scoring points with a highly accurate outside shot. The desired resolution is to stop or at least reduce the points scored from that shot. Possible solutions may include guarding him more closely, attempting to keep him from getting the ball, and players waving their hands in front of his eyes to interfere with his seeing the basket clearly. Next, the players try all the possible options and evaluate the success of each. Finally, determine which solution or set of solutions best solves the problem. If none have succeeded, more potential solutions must be found and tested.

An important task for a teacher when developing students' problem solving abilities is to provide meaningful problems for students to solve. A teacher with sufficient understanding of the students' previous knowledge and experience is in a better position to design appropriate problems. Problems that are too simple or beyond the students' knowledge have little chance of promoting student learning. When presenting problems to students, teachers should review problem solving strategies as well as identify the knowledge resources students may find helpful in solving the problem.

Experiential Learning: Your Problem, Your Solution

In a recent study, teachers were asked where they learned the greatest amount of information for their day-to-day teaching practice. Their overwhelming response was simple: experience (Fincher and Schempp 1994). Experience is a wonderful teacher, and skillful teachers help students turn experiences into lessons.

Unlike guided discovery and problem solving, the outcomes of experiential learning are less important than the process itself (Kolb 1984). A fundamental assumption in experiential learning is that ideas and knowledge are not fixed. Each new experience brings change to those ideas. Learning is conceived as an emergent process in which the outcomes are merely historical artifact and not the knowledge of the future. Knowledge is constructed from the experiences we hold and becomes reconstructed, expanded, and developed with additional experience. In the words of John Dewey, "the principle of continuity of experience means that every experience both takes up something from those which have gone before and modifies in some way the quality of those which come after" (1938, 35).

In experiential learning, the student comes to the teacher not only ready to learn but also with a plan for learning. The plan may be a bit unstable and in need of some refinement, but within the plan a student identifies the skills or knowledge to be gained and a proposal for gaining that knowledge. Together, the teacher and student review the plan of action to search for ways to improve the project. Once the student and teacher are satisfied that the learning plan appears sound, the student executes the plan. Changes in the program, when and if necessary, are normally determined and made by the student, perhaps after some consultation with the teacher. In the final phase of learning, the student evaluates her performance and the quality of her plan. The learner may consult the teacher, but it's the learner who makes the decisions about learning objectives; time allocations and practice schedules; resources, equipment, and facilities; information sources; practice activities; program changes or modifications; and evaluation criteria. Experiential

learning gives the student independence to design the topics and questions to be studied as well as to assess the quality of the learning.

This type of learning can focus on the learner devising a fitness plan, selecting skills or an activity to master, training for a competition, or discovering an effective game strategy. Many elite athletes use this learning strategy when their coaches aren't readily available. Experiential learning has also proven an effective strategy for someone attempting to learn and master a new sport or physical activity. Because of the necessary maturity and motivation, this style of learning is best reserved for more advanced students. Advanced learners already have some knowledge and experience in the subject, which is helpful for identifying what they need to learn. They are also better able to make informed judgments about the quality of the learning experience and the outcomes.

In this style, the instructor's role is most critical in the planning phase. Ensuring the learner identified appropriate resources, planned a progressive and appropriate series of learning tasks, set realistic goals, and is ready in terms of motivation and background are key elements for the success of experiential learning. Once the student begins the program, the teacher continues the consultation role by periodically checking progress and discussing modifications or changes in the program. However, the primary responsibility for learning rests with the learner.

Critical Pedagogy: Learning As Social Change

Sport and physical activity, particularly in modern culture, have come to represent more than fitness, skills, or friendly competition. With the attraction of millions of dollars from commercial sponsors and the use of physical activity as a prime medium in advertising, a host of social values and cultural codes are embedded in human movement. Like other areas of society, sports are not immune to the social ills of racism, sexism, economic disadvantage, and other forms of social oppression and injustice. Because teaching is a human social interaction, the act of teaching holds social and political consequences. Teaching can thus be an opportunity to endorse or challenge social conditions and characteristics.

The seminal work of Paulo Freire (1970) in teaching literacy in his home country of Brazil is often cited as providing the cornerstone of critical pedagogy.

Freire wrote, "It is my basic conviction that a teacher must be fully cognizant of the political nature of his/her practice and assume responsibility for this rather than denying it" (Shor 1987, 211). As a critical enterprise, critical pedagogy seeks to enhance and transform participants' self-understanding (students and teachers alike) in ways that affect the way we live (Landau 1996). Critical pedagogy involves three phases: listening, dialogue, and action (Shor 1987).

Listening serves as the avenue for investigating the significant issues or themes pertinent to the class participants (Oliver and Lalik 2000). It's common for a teacher at this stage to not know precisely what to listen for. Listen for the issues or topics that have high emotional impact in students' lives. What are the students worried about? What brings them joy, sadness, anger? Emotions, particularly fears, are often difficult to draw out because they can be cloaked in quiet voices. Listening can take place in both formal and informal settings, in class or outside of class. You can listen to spoken, written, and represented words. To truly listen, therefore, the teacher must not only hear what students say but also read what students write and appreciate what students draw, sing, or move to. Teachers can also listen by observing what students wear, the objects and activities they value, and the interpretations they give to the events of their everyday lives. By critically listening to each other, students and teachers identify the issues to be brought forward for discussion and subsequent action.

Once an issue or issues have been identified, dialogue can then follow. Because of the deep-seated social and emotional nature of oppressive beliefs and practices that form the issues in critical pedagogy, it's unlikely that an immediate solution will be found. It's therefore important to structure a positive dialogue so that the participants don't easily give up in frustration over what they see as a hopeless or endlessly contradictory issue. By using "codifications" (Freire 1970) and inductive questions, teachers can have students base their discussion in personal experiences, integrate those experiences into a broader social context, and explore alternative strategies. Codifications are ways of naming common objects or concepts identified in the listening stage. They can take the form of a written dialogue, pictures, a told story, a collage, poems, or songs. In the Martial Arts Club, *membership* is an important code that gets discussed, interpreted, evaluated, and lived (figure 11.1).

Regardless of the form, a code represents the students' reality and allows them to project their social and emotional responses in a focused manner. However, direct discussions may be too threatening or overwhelming for many students because of the private nature of many of these issues. A codification on social responsibility in sport participation (Hellison 1995), for example, permits the group participants to project their thoughts and concerns on the topic but remain one step removed from per-

© Sport The Library

Figure 11.1 Like many activities, the martial arts welcome understanding about their respective cultures and histories, as well as discussion of issues pertaining to them.

sonal revelations. They can discuss incidents they may have witnessed or tell stories of a "friend who had that happen to them" without the risk of revealing an embarrassing personal experience.

There are no clear-cut solutions for many social issues in sport participation. Because of the depersonalized nature of discussion codifications, students are free to critically reflect on, discuss, and offer their own options for action. The role of the teacher in group discussion varies, but initially, the teacher provides structure and stimulates discussion through problem posing or introducing questions about the codifications. As students become comfortable with sharing experiences and dialogue, the class environment changes. The students begin posing problems, asking questions, extending discussions, and seeking alternatives. At this point, the teacher may provide the group with additional information that will promote critical thinking. In the case of gender equity in sports, for example, a teacher might provide data on opportunities for boys and girls in sport or court cases on equity issues.

The final phase in critical pedagogy is action. The actions draw directly from critical reflections and group discussions. Student action means learning to see themselves as social and political beings with rights and a voice. Plans for action stem from the students' understanding of the root causes of problems and their visions for a more just society—a society in which they feel both responsible and appreciated. Actions vary from building a supportive community of friends to making the problems known to a larger social circle (e.g., a school or community) to changing unjust social practices, rules, or laws. The ultimate decision for action and the forms that action will take rest with the group participants. For a teacher, the final evaluation of critical pedagogy is measured in the students' needs for language, self-expression, sense of justice and purpose, and control over their own lives. In the sidebar, Don Hellison (1995) describes his work with the Martial Arts Club. In the context of his story, you can find the three-step critical pedagogy process of listening, dialogue, and action.

The Martial Arts Club

Don Hellison

Don Hellison is a talented and dedicated physical education teacher. In the world of physical education, few others have directly or indirectly influenced more students or more teachers. Although he holds the well-earned position of professor at the University of Illinois at Chicago, his heart and soul go into his work with youth. The story of the Martial Arts Club provides a fine example of a skilled teacher using critical pedagogy. As you read the story, try to identify the processes of listening, dialogue, and action. I've known Don for more than 20 years and in that time have learned a great deal from him about teaching. The following story, told in his words, is just one example of why.

The Martial Arts Club is based on a progression of lesson plans. At first, when everyone is a rookie, club meetings consist of teacher-directed martial arts and fitness activities. At the end of the first lesson, students are given a journal (which I keep) that has the Martial Arts Club Levels on the cover. The journal contains a checklist and comments for each day in the program. Thus, reflection begins immediately.

As soon as the student shows self-control (Level I) and is on task (Level II) most of the time, based on the student's journal and my observations, the student is formally promoted to club member. The second half of the lesson is for club members only. After the rookies leave, the club members begin to learn kata, point karate, and kickboxing.

As soon as students become club members, group meetings begin. The first order of business is to discuss new members. Unfortunately, this causes (me) many headaches because students who have been promoted are reluctant to vote new members in. A victory: The group voted in a very overweight boy they love to make fun of but who clearly met the criteria. A defeat: They didn't vote in a fifth grader who had been a problem but settled down and met the criteria. "He only does it 'cause you're looking at him," one student claimed. Others agreed. I argued for him but lost. It was my job to tell him. He was tough,

(continued)

(continued)

perhaps in a gang already (I saw him flashing gang signs), but he cried silently when he heard the verdict. I couldn't stand it. I pleaded his case at the next group meeting. "No problem," they said. The only consistency is inconsistency.

Group meetings provide time for students to evaluate the lesson, the program, each other, and me. Although students have a lot to say about who should be in the club, they are, in general, slow to share their opinions and thoughts. Their worlds at home, at school, and on the street are not very democratic. But once they get the idea (and believe that I will listen), sharing is no longer a problem.

On the front of their journals, in addition to the Levels, is a quotation from Randall Bassett that I use to introduce Level V, true martial artist:

> *Great self-defense technique largely consists of obtaining a keen insight into the limitations of force as a way of resolving human conflict. . . . Aggression cannot be understood without fathoming just how far men will go in order to prove that they are not "nobodies." It is this inner doubt, this lack of authentic self-confidence, that fuels most violence. . . . The essential question is who and what you would be if you could go beyond your deepest fears. (Hellison 1995, 78-81)*

—Don Hellison, Professor, University of Illinois-Chicago

Summary

In this chapter, several instructional strategies were explored. There is no single best method of teaching all students a given skill or concept. Which strategy is most effective depends on the teacher, students, tasks to be learned, and conditions for learning (e.g., time, equipment, goals, resources).

In this chapter, instructional strategies were explored that ranged from the students' heavy dependence on the teacher for information, goals, and practice activities to instructional strategies that emphasized the students' independence as a learner. In the range of instructional activities provided, a host of methods for presenting information and devising instructional activities were offered. Task cards and contracts, for example, are often underused in physical education classes, but provide a proven method of individualizing instruction, even in large classes.

No one strategy should be used for all students in all situations. As students, subject matter, and the learning environment change, the teacher should seek strategies that make the best use of the learning conditions to maximize student learning. Additionally, using a variety of instructional strategies keeps the teacher fresh and the learning environment invigorated.

Discussion Questions

1. Have you had personal experiences with some or all of the instructional strategies described in this chapter? If so, what were your impressions of each? Which did you believe stimulated effective learning?

2. Critique the six strategies presented in this chapter. What do you see as the strengths and limitations of each?

3. Which strategies would you use most often and which would you use least often? Why?

4. Select three strategies and describe how you would use these strategies to teach a sport or activity of your choice.

Chapter 12

Checking for Learning

If the only tool you have is a hammer, you tend to see every problem as a nail.

— Abraham Maslow

DISCOVERY

One of the significant differences between highly skilled teachers and their less accomplished counterparts lies in understanding what the students have learned. Good teachers constantly analyze and assess their students' learning. They find this knowledge invaluable for deciding which activities, skills, and concepts are best suited for the learner at a particular point in the lesson or learning progression. The ability to check for learning is, therefore, a critical skill for anyone wishing to become an effective teacher.

This chapter identifies several techniques teachers use to check learning and assess learner progress. These techniques are often used in combination, and no one technique is superior to another. Good teachers effectively use any or all of them depending on context, student, or instructional goal.

Assessment Defined

Assessments require two steps: a measurement and an evaluation. A measurement or evaluation can be made singularly, but when combined, they form an assessment. That is, something can be given a numerical value without a judgment being made, and a judgment can be made without the benefit of tangible evidence.

Measurement is the process of quantifying a characteristic or property. In other words, in the process of measuring something, you assign a number for the purpose of comparison. Stand on the scale and you receive a number descriptive of your total body weight. In taking an exam for a driver's license, you are assigned a number intended to measure your understanding of traffic laws. Run times, basketball free throw percentages, softball batting averages, and percentages of successful first serves are all examples of measures used in sport and physical activity. Seldom is a single number enough to take the next step (evaluation). Multiple numbers provide comparisons, and comparisons allow for judgments. If I run a mile in 10 minutes today but ran the same mile in 9 minutes yesterday, the better run was yesterday. If I run the mile in 10 minutes and you run the same mile in 9 minutes, you are the better runner.

Measures can also take the form of words or text—things that students say or write. Spoken or written words not only reveal what students know but also describe the thought or emotional process involved in the learning. Whether using numbers or words, judgments of student learning must be based on some form of measurement or solid evidence.

Evaluation is the process of making judgments about a property or characteristic. While a number represents a quantity, and words describe an event or information, evaluation is the process of determining quality. Judgments are decisions about success or failure, better or worse, improved or deteriorated, adequate or inadequate, sound or unsound, as well as the degree to which something is good or bad. People constantly evaluate the things they see and do. Judgments help determine the success, or lack of success, in previous actions and help plan the next course of action. If teachers and students work toward specific learning goals such as increasing understanding, improving performance, or enjoying an activity, then evaluating the progress toward those goals determines the adequacy of the decisions used to construct the lesson.

Evaluations can be based on beliefs, impressions, or indirect evidence, but the best judgments are based on direct evidence. Put another way, a teacher might judge a student's performance based on a belief about the person's appearance, an impression gained from watching a warm-up, or evidence from a previous experience with that student. However, higher quality evaluations come from direct evi-

dence. Seeing a student perform or hearing the student discussing her understanding of a topic yields more convincing evidence and provides the basis for a more credible evaluation.

Assessment requires both evidence and evaluation. That is, you must take a measure or sample of some kind and judge the quality or standard of that measure. In the strictest sense, assessments are the most formal process of checking learning, but they also tend to reveal the most valid and reliable judgments. Evaluations based on evidence are often critical for making reasoned and informed decisions about the effectiveness of the teaching and quality of the learning. Assessments further provide useful information for planning future instructional activities.

When students practice and see their scores increase in sports such as basketball, tennis, and softball, or when fitness measures such as heart rate, body composition, or strength show progress, it can be said that the teaching was adequate. When scores go down in track, golf, and swimming, learning may also be taking place. Likewise, learning has occurred when student descriptions reflect deeper levels of understanding, motivation, or enjoyment. When no changes are noted or the change is judged to be too little, the practice or instruction is ineffective and needs adjustment. Skillful teachers use the information generated through assessments to guide and monitor the instructional process.

Purposes of Assessment

Learning assessment serves a variety of purposes. You may have one reason or multiple reasons to assess learning. To a large degree, how you check for learning depends on what you are checking for. In this section, common reasons why teachers assess learning will be identified and explained.

Identifying Current Knowledge

Determining what the students already know is useful for setting instructional goals best suited to the students' current understanding, aspirations, and abilities. The most skillful teachers often begin an instructional episode, class, or season by first determining the present capacities and knowledge of students so that instruction is neither redundant nor too challenging. Understanding what the students would like to learn and why they want to learn it also provides invaluable information for teachers to motivate students.

Diagnosing Difficulties

Assessment is a necessary part of identifying a student's limitations, or difficulties with performance. Understanding where a student is having problems with a subject is critical for determining what needs to be learned. With this information, the teacher can structure an appropriate lesson to remedy or circumvent potential difficulties.

Grouping Students

There are times when a teacher wishes to group students according to certain characteristics (figure 12.1). For example, a teacher may wish to segregate a class by fitness level so the appropriate level of challenge can be given to each group. Coaches are often faced with the difficult task of selecting a small group of athletes from the multitude who try out for a team. To ensure fairness and accuracy, assessment should be a critical element in the selection process.

Measuring Progress

The measure of any good teaching is the progress a student makes in learning. It's therefore important for a teacher to accurately assess the progress of the students to determine how much has been learned. Measuring progress also helps to identify goals for the next learning activities.

Figure 12.1 Students can be grouped together by skill level to better obtain assessment of their understanding of the skill.

Providing Feedback

In chapter 10, the importance of feedback for student learning was described. To provide accurate feedback about a skill performance, an accurate assessment of the strengths and weaknesses of the performed skill is useful. Generally, the results of any assessment provide a student with constructive feedback regarding learning and performance of the skill, sport, or physical activity. Feedback generated through assessment can be offered in a variety of forms: written, verbal, or nonverbal (e.g., videotape, demonstration).

Making Comparisons

Performance differences between students are sometimes useful information for both students and teachers. For example, if a student knows how she rates on a fitness test in relation to others, it identifies her present level of fitness and helps her establish future target goals. A public school teacher is often required to grade students in physical education class. Measures of performance and comprehension differences are vital information for identifying those who have learned the greatest from those who have learned the least.

Evaluating Programs

The purpose of program evaluation is to determine the effectiveness of the program (Stillwell and Willgoose 1997). Is the program meeting its objectives and doing what it is intended to do, or are changes needed? These are the questions that drive program evaluation. To develop a sound educational program, you must devote time to determining its strengths and weaknesses. Two criteria should be the target of program evaluation: (a) student performance and satisfaction and (b) program components. Student performance and satisfaction should be the primary goal of any educational program. Therefore, assessing quality requires judging student improvement. Knowing if students are satisfied enough to stay in the program and recommend the program to others can be critical to the long-term health of any instructional program. Assessing programs also requires an honest analysis of the administration, staff, facilities, equipment, and program design and offerings, as well as objectives, goals, and philosophy. Program improvement is dependent on knowing what needs improvement.

Types of Assessments

There are two times when a teacher may wish to check learning. Formative evaluations are made while learning is taking place, and summative evaluations are taken at the end of the learning episode to determine overall improvement. To be most effective, formative evaluations should begin early in the instructional unit and continue throughout the unit so that learning can be continuously monitored and new goals set or former goals adjusted as students make progress. In fact, most good teachers constantly take measures and make judgments about the quality and quantity of the learning. Formative evaluations are also important for determining the types and amount of feedback learners require during the practice portion of the lesson.

Summative evaluations are conducted after the student completes the learning activities. Such evaluations are useful for determining the degree to which program objectives have been met and for assigning certifications or grades. Identifying the satisfactory level of skills and knowledge required for a particular task, such as lifeguarding, can only be determined at the conclusion of the program.

Evaluations come in two forms: subjective and objective. A subjective evaluation requires the teacher to make a value judgment without the benefit of a number score or standard. Instead, they are based on a teacher's knowledge of particular criteria for a "good performance." If those criteria are present and observed in some fashion by the teacher, then a favorable judgment is rendered. Teachers often use subjective evaluations when viewing student performances and then relay their judgments to the performer through feedback and evaluative comments. A subjective evaluation can result in a score, but the score is assigned after a judge, as in gymnastics, makes the evaluation.

Objective evaluations yield a score for a particular performance. In this evaluation process, a test of some kind is used to measure a student's performance. A fitness test may use pull-up counts, timed distance runs, and flexibility measured on a numeric scale. These are all examples of objective measures. A coach may use a free throw percentage score to determine whom she will send to the line in critical game situations. Objective evaluations are based on clearly defined scoring systems.

Areas of Assessment

Learning takes place in four domains: cognitive, social, emotional, and physical. It makes sense, therefore, that if a teacher or coach wants to check for learning, he should analyze each of the domains in which there is some instructional goal.

Cognitive Domain

Cognitive instruction in sport and physical activity traditionally takes the form of memorizing concepts (e.g., the components of a skill), understanding rules, developing strategies, ingraining pre-shot or pre-game mental routines, and gaining knowledge of the social, political, or historical factors of the sport or activity. Knowledge of the social and cultural significance of physical activity is important to people who appreciate and promote the activity. Understanding the movements necessary for performing a skill and the purpose of the skill in the context of a sport or performance is essential for continued improvement. If students can't remember the proper sequence of a skill or the rules of the sport, they have little chance to improve their present performance level.

Written responses or tests are more formal ways of identifying cognitive changes and learning; a less formal method is to interview the students. Written tests take two forms: mastery and discrimination (Baumgartner and Jackson 1999). Mastery tests determine if the student has sufficiently learned the required information, whereas discrimination tests determine the level of understanding. Interviewing students provides useful evidence for assessing student knowledge, thinking, and understanding. This technique is addressed more thoroughly in the questioning and listening sections of this chapter.

Social Domain

Sport and physical activity have a strong social component. Concepts such as team cohesion, fair play, cooperation, and leadership are often identified as instructional goals (figure 12.2). Team cohesion scales and measures of fair play are available for more formal analysis (Safrit and Wood 1989). When the main purpose behind the sport or physical activity program is the development of social skills, it's important to monitor social development as a means of assessing student learning and program effectiveness. For example, Hellison (1995) stresses the development of social responsibility through physical activity programs. He uses student interviews, journal keeping, and other records to assess the social responsiveness of the students with whom he works. Direct, focused observations by a teacher are often a simple yet effective way of assessing social skill development.

Figure 12.2 Team leadership is an important social domain in physical activity and sport.

Emotional Domain

People often hold very personal reasons for participating in sport. Enhanced physical appearance, activity participation, and performance competence may boost self-esteem. Motivation, self-esteem, self-control, and perceived competence are emotional factors often identified as instructional/developmental goals. Factors such as anxiety and arousal that potentially affect performance may also need assessment. In team sports, students and teachers often consider issues of attitude, team cohesion, and leadership. Sport and physical education programs have proven effective for helping students or athletes develop self-control and personal responsibility, as assessed through record keeping, student writing, and teachers' observations (Hellison 1993; Hellison and Templin 1991).

Physical Domain

Physical fitness and skill development are two common physical capacities assessed by teachers and coaches. When assessing learning in the physical domain, the teacher must have an accurate measure of the attribute or skill being assessed. Valid and reliable tests of fitness and physical skills are available in contemporary measurement books (e.g., Baumgartner and Jackson 1999; Hastad and Lacy 1998; Safrit 1998). The assessment procedure must be appropriate for the participants. Making the experience enjoyable goes a long way toward moti-

vating students to produce good scores and achieve even better performances in the future.

Methods for Assessing Learning

There are many ways to evaluate students' knowledge, attitudes, skills, or learning. It's often merely a lack of knowledge and ingenuity that prevents a teacher from making adequate assessments. In this section, several techniques are described that have proven valuable to teachers.

Evaluation

One problem is frequently cited when conducting assessments: Who will do them? Teachers often have so many other responsibilities that taking the time to also assess learning is seen as just one more task to do. Students are often perceived as lacking the knowledge or honesty to conduct accurate assessments. And people outside the class are seldom considered. The reality is that anyone can conduct a useful assessment: teachers, students, peers, or others.

Teachers As Evaluators

Whether they realize it or not, teachers constantly assess students and their learning. Expert teachers seldom begin a lesson or practice without first assessing the students' current skill level, knowledge, fitness, and motivation. These assessments can be completed with a few simple questions or some quick observations of the students' performance on the skill to be developed.

At times, more formal assessments are necessary. In these cases, teachers must find ways to collect the necessary information without sacrificing potential instructional or practice time. To hold up an entire class of 30 or 40 students so the teacher can count the number of sit-ups or pull-ups 1 or 2 students can perform is a waste of important learning time. Skillful teachers find ways to integrate assessment strategies with instructional practices so that learning progress can be measured without stopping the learning.

Students As Evaluators

Students are more than capable of recording information about their learning, and they can also reliably judge their progress. Students can be invaluable during practices in which the teacher isn't always available. For example, a teacher may be unable to observe every student in a large class, and it makes little sense to interrupt everyone's learning for a teacher to focus his attention on assessing a single student's skill performance. The same may be true in situations where students practice away from the instructional setting. If teachers and students are mutually committed to the instructional goals, students will want to know their progress in achieving the goals and will be motivated to undertake accurate assessments.

One key to successful student self-assessment is making it regular and progressive. If students keep a daily record of their heart rates, swimming lap-times, distances run, or some other measure, they will see the progress in their performances and become accustomed to taking the responsibility for self-assessment. Conducting assessments sporadically is usually a less successful strategy.

Students are also capable of assessing other students. Students can work in pairs or in small groups with one or two students assessing the performance of the other students. Depending on the students' level of knowledge, they may need to focus on quantifying, or counting, the performances rather than attempting to qualify them by making judgments relative to performance adequacy.

Other Evaluators

People outside the class are often willing to help with assessment. Parents, supporters, other teachers, and students from other classes can all take data and provide evaluations. Once teachers and students decide what they would like assessed, a little energy spent outside class usually results in finding helpful assessment assistance. Keep in mind, however, that assessment techniques used by people from outside the class or lesson should require little training and be relatively easy to use.

Instruments and Techniques

Just as there are many ways to teach a skill or concept, there are many ways to assess skill or concept learning. Some of the more typical methods include paper and pencil tests, direct observation, authentic assessment, and videotape analysis (figure 12.3).

Figure 12.3 Videotaping and taking notes during practice sessions can aid teachers in assessing a student's ability.

Paper and Pencil Tests

One of the most traditional, and still effective, techniques for assessing student knowledge and understanding of a subject or topic is the paper and pencil test. These tests are particularly useful for assessing the students' understanding of game rules, strategies, attitudes, and knowledge of skills and game concepts. In constructing tests, consider making them brief while still obtaining the necessary information. In a sport instruction environment, it's preferable to have the students moving more than just their pencils. Data may also be gathered using checklists or rating scales, journals, or student reports. Written documents of almost any type can be useful for assessing student progress and development. One advantage of written documents is that a teacher can analyze the information after class, so she doesn't need to sacrifice instructional time to assess student learning.

Direct Observation

Instructors continually use direct observation to monitor and evaluate students' progress as they perform the skills and execute the strategies of a particular activity or sport. The trick here is to effectively use these observation periods as assessment techniques. Learn to look for the same skills or points provided in the instruction as students go through their practice. If a grip, stance, or follow-through was explained or demonstrated, focus attention on this skill. Experts monitor practices to identify the atypical, then devise ways to reteach the skill to eliminate the error. They also focus on the positive aspects of the performance and let students know what they are doing correctly.

Authentic Assessment

Collecting work samples and displays of student progress in real-life learning or performance settings is characteristic of authentic assessment (Meyer 1992). For example, monitoring the number of successful backhands in a tennis match is a more authentic assessment of someone's learning than counting the number of backhands made during a test situation. Authentic assessment represents an ongoing process by monitoring the learner's progress throughout the instructional program. Work samples used in authentic assessment might include developmental checklists, peer reviews, student portfolios, videotape analyses, logs, self-evaluations, projects, tests, and summary reports (Melograno 1996). In authentic assessment, the teacher or coach plays the role of facilitator, helping students select

the assessment criteria that best represent and document the students' learning.

Videotape Analysis

With the increased availability of technology, videotape assessments of an individual or team performance have become commonplace. Virtually any physical activity or sport performance can be recorded on tape and analyzed by the teacher, student, or both. Keep in mind, however, that beginners may need more assistance from the teacher to analyze their performances and devise instructional cues and goals from videotape. Video analysis is also more effective when used over time rather than once or twice in the learning progression. The more accustomed a learner becomes to viewing a videotape, the more cues she can derive from the tape. With practice, students become more astute at analyzing their performances, judging developments in their performances, and detecting nuances or changes that might signal the necessity of a correction.

Asking Questions

No clear connection seems to exist between a teacher's questions and student achievement (Gall 1970). Simply asking questions does not necessarily promote student learning. However, asking questions serves three functions by "enabling the lesson to proceed as planned, helping children learn how to accomplish an academic task, and helping the teacher assess their learning" (Cazden 1986, 441). Questions are an excellent method for assessing students' understanding of the material under study without interrupting the learning process.

Gaining Useful Information

In a recent study, Schempp (1999) found that expert teachers ask students many questions, particularly at the beginning and end of the lesson. The questions asked at the beginning of a lesson take the form of a friendly conversation between the teacher and the students. Teachers use questions at the start of the lesson to shape the instructional content and teaching style. Opening questions should focus on a variety of issues, including physical activity experiences and knowledge directly related to the day's topic, experiences and knowledge indirectly related but pertinent to the day's topic, motivations or inhibitions in learning, and injuries or physical limitations. Information on students' academic interests, professional aspirations, recreational activities, and hobbies can prove useful for a skillful teacher looking to make learning experiences relevant for students.

To construct meaningful and personalized lessons, skillful teachers apply knowledge gained from asking questions. Information on previous activity experiences can be used to draw connections between mastered skills and the skills being learned. For example, if students can throw a ball overhand, the same mechanical fundamentals can be applied when teaching a tennis or volleyball serve. Understanding students' previous experience with the topic at hand helps the instructor determine the students' skill, knowledge, and learning potential. From there, the teacher can determine an appropriate level of challenge for the lesson. The students' motivation for learning (as well as their perceived resistance to a topic) helps a teacher set the tone of the lesson. For example, if students see social value in learning the activity, the teacher can take a more relaxed approach to the lesson than if they had competitive aspirations for the same activity. Finally, knowledge of injuries, health conditions, or fitness levels lets teachers know the stamina of the students as well as whether they must compensate for physical limitations.

In summary, decisions about the content to be taught, tone of the lesson, and feedback to give as students practice can all be enhanced by a teacher asking questions. The friendly, personal nature of the questions helps to relax apprehensive students and establish a positive, accepting atmosphere. Finally, asking questions at the beginning of the lesson gets students talking about the topic, which in turn lets them feel free to ask subject-related questions and make comments throughout the lesson.

Some teachers find it helpful to prepare ahead of time several questions pertinent to the main points. Asking frequent but brief questions about the main points of the lesson, supplemental points, and the learning process itself is an effective method for monitoring the learning pulse of the students. It's particularly helpful to ask students to summarize, in their own words, the main points of the lesson at its conclusion. This lets both teachers and students clearly understand precisely what was learned.

Getting Correct Responses

Most questions teachers ask should elicit correct answers. Students who experience success in answering questions are more likely to continue answering them. One helpful technique for constructing these questions is to think of the answer first (usually a point you want to make in class) and then structure the question so students actually make the point with their answers.

Asking questions that students can't or won't answer is ineffective. If students experience failure in answering questions, they tend not to answer very often. Seldom do people like demonstrating their ignorance on a regular basis. If students discover that they're very often wrong, they wind up believing that they really don't know anything. Also, asking questions such as "What's the matter with you?" "Who made that noise?" or "Do you want to be sent to the headmaster's office?" makes students apprehensive to answer any of your questions, even the most academic ones. The impression they gain is that although it sounds like a question, it isn't, at least not one they can answer with any level of safety or comfort.

Skillful teachers avoid vague and ambiguous questions. Clear questions are more easily answered. Knowing what kind of answer you are looking for sometimes helps in formulating clear questions. Vague and ambiguous questions tend to turn students off of answering even clear questions because they're never really certain of the answer, even when they know it.

Questions are more manageable when they come one at a time. At times, teachers get carried away and ask several questions all at once. Students become overwhelmed and don't know which question the teacher really wants answered or even in what order, so they simply remain silent.

Research indicates that most teachers wait less than one second after a question before speaking again (Cheffers and Mancini 1978). This is easy enough to understand since teachers are used to talking and unaccustomed to silence in their lessons. On the other hand, students aren't used to talking, so it takes them a second or two to think of the answer and then formulate a response. Therefore, it's better to wait at least three seconds after a question before calling on a student for an answer.

As questions become more complex, increase wait time in proportion to question difficulty. More complex questions require more time for students to assimilate information and construct a thoughtful response. Teachers need to be patient. Telling students "This is a tough question, so I'll give you a few seconds to consider an answer" may help them formulate a better reasoned response and reinforces the message that you do indeed expect an answer.

Questioning Strategies

Questions serve little purpose in instructional environments if they aren't intended to elicit a response. Over the years, however, most students have been conditioned to listen and not talk when learning.

Teachers' questions may therefore go unanswered, at least at first. Preformulation and reformulation are two strategies that help draw answers to important questions.

Preformulation gives orientation and clarity to a question. It cues the student that a question is coming and provides the context for answering it (Cazden 1986). The following questions illustrate the point. The first question is asked with no preformulation, whereas the second makes use of the strategy.

Question One: "What is the first thing a basketball player should do upon receiving the ball?"

Question Two: "If the object of the game is to score, what is the first thing a basketball player should do upon receiving the ball?"

Reformulation reworks an original question and offers greater specificity. The original question may have been too challenging, ambiguous, or general for the students. Reformulation narrows the question to align it more closely with a desired answer. The questioning strategy shouldn't be abandoned because the next time a question is asked, the students may simply wait until the teacher supplies the answer. Reformulation therefore repackages the question until only the simplest response is necessary. The following is used as an illustration.

Original Question: "What is the fastest method of moving the basketball from your opponent's goal to your own after a rebound?"

Reformulated Question One: "What was the transition play we practiced last week?"

Reformulated Question Two: "Who gets the pass after a defensive rebound?"

Reformulated Question Three: "Can anyone explain a fast break?"

Reformulated Question Four: "A fast break quickly moves the ball from the opponent's goal to our own, doesn't it?"

The Power of Questions

An accomplished teacher uses questions often and purposefully. Questions serve multiple purposes in a lesson, but whatever their intention, they are critical for teachers to receive a clear idea of a learner's understanding of the subject matter. Teaching and learning go hand in hand. Teachers can be reasonably sure they are teaching, but only by asking questions can they be sure the students are learning. And once a question is asked, listen. At times, a teacher becomes so used to talking that listening becomes a seldom used and neglected

skill. The best teachers recognize that the power of questions can only be realized by listening to the comments and responses of their students.

Be a Good Listener

It does little good for teachers to ask questions if they are unable to listen to the answers. Listening, however, takes time, effort, and some skill. Teachers can develop a routine in their teaching for communicating with and listening to their students. Good teachers ask questions and listen intently for the answers. They listen to gather facts so they can understand what their students are thinking, feeling, and understanding. Listening becomes an integral part not only of assessing students' learning but also of building the relationship between teacher and students.

Proactive Listening

Good teachers see value in gathering student input and gaining a student's perspective on the learning experience. They are proactive listeners. That is, they don't merely wait until students speak up but rather make a sustained effort to understand students by getting them to talk. Oliver and Lalik describe this process as active listening and encourage teachers to continually ask themselves the following questions: "what is this student trying to say; how can I help her or him to explain what they mean in greater detail; and how can I help this student to better articulate what they mean so I can more fully understand and appreciate their view?" (2000, 106).

Listen to Understand, Not Just to Reply

Listen to understand what the students know, their perspectives on their learning, and what they are trying to say before you even consider a reply. This is fundamental to productive communication (Nichols 1995). Lynn Marriott's story (see p. 140) reveals the power in being able to listen like this as a teacher and coach. Effective listening requires actively accepting the students' remarks rather than making reactive judgments. Some call this keeping an open mind. Students are far less prone to provide teachers with information if they believe the teacher is constantly judging them. When they feel that the teacher truly seeks to understand and accept, students are more inclined to honestly share their thoughts and feelings. Expert teachers believe that understanding students' thoughts, beliefs, and knowledge is absolutely essential to teaching well.

The Power of Listening

Lynn Marriott

In the fall of 1997, the Sport Instruction Research Laboratory at the University of Georgia received a grant from the Ladies Professional Golf Association (LPGA) to study their top teachers and coaches. As part of that study, we videotaped the participants teaching a lesson. As we studied the tapes, one teacher struck us with the energy and enthusiasm she put into listening to her student. She asked a question and listened intently as her student responded. Her eyes were tightly focused on the student, and her head bobbed continually in acknowledgment of the student's thoughts, words, and feelings. The warm rapport she established with her student and the success they achieved in the student's learning seemed directly tied to the teacher's skill as a listener.

We later learned that this teacher, Lynn Marriott, was the 1992 LPGA Teacher of the Year, one of *Golf Magazine*'s Top 100 Golf Instructors in America, and the coach of several leading professional and amateur golfers. She is also the cofounder and director of Coaching for the Future in Phoenix, Arizona. Because the power of listening in her teaching and coaching so impressed me, I asked Lynn to share a story for this book. Here is what she generously wrote:

One of the junior girls that I coach was having some challenges with her college team coach. Mary was a freshman at a top-ranked university. She thought that she had qualified for a couple of college events but wasn't picked to go, and she didn't know why. Mary's mother also got involved and felt that her daughter was being treated unfairly. Mary and I had communicated a bit via phone and e-mail. During spring break, we finally got a chance to meet. The intention of the coaching session was to help. Mary needed to sort out the situation and make some decisions as to what to do next.

My strategy was to genuinely listen to what Mary had to say and ask some open-ended questions. When I say genuine listening, I mean that I truly listen from my heart. I don't think about solutions or about my own opinions. I am present with the player and listen to what she has to say. While I was listening, I also wanted to be present to observe all her nonverbal communication. I had given Mary some questions to answer even before we met:

- Where do you want to be 10 years from now?
- Make an asset and deficit list of staying at the school and another asset and deficit list of transferring to another school.
- Make a list of those things you can influence about your situation and those you cannot influence.

We started going through Mary's answers and thoughts about her golf and school situation. It became very obvious to me as a coach that she loved her present school and the friends she had. She also liked everything about the golf part, except a couple of coaching experiences. But it's still the player who needs to come to conclusions and solutions, and not me as a coach! I continued asking her open-ended questions and just listened to hear what she was feeling, experiencing, and thinking. She ended up deciding to stay at her present school and to keep focusing on the things she could influence. Even if the coach never, ever picked her for a tournament again, the positive outweighed the negative. She knew to focus on the things that were under her influence.

Mary went back to school after her spring break. She kept her focus and kept improving her own game. Mary finally got picked to play. She responded by being the best performer on the team. Mary's success led to her playing in both the regional and national championships later that spring.

—Lynn Marriott, 1992 LPGA Teacher of the Year

Summarize What You Hear

Hearing the words and showing interest do not ensure that the listener understands. Effective listeners develop the ability to concentrate on the statements their students are making and mentally summarize what they said. Good listeners mentally review what they just heard, seek clarification on points not well understood, compare and contrast the ideas presented, and then seek ways to put the ideas expressed to good effect in the lesson.

Summary

To teach well, teachers must firmly understand what their students know, think, and feel. The techniques used to gather and analyze this information make up the process of assessing student learning. Assessment involves a measure of some kind, evidence if you will, and an analysis, or judgment, based on that evidence. Teachers assess student learning for a variety of reasons that range from identifying students' current knowledge and potential to measuring progress and predicting future success. Formative assessments are made while students are learning, whereas summative evaluations determine the amount of learning resulting from the completed instructional program.

Most skilled teachers view their students as people, not performers. Therefore, they are concerned about the people they teach and monitor their social, emotional, intellectual, and physical development. Assessing student learning and development is a considerable task, so teachers use a variety of methods to gather the information they need to make informed judgments. Paper and pencil tests, direct observation, authentic assessment, and video analysis all provide useful data from which a teacher can draw conclusions. One of the most useful and often used techniques for assessing learning is asking questions and then listening to the responses students provide. Interestingly enough, it's usually only the more skilled teachers who use this relatively easy and cost-effective technique. Perhaps this is because the most highly skilled teachers have the strongest interest in knowing what their students have learned, need to learn, and want to learn.

Discussion Questions

1. Identify at least four reasons for assessing student learning. Describe how you might use each of these to provide better learning experiences for your students or athletes.

2. If you were a physical education teacher, what measures would you use to assess your students' cognitive, social, emotional, and physical learning?

3. Select a sport or physical activity and identify the work samples and exhibits of student learning that you might use to assess the quality and quantity of a student's learning.

4. How would you use students to assist in gathering assessment measures in your classes?

5. Research reveals that expert teachers are highly skilled at asking their students questions. What role do you think questions will serve in your teaching?

6. How can you become a better listener?

Part V

© Joe Rogate

Development
Becoming a Better Teacher and Coach

The only way to get better is to believe that you can. As you have learned in parts I to IV of this book, improvement begins with desire, then knowledge, and then the application of that knowledge with sufficient vigor for it to make a difference. In the final section of this book, ideas are presented for developing the influence you have as a teacher or coach. Promoting your program (chapter 13) is the first topic in this section. Included in this chapter are ideas for "getting the word out" about what you do in your classes and practices.

In an age of unprecedented technological advances, new tools and techniques are available for helping students learn, both in class and out. Chapter 14 discusses many of these innovations and how they can improve your teaching and coach-

ing. Teachers and coaches don't automatically improve as their years of experience add up. If a teacher or coach stinks, time alone will not sweeten the smell. However, many techniques can steer a teacher toward the path to improvement. Chapter 15 reports on many of the techniques teachers have successfully used to become better. The final chapter, chapter 16, closes the book with a discussion designed to encourage all teachers and coaches to elevate their expertise. People are not born great teachers. Great teachers are the product of extensive learning and prolonged practice. In the final chapter, the characteristics of teachers at varying levels of expertise are identified, and suggestions are offered so that you too can move along the road to teaching and coaching excellence.

Chapter 13

Going Public: Promoting Your Program

You have got to use every field of
publicity to force the truth into their
ears, and before their eyes.

— W.E.B. Du Bois

DEVELOPMENT

Teachers and coaches work hard to develop quality programs, but often only those directly involved in these programs know of their efforts and achievements. A wider public stands to benefit by being informed of the goals, activities, and achievements of successful sport and physical activity programs. In turn, the better publicity a program receives, the greater the likelihood of its growth and increased support.

Effective program promotion brings many benefits. For one, increased public awareness heads off misperceptions, misinformation, and rumors. Promotion of an educational program also builds the public support necessary for financial health. Helping the public understand the purposes, activities, and accomplishments of a program creates goodwill, respect, and support. Working and amicable relationships with news personnel can also ensure fair and adequate treatment in the press (Cutlip, Center, and Broom 2000).

Good publicity begins with a good program. It's difficult to consistently promote a program that lacks high standards, contemporary practices, or recognized achievements. The greater the quality of the program, the easier it is to promote and the more people want to hear about it. A good program alone, however, will not be enough to ensure its promotion to the public. True, students and participants in good programs may (or may not) spread the word to those they know, but that is a limited range of eyes and ears. Reaching a larger audience takes time and effort.

In the information age, teachers are finding it increasingly more important to "get the word out" about their programs. Fortunately, a number of avenues are available to convey information about what you're doing, why, where, and to what effect. This chapter presents several of these avenues, including the media, technology, demonstrations, and community activities. Before beginning the process of promoting a program, however, it's crucial to know exactly what is being promoted.

Defining Your Program

Program promotion begins with knowing two things: what you want to say and who you want to hear it. Promoting a program is a communication process. It involves both a message transmission and a message reception. To be effective, that means sending a clear, purposeful message so that the intended party appropriately and efficiently receives it.

What Do You Say About Your Program?

The history and mission of a program is a good place to begin. Biographies of program participants, certifications, and achievements all provide basic information that conveys important messages about who is involved in the program, what they do, and how well they do it. Awards, honors, or recognitions received are particularly important because not only does such information appeal to program participants and potential participants, but identifying achievements also conveys the mission and standards of the program. For nonparticipants, descriptions of services, resources, facilities, upcoming events, and recurring activities let people know what the program has to offer.

Identifying what you want to say about your program is a critical step in the promotional process. This is your chance to determine the public image you want to project. Consistencies must be evident between the purpose of the program and the program activities. The teachers and staff must, at all times, portray a professional, competent image. It's also important that the values espoused in the promo-

tional materials be consistent with the program itself. If the program promotes fitness and a healthy lifestyle, it's imperative that the staff be fit, neatly groomed, and appropriately dressed. Rather than a single individual selecting the content for promotional materials, relying on program participants and an advisory board to determine what to say about the program can yield invaluable insights and perspectives on the virtues of the program and its activities.

Who Should Hear About Your Program?

Define your target populations and your purpose for wanting to contact them. In any instructional program, students represent a natural target population because they need information about the aims and practices of the program in which they are participating. Students also like to receive a calendar of events and to read about their accomplishments and the achievements of other participants. For teachers who work with children, parents also represent a target population. Parents learn the greatest amount about a program from their children, so keeping children informed, as well as parents, is a key to promoting a program. Program staff and alumni are also important constituents who appreciate being kept in the loop by receiving promotional materials.

When promoting an instructional program, target groups within the community include business people, program sponsors, school boards, taxpayers, potential students, and news media. Effective program promotion involves providing information that target groups will find useful or enjoyable. To determine the needs of the target audience, a teacher might use personal contacts, key informants, or selected community forums to solicit ideas on details that would be beneficial to distribute. Potential funding agencies or program sponsors will require specifics about the value and quality of the program as well as the participants. As the competition for funding becomes increasingly stronger, nothing substitutes for clear, timely information about a good program to sell a sponsor. Regardless of the target group, don't forget to include contact information for program personnel. Surprisingly, this is often overlooked in promotional materials.

Make Use of the Media

The purpose of publicizing your program is to gain local support so that people will believe in what you are doing and help make it continue (Cutlip, Center, and Broom 2000). Promoting your program should therefore begin with local promotion. Let those most affected and able to affect your program get the word.

Newsletters

With the availability of computers and sophisticated software, it's now relatively easy and economical to provide your constituency with regular, pertinent, and detailed information about your program and its participants. Newsletters serve to keep people informed of events, results, accomplishments, and other items related to your program (Milo 1997) (figure 13.1). People not directly involved with your program can get a thumbnail sketch of your activities, and newsletters are a great way to educate the public about the goals and accomplishments of the program. Particularly in tax-sponsored public programs, people want to know what's going on. Newsletters can also ease the administrative burden by providing information to participants or potential participants about the procedures and policies used to manage the program. Deadline reminders, medical requirements, upcoming events, and registration procedures are just a few examples of items for inclusion in a newsletter.

Teachers often write articles, but contributions from students, administrators, organizers, parents, or community members may also be welcome if they contribute to the purpose and goals of the program and project its positive attributes. Having several authors spreads the ownership of the newsletter over several people, and combinations of perspectives increase the appeal of the newsletter. Articles should be kept succinct yet potent and readable. Newsletters aren't normally more than a page or two, so each word must count. Pictures, drawings, graphs, and tables not only present information concisely but also add to the attractiveness of the newsletter by increasing the visual presentation beyond the printed word. An attractive newsletter is more likely to be read than one that appears dull and uninspiring—even with the same information.

Newsletters can be distributed in a variety of ways. Students and program participants can give them out to target audiences like parents, family, or friends. A stack of newsletters may be left in certain public places that allow for their distribution (e.g., stores, supermarkets, sporting events, conferences, public meetings). Mailing is a third, but more expensive, option. Mailing does ensure a wider circulation, however. Considering its effectiveness for

informing people about a program and its events and the relative ease of writing one, every teacher should consider publishing and distributing a newsletter.

Newspapers

Sport, school, and community programs are all interest items for regional or community newspapers, which are always receptive to a good local story. Therefore, cultivating relationships with personnel from the local papers is imperative for getting your program in print. A newspaper is often willing to send a reporter and photographer to special events or interesting activities. Papers will also consider running submitted stories and photographs, particularly if the story has broad appeal to the newspaper's readership. An additional benefit of newspaper coverage is that it is cost-free advertising.

Although there is limited benefit to running a story about a school or instructional program more than perhaps once per year, special events are always newsworthy. If an organization, particularly one with wide community appeal, holds a special event, newspapers often cover the occasion. Fundraisers, program promotions, groundbreakings, open houses, anniversary celebrations, dedications, organized protests, award ceremonies, demonstrations, and activities involving local, regional, or national celebrities are all attractive news items. Events that feature and focus on children are particularly attractive to hometown newspapers.

Television

Much like newspapers, local television stations are continually on the lookout for community and newsworthy activities to air on their news and special interest programs (figure 13.2). Television holds several advantages as a medium for publicity. First of all, a television broadcast can potentially reach many viewers. Television also provides visual movement, whereas a newspaper provides news text and perhaps a photograph, and radio offers voice only as the medium of communication. For sport and physical activity—movement-based activities—television is an ideal avenue for public relations.

Contact the local station manager or cable operator to find out how program material is selected and how you can advertise your program on television. Because of the high cost of producing and airing televisions programs, it's more difficult to receive

. . . on the MOVE

News from Roswell Middle School Physical Education Department

Up the creek without a what?

Our eighth graders have been paddling like crazy lately as they prepare for our annual fall canoeing trip down the McKenzie River. In preparation for the trip, students in Ms. Lynn's outdoor education class have been practicing their paddling, canoe craft, and water safety skills to be fully prepared to navigate the scenic waters of the McKenzie. The class will put in on Saturday, October 23, at Eagle Butte point at 8:00 A.M. and take out at Thompson's Landings. Please be at the school ready to go no later than 7:00 A.M. This year, Mr. Braintree will lead us in water quality testing experiments along the trip. Please get permission slips in, because students cannot go without them. For more information please check our Web site: www.roswellmschool.org/pe or call Ms. Lynn at 259-6528.

Roswell Road Rats: Four members of the RRR recently ran in the Pink Ribbon 5K Run for a Cure. All finished in under 25 minutes! Congratulations to Andy, Alison, Erin, and Alex!

Open House!
The physical education staff will be on hand Thursday night, September 4, during Open House to answer your questions and explain your child's program. We also value your opinion and would love to hear from you. Please stop down and see us!

For the latest info on physical education, health, sport, and physical activity, check out **www.roswellmschool.org/pe**

Eat Fat = Get Fat

The latest statistics show that obesity continues to be a problem for American teenagers. Although most teens agree that getting fat is not fun and certainly not healthy, few seem to know how to curb this "growing trend." To help our students fight the fat fad, we've introduced a new unit in the sixth-grade personal fitness classes. Students will learn exercises and activities that will keep them healthy, and they will participate in a new unit called "Eating Your Way to Good Health." Studies show it isn't always how much you eat but what you eat. Did you know that you'd have to eat five apples to equal the calories in one bag of french fries (and the apples have a lot more nutrients)? You don't need to starve to maintain healthy weight; a smart diet and a little exercise is all it takes.

Get healthy and wealthy? Yep! Students who bring in their personal fitness goal sheets to East Street Sporting Goods will receive a 10% discount on all workout apparel (includes shoes, shirts, shorts).

Figure 13.1 Newsletters are an excellent way to keep people aware of what you are doing in your physical education program.

Figure 13.2 Savvy teachers and coaches can use the media to help showcase their programs. In this photo, a local TV station covers a roller hockey tournament.

television coverage for events and activities than radio or newspaper coverage. However, local stations usually cover school physical education or sport programs as part of their news programming. A special event or a distinctive program feature of general or human interest might appeal not only to local television but also to public television or national networks. If there is something special about your program, and there should be, don't hesitate to contact the television media in your area. If they can't help you, perhaps they can recommend someone who can.

Radio

Radio, especially local radio, offers several opportunities for promoting sport and physical activity programs. Radio talk show hosts need a continuing stream of people to fill airtime. If you have a quality program that appeals to the listeners of the talk show, you stand a good chance of being invited on as a guest. In addition, each radio station (and television station or cable company, for that matter) is required to broadcast a given number of minutes of Public Service Announcements (PSAs). PSAs deliver information from nonprofit organizations that might be of general interest to the community. Sign-up days for your program, significant accomplishments by students, and upcoming events are a few examples of items a radio station will broadcast as a PSA. For information on being a guest or making a PSA for your program, contact your local

radio stations. There is usually no charge to the organization for making or broadcasting the PSA or for being a guest on a talk show program.

Like newspapers and television stations, radio stations also have news departments and programs. Most radio stations are receptive to including "spots" for local events if they appeal to the listening audience. The radio news spot must be newsworthy, rather than an advertisement, if it is to have a chance of reaching the airwaves. Radio stations make their money from advertising, so they will not advertise a business venture for free. However, nonprofit activities or newsworthy achievements are a different matter.

Make Computer Technology Work for You

With a computer and a modem, you have access to a vast amount of information and information outlets. Information can be sent or received in an instant. Computers with access to the Internet offer several features that can be attractively incorporated into an effective promotional initiative.

Electronic Mailing Lists

An electronic mailing list (EML) is a collection of e-mail addresses of people who share a particular interest. These people wish to receive regular correspondence about a specific topic or program and often participate in interactive discussions with other list members. An EML is an efficient, cost-effective method of sending regular newsletters to a group of people interested in your program. It also allows for the distribution of personalized, direct e-mail to targeted groups within the list. A major advantage of an EML over conventional postal mail is the interactive function. That is, list members can interact with anyone or everyone on the list. This function is particularly useful for stimulating discussions on pertinent questions, seeking solutions to common problems, coordinating events and projects, offering technical assistance, and promoting connections among list members and through the program.

A mail list manager (MLM) is a great device for handling the administrative functions of the list. MLMs are software programs designed to handle such tasks as adding and removing subscribers, distributing submitted messages, and sending topic-related information. One of the best-known MLMs is Listserv (www.lsoft.com). MLMs are best for managing large electronic mailing lists (i.e., lists over 100 subscribers). For smaller lists, teachers may manage their own mailing lists by simply collecting the appropriate addresses in one file and then sending the desired information by typing in a single key word.

At present, many electronic mailing lists for teachers and coaches are available, as well as for people interested in particular sports, physical activities, or health and fitness ideas (see appendix I for recommended Web sites).

Web Sites

A Web site or Web page is space on the World Wide Web (WWW) containing information of a particular nature. Web sites are created by individuals or organizations and serve a variety of purposes. Governments and institutions have Web sites, as do professional and special interest groups, but anyone can establish a Web site, including teachers of physical activity (figure 13.3).

A Web site is an effective, economical way to offer extensive information about a program, activity, or group, and it can reach thousands, if not millions, of "Web surfers" (i.e., people who regularly search the Internet for information of interest). A site can provide a database for those interested in various aspects of a topic or program, as well as related (or "linked") sites for those interested in

Figure 13.3 Teachers can now use the World Wide Web to connect with colleagues and stay abreast of developments in physical education.

sport, physical activity, or physical education. Photographs, charts, drawings, and tables can all be loaded onto the Web site. Upcoming events or descriptions of recent activities can be included, as well as information about the current members of your program, policies, history, or any information you care to share with those exploring cyberspace. A Web site brings the added bonus of projecting the image that a program is up to date and using the latest trends and developments in the industry (Baker 2001).

Web sites are developed using Web-editing software programs to combine text, graphs, photographs, video clips, or any combination thereof. Once constructed, the document is saved as a file on a computer server, much like an e-mail message. The homepage, usually the first page a person is directed to when visiting a Web site, describes the purpose and contents of the site, provides a site map, and often has some distinctive logo or picture. Web sites are maintained by periodically updating or adding information. They usually provide a method by which a visitor can contact the author or other people associated with the site. Although many businesses specialize in developing professional Web sites, with a computer, Internet access, and the available software, it's easy for anyone to construct and maintain a Web site. Examples of instructional and educational Web sites are identified in appendix I.

Spreading the Word About Your Program

Media
- Newsletters
- Newspapers
- Television
- Radio

Internet
- Managed mailing lists
- Web sites

Demonstrations/Exhibitions: Seeing Is Believing

Sport and physical activity encompass both participation activities and spectator events. People can watch what you do as a teacher, and they can watch those you teach. Inviting local elected officials, members of the media, parents, and civic groups to view exhibitions or demonstrations of your program gives them a firsthand experience. Local businesses are often willing to provide financial or material sponsorship for local demonstrations or exhibitions. The events also offer good photo opportunities, with the photographs being distributed to the local community through newspapers, newsletters, or a Web site.

Jump rope or gymnastics demonstrations at the local shopping mall, a sport day or team day at a local school or business, dance recitals, and workout exhibitions at a civic meeting or game half-time are all examples of ways you can get the message out in a tangible manner. Being available after the exhibition or demonstration to answer questions or provide autographs (if appropriate) is an essential part of the effectiveness of these programs as public relations activities. In public schools, physical education teachers can participate in school-wide activities and collaborate with teachers of other subjects. One of the best ways for a good physical education program to gain its deserved recognition from other teachers in the school is through collaborative programs (Feingold 1994). Give people a chance to see what you do and get to know who you are.

Static displays of your program can also be effective. A booth or pictorial display at a local shopping center or public institution can enhance your program. Stationing informed participants in a booth or beside a display can be effective for providing a human touch, as well as for answering questions and providing additional information. Displays at community events during public holidays may be a particularly timely method for identifying with the community and promoting your program.

Community Activities: Make a Difference

Sport and physical activity programs appeal to communities—be they residential, special interest, or professional. Local communities have historically taken pride in and actively supported sport and physical activity. Civic-minded individuals enjoy the opportunity to assist causes they believe enhance the community's standard of living. Sport and physical activity programs represent such causes. But the public can't get behind programs it knows little about, so promotion becomes an important element of program support and enhancement. But just as it is important for a program to receive something from the community, as a part of that community, that program owes something back. Because of the educational and influential roles they play, physical education teachers, sports instructors, and athletic coaches must be contributing and responsible citizens in their communities.

Supporting a charity event or sponsoring an activity to benefit a local cause or civic group is both a method of showing appreciation for community support as well as a way of gaining positive public attention for your program. Sponsoring a 5K or 10K road race promotes the benefits of physical activity and at the same time serves as a fundraiser for a deserving community cause. Having your team or program participants volunteer for a community project such as Habitat for Humanity; cook for or help out at a homeless shelter; and read, sing, or perform at a senior citizens' home are all positive community activities that can enhance your program. In such activities, not only do the people involved with the charity or local group benefit, but your program benefits from positive public relations, and your program participants benefit by feeling like they made a difference in their community.

A community appreciation day is another way of "giving back" while at the same time letting people know about your program. Such a day can take on a variety of forms. In schools, a parent or family appreciation day for a school team or an open house that allows parents and other community members to meet your staff, view your facilities, and talk with people about the program can open lines of communication and support. For private instructional programs, community days that invite members of the public in free of charge or at reduced fees for the purpose of learning about their neighbors may not only be good politics but may also bring in some new sponsors and students.

Whether the educational institution is public or private, connecting with families is an important consideration (Baker 2001). Children provide a direct link between the teacher, the parents, and the community. What children say about the teachers and the instruction strongly shapes impressions parents form of the instructional curriculum. These impressions become the fundamental building blocks for later interactions between parents and teachers. If the initial impression is anything but positive, the teacher has a great deal to overcome. The goodwill that develops between teachers and parents spreads to relatives and friends and, like ripples on a lake, spreads out across the community. As this goodwill builds, the program receives invaluable long-term support because it's viewed as an important community asset.

Summary

With funding decisions and program participant recruitment so heavily dependent on good public relations, teachers need to assume greater responsibility for projecting the image and substance of their programs to the general public. Fortunately, increasing outlets for information make this a relatively easy task. This chapter described effective program promotion strategies through the media, computer technology, and community involvement. Good public relations, however, be-

gin with a sound high-quality program. In other words, good programs make for good public relations. Once the program is in order, the ability to effectively use as many of the appropriate tools of publicity as possible determines the level of participation, funding, and support that physical education, physical activity, and sport programs receive.

Discussion Questions

1. As a teacher or coach, what are some of the things you would like to say about your program, and what groups would you target to receive this information? Why would it be important for these people to receive information regarding your program?

2. Given the variety of outlets for promoting a sport or physical activity program (e.g., newsletters, Web sites, newspapers, television, radio), as a teacher or coach, which forms do you believe might best suit your purposes and why? How would you go about making use of these outlets?

3. Discuss the role of a demonstration or exhibition in promoting a program in which you are currently involved or for a program you would like to be involved with. What would the demonstration or exhibition consist of and how would you go about planning for it?

4. How would you get your students or athletes involved in their community? What activities or projects do you believe to be worthy causes to which you and your students might contribute as responsible citizens?

Chapter 14

Technology for Teaching

Technology, like art, is a soaring exercise of the human imagination.

— Daniel Bell

DEVELOPMENT

The dramatic increase and improvement in technology in the latter half of the 20th century have resulted in a multitude of tools for several key areas of teaching. Electronics and computer-based equipment offer an informed, creative teacher innovative ways of stimulating learning. Technology now places a virtually endless world of information in the hands of teachers. This chapter examines technology as a tool for providing information, analyzing student performance, instructing, communicating, and assigning student projects.

Tools for Finding Information

Teaching well requires a constant stream of information. Good teachers and coaches closely monitor new developments in teaching, teaching aids, training techniques, nutrition, or trends in a particular sport. Technology has not only made such monitoring easier but has also provided access to new information that has never before been available.

The Internet

As the name implies, the Internet is an interconnected network of computers. Large-capacity computers called servers continually assist one computer to connect with another for the purpose of ushering along information. When a person connects a computer to the Internet, they are logged in (electronically attached) to a server and are online (i.e., can send and receive information). Internet access is gained through the use of a personal computer with a connection to an Internet Service Provider (ISP). Usually, this connection is established through a telephone line coupled with a computer modem. Several commercial servers are available for a reasonable monthly cost. America Online (AOL) is perhaps the largest and most widely known ISP. People affiliated with universities, governments, or other large institutions often gain access to the Internet by connecting to the institution's main computer. For people unfamiliar with Internet connections, a visit to a local computer shop is a good place to start. Connection to the Internet brings a host of services such as e-mail and access to the World Wide Web.

The World Wide Web

As a subset of the Internet, the World Wide Web (WWW) presents a virtually inexhaustible well of information for the savvy teacher (figure 14.1). Once connected to the Internet, a teacher can search, or surf, for information of interest. The software used to connect to the Web will contain one or more search engines (computer software used to locate desired information). Typing in the category of information or keywords sought and hitting the "go" button brings a range of potentially useful Web sites. Keywords include such terms as *fitness, nutrition,* or *lesson plans* or more activity-related terms such as *running, basketball,* or *aerobics.*

Web sites are the computer locations for a particular topic. The Internet address for such a site normally begins with *www.* Web sites are created and maintained by various groups or individuals. Equipment corporations, professional organizations, or other teachers can create Web sites of interest to teachers. Most Web sites contain information on a particular topic, photographs or videos, and links to other similar sites.

Many Web sites offer "chat rooms" that allow people logged on to the site to interact with one another about topics pertaining to the Web site. Chat rooms are designed to facilitate electronic conversations; one person types a message into her computer and the person or persons also logged into the chat room can immediately respond to the message. Teachers who use Web sites for instructional purposes often designate chat room hours when students interested in conversing with the teacher or other students in the class can log in. As technology develops, there will be an increasing number of useful new tools for teaching.

Professional associations frequently establish sophisticated Web sites that provide their mem-

Figure 14.1 Computers are a valuable tool for teachers that want to stay current, connected, and organized in their profession.

bers with up-to-date information to keep them informed and to improve their teaching. Teachers of specific sports and physical activities find Web sites tailored to their needs increasingly useful for improving the quality of their teaching. In the field of physical education, for example, a teacher can log on to PE Central (http://pe.central.org) and find well-developed lesson plans, announcements of upcoming conferences, links to other physical education programs, and job announcements and can even send PE greeting cards.

Launching Physical Education Into Cyberspace: The Story of PE Central

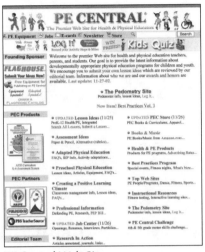

PE Central Web Site
Used by permission of PE Central (www.pecentral.org), the premier Web site for physical educators.

A common fixture in graduate schools, seminars usually produce a flood of enthusiastic debate and dynamic activity. Their main mission is to bring together graduate students and a major professor to analyze a current trend, discuss shared scholarly readings, or undertake a pertinent academic project. The students who found their way to Dr. George Graham's Special Topics seminar at Virginia Tech in the fall of 1995 had no way of knowing that it wouldn't be an ordinary seminar. They were about to make history.

Dr. Graham and the 10 doctoral students began discussing the idea of establishing a Web site for physical education teachers—an Internet site where the teachers could find useful information and resources for PE classes. They considered the far-reaching potential of the Internet and the growing accessibility teachers around the world had to the World Wide Web. In doing some exploration, they found few sites of any quality or substance for physical educators.

If the site was to serve teachers, the group members reasoned that they should talk with teachers about what would be of value on such a site. Using a scenario-based design, they asked teachers to think through and write out what should be included. They also had the teachers explain the best way to navigate the site to get to the needed information. The seminar group was pleased to find that the teachers' ideas meshed well with those of the group.

Being located at Virginia Tech, a premier institution of technology, was also useful in developing the Web site. A working relationship with the instructional technology department was established. It was agreed that the seminar group would develop the content and write the HTML pages while the technology crew would provide the server, consult on design features, and offer technical assistance.

As the school year drew to a close, there was much work left to be done if the good idea and previous hard work was to result in an operational Web site. Mark Manross, one of the original seminar participants, carried the work forward and designed, built, and provided the content for the early pages of PE Central using ideas developed over the previous year as well as a few of his own. Along with Dr. Graham, they designed and edited the first draft of PE Central. Other students also continued their contributions, and steady progress was made throughout the summer. On August 26, 1996, PE Central debuted on the Web.

Since that debut, PE Central has been accessed by millions of visitors and has received a number of prestigious awards. With the growing success and increased demand for content and innovation, PE Central needed both financial and information resources. FlagHouse, Inc., a marketer of sport and physical activity products, became the founding sponsor, bringing the necessary financial base to the operation. An advisory board made up of physical education teachers and scholars was established to ensure a vibrant and continual flow of new ideas and materials for the site.

From a series of discussions in a seminar room on a college campus, PE Central has grown to become the most popular destination on the Web for health and physical education professionals. At present, 15 managing editors and 80 advisory board members are responsible for acquiring, organizing, and presenting the site's content. Averaging over 50,000 unique visitors a month, the site has published

(continued)

(continued)

contributions from over 700 health and physical education professionals and currently features over 1,000 developmentally appropriate lesson ideas. The resources of PE Central include health and physical education lesson ideas, ready-to-print assessments, adapted physical education information, classroom management strategies, a job center, a book and music store (in association with Amazon.com), equipment discounts, links to other relevant sites, information on best practices in physical education, and programs designed to motivate children to improve their motor skills and understanding of the importance of physical fitness. Future plans include useful physical fitness and movement information for parents and motivational and interactive sections for youngsters. For anyone teaching sport and physical activity, the site is well worth the visit.

Literature Searches

Through the use of computers at a local or university library, a teacher can now access lists of books and articles on any subject of interest. Similar to a search engine on the Internet, library literature searches use a computer program that searches out a topic based on keywords. Keywords in a literature search can focus on the subject, author, or publication year (or a combination of the three). Some literature searches contain abstracts of the publication to give the searcher an idea of the full text of the book or article, but many simply list the reference (author, publisher, title, and copyright date). Once the literature search is completed, the publication can then be located within the library. Although more time consuming than a Web search, it's far more efficient than simply browsing the library bookshelves.

Libraries or Internet providers subscribe to several databases that maintain lists of publications. Educational Resource and Information Clearinghouse (ERIC) contains extensive publication resources of interest to teachers. Canada's Sport Information Resource Center (SIRC) is a comprehensive listing of information specific to sport and sport-related topics.

Courses and Workshops

Universities and professional organizations are beginning to offer coursework and certification programs online. Students can log on to a class in session or participate in a teleconference course when the teacher may be hundreds of miles away or even around the world. The Internet also allows teachers to advance their education through distance learning (St. Pierre 1998). That is, a teacher with limited time or located a long way from a university or other educational site can now take courses and, in some cases, even degree programs

through the Internet. Emporia State University, Virginia Tech, and West Virginia State University are among those universities currently offering online degrees in physical education and sport studies. A teacher with a computer, printer, and modem now has access to resources and opportunities heretofore unavailable.

Tools for Analyzing Performance

Teachers frequently assess student skill performances. Coaches have long used film and videotape to analyze the offensive and defensive strengths of upcoming opponents, and elite teachers often use videotape to pinpoint minor flaws in otherwise expert performances of top athletes. Whether you are attempting to rate potential performance levels, assess learning progress, or diagnose performance problems, technology can help (figure 14.2).

Figure 14.2 Cordless microphones are an example of a way teachers can use technology in relatively simple ways to improve their instruction settings.

Video Recordings

Using video cameras to tape and subsequently ana-lyze an individual or team performance has been a common practice in teaching and coaching for decades. Equipment innovations have made the practice far less expensive and thus more common than ever before. Currently, two types of cameras are available for capturing performance images: video cameras and digital cameras. Digital cameras capture images that are stored and viewed on a computer, whereas video cameras capture images on videotape for viewing on a monitor. The advantages of digital cameras are that film isn't necessary, the camera is smaller and lighter, and the images can be stored in a computer file and are transferable over the Internet. The advantages of video cameras are that they are usually less expensive and more durable. Regardless of the camera used, video records have proven useful tools for analyzing sport and physical activity performances.

A video recording lets a learner view his performance from a perspective he cannot otherwise see. Watching a taped performance lets an athlete actually see the particular aspects and mechanical movements. Reality does not always match perception, and therefore, a learner may believe he is doing one thing when, in fact, he is doing something altogether different.

Skillful teachers use videotape to identify the particular components of a performance that are being done well (and thus reinforce proper technique) as well as aspects in need of correction or additional practice. Charles Sorrell, the 1990 PGA Teacher of the Year, goes one step further and uses a telestrator to draw colorful lines and diagrams over his students' golf swings so they can clearly see what he is attempting to explain to them. This technique allows Mr. Sorrell not only to clearly describe the proper mechanics of the performance but also to personalize it directly to the student with whom he is working. Additionally, Mr. Sorrell audio records his analysis on the tape, offers practice suggestions, and then gives the student the tape to take home and review. The student can then watch the tape whenever she feels it necessary or appropriate.

Research reveals several points about videotapes as feedback that are pertinent for teachers (Schempp and St. Pierre 2000b). First, the effectiveness of videotaping does not appear to be dependent on the activity. That is, a teacher of gymnastics may find videotape as effective for helping learners as would a teacher of swimming, volleyball, dance, running, or basketball. Second, intermediate and advanced athletes get more out of viewing videotapes than do beginners. Beginners need greater assistance from a teacher to analyze their performances and devise instructional cues and goals from a videotape. Finally, video recordings provide more useful feedback the more often videotape is used. That is, the more accustomed a learner becomes to viewing videotape, the more cues he can derive from the tape. Used only once or sparingly, the effectiveness of videotape as a feedback source for the learner is limited. The more students see themselves on tape, the more astute they become at analyzing their performances, judging developments in their performances, and detecting nuances or changes that might signal the necessity of a correction.

Photographic Images

Still photographs can serve as representational images that either depict what a current performance looks like or what a performance should look like. Like video, photographs can be taken with either a traditional film camera or a digital camera. However, there are times when a sketch or line drawing can substitute for a photographic image. A student and teacher seeing a clear picture of a current performance can often identify both appropriate and inappropriate technical aspects of the performance. An image of a well-performed skill provides relevant learning cues and an accurate visual image for students attempting to master a new skill. Sport magazines, such as *Golf Magazine* and *Ski*, make extensive use of photographs to depict the important performance cues presented in the text of their instruction articles. These photographs combine with clear, concise text to provide helpful tips to amateur athletes.

In order for an image to assist learning, two conditions are necessary (Leshin, Pollock, and Reigeluth 1992). First, the images must be placed in a meaningful context. Contextual distortions of a skill or its performance interfere with the interpretation of the image. Simplicity is also helpful because too many details are difficult to process and provide too many distractions. Second, the student must interpret the image so that the information can be properly processed. Normally, this involves reviewing the image or images with a teacher so that the appropriate cues and topics can be identified. More advanced performers and those with experience analyzing their own performances may be able to make appropriate and meaningful interpretations without the assistance of a teacher. In general, however, it's better to involve the eye and mind of a teacher experienced in image interpretation.

Computer Analysis Programs

Although the cost is considerable, computer software and hardware packages are now available to biomechanically analyze a student's performance. Instructors working with elite performers often use this technology to detect minor flaws and nuances in an athlete's performance that may be undetectable to even a trained eye. Therefore, the advantage of these programs is that the teacher doesn't have to rely solely on his analytic ability. He can now critique a learner's performance with a computer program that bases its analysis on accurate and appropriate biomechanical principles. These programs are currently available for instructors of sports such as track and field, tennis, skiing, rock climbing, soccer, and golf; they are likely to grow in popularity as technical innovations increase and computer-related equipment decreases in cost (Mohnsen 1998).

Virtual Reality

People learn physical and sport skills best if they practice in conditions closely approximating the environment in which those skills will be performed. Virtual reality (VR) is a computer-generated, three-dimensional environment that allows people to experience multisensory immersion and interact with selected events as they would in the physical world (Heinich et al. 1999). In VR, the student wears a special headpiece containing a video display and headphones. The student practices the preprogrammed skills by manipulating a peripheral device such as a joystick, glove, club, bat, or other equipment. The peripheral device is used to manipulate objects and direct the student's movements in the virtual world. The student might practice tennis strokes, play a round of golf, take batting practice, or shoot basketball free throws.

VR creates a realistic environment that is safe from the normal hazards of the sport or activity area. Through VR, students can explore opportunities not feasible in the real world (e.g., participate in an Olympic event, take a penalty kick in a World Cup soccer match). Because the environment can be manipulated so thoroughly, the student has opportunities to experiment with a variety of scenarios in the virtual environment.

There are significant limitations to the general use of VR for teaching sport and physical activity, however. The equipment is expensive and the technology complex. At present, a limited number of software "realities" exist. But given the potential of VR to enhance sport and physical activity learning,

this is one technology that seems destined for development and implementation in instructional programs.

Tools for Instruction

Technology offers teachers countless possibilities for presenting information. With advances in computer software and hardware, the development of the Internet, and the availability of computer peripheral devices such as cameras, monitors, and disk drives, more options are available than ever before for bringing information to learners in purposeful and attractive ways. Contemporary technology allows teachers to deliver multimedia messages that include striking blends of text, video, graphic images, sounds, and animation.

Technology can easily be integrated into almost any instructional environment. In addition, technical innovations offer the teacher and learner an option that is seldom available in traditional forms of teaching: learner control. With the appropriate technology, students can make their own decisions about learning content, sequence, feedback, methods, and pacing. If the instructional program calls for students to make decisions about their learning or have access to supplemental information, technology offers an attractive option. Whether a teacher uses a computer and printer to produce a simple handout or integrates multimedia to conduct an interactive Web conference, technology represents an important tool for a skillful, knowledgeable teacher.

Desktop Publishing

Creating professional looking publications is easy and economical with modern word processing programs and laser printers. Posters, handouts, task cards, flyers, and newsletters all add flair to an instructional program and require only a bit of time and money with today's technology. With a computer, a word processing program, a good quality printer, and a little creativity, a teacher has all the resources she needs to produce printed materials that enhance her teaching.

Printed materials reinforce important points or principles in a lesson or program. Making take-home materials available for learners gives them a chance to review the key concepts from the lesson, seminar, or practice. Quality supplemental materials emphasize the importance of the instruction and reflect the quality aspired to by the instructor.

Slide Show Software

Computer software programs now make it simple to create interesting slide show presentations. A slide might include text, graphs, diagrams, drawings, or photographs. Slides can be created in a multitude of colors and patterns, allowing the creator to highlight important information in attractive ways. With appropriate software and sufficient computer capacity, it's possible to integrate video, photographs, music, voice, and background sound into a slide presentation. One of the more popular slide show programs available is Microsoft PowerPoint. The software is relatively easy to learn and use and has a wide assortment of options for crafting attractive presentations. Keep in mind, however, that too many words, pictures, or sounds flying at your listener all at once are more likely to cloud the message than clarify it. Use the technology to display your message, not your message to display the technology.

Depending on the presentation, a slide show might be as simple as a single slide depicting a diagram or summarizing learning cues or a series of slides to supplement a lecture or demonstration. Using computer slide show software permits several options in terms of presentation. The most common is to project the images from the computer through a projection system to a large screen. The slide show can also be projected directly from the computer monitor. Still, a teacher may want to print out the slide show and make transparencies to be placed on an overhead projector or convert the computer-generated slides to traditional film-based slides.

Instructional Videos

If a picture is worth a thousand words, consider the value of a videotape that comprises over a thousand pictures. Instructional videos focus on particular skills or knowledge students need to master a sport or activity. They are useful for learning a fitness routine, fundamental sport skills, or the rules and etiquette of a game. Videos can be shown to large or small groups. An added advantage of videos is that they can be reviewed from time to time as students feel the need to revisit various points.

Instructional videos are available commercially and often feature leading authorities in the activity. For example, Human Kinetics Publishers offers instructional videos on topics such as strength and conditioning, sport nutrition, training, dance, baseball, and tennis. Professionally produced videos

also take care of the setting, actors, and script, resulting in a video that conveys a clear message in a motivating way. Depending on the need and the equipment available, teachers may decide to produce videos to use in a class or lesson. Most video cameras now permit editing and title creation right on the camera, and a camera can serve as a second monitor when attempting to create a fresh tape from sections of another tape or tapes.

Interactive Multimedia Programs

With the development of speedy microprocessors, mega-capacity hard drives, and CD-ROM technology came the ability to blend text, images, animation, audio, and video into powerful learning environments. Interactive multimedia programs are computer-based programs that give students a degree of control as they interact with the variety of sources brought together in the program. They are designed to build skills (e.g., problem solving, strategic decision making, analytical skills), explore knowledge (e.g., rules, history, strategy), plan programs (e.g., a practice plan for developing hockey skills, a training timeline for a swim competition, a wellness program), or serve as a reference (e.g., encyclopedias, dictionaries, atlases, collections) (Hackbarth 1996).

The interactive portion occurs as the learner navigates the program by selecting the content areas and activities to be explored. The selection process is registered in the program when the student clicks on an icon. Clicking an icon allows the student to print a file, hear a narrated account of an event, view a film clip, take a test, move to another topic, or terminate the program. The obvious advantage of these programs is that the student can continue to learn when the teacher is unavailable. Learning is no longer confined to class or lesson time only. Additionally, if the teacher is working with one or more students on a special topic or is unavailable for other reasons, students can use the computer programs to continue their learning independently.

Depending on the topic, these programs may be available commercially or can be developed by a teacher using any number of author programs. Teams made up of experts in the subject, instructors, and computer programmers assemble commercially available programs. It's difficult for a teacher to compete with those resources. However, there may be no interactive media programs available in the teacher's subject of interest. Teachers can produce the programs themselves, although it usually takes considerable knowledge, skill, and time. Multimedia authoring tools such as HyperCard, Hyper Studio, Multimedia Toolbook, and Authorware produce attractive, effective learning programs.

Video Conferencing

A quickly advancing technology that holds significant potential for sport and physical activity instruction is video conferencing. Using video streaming through an Internet connection along with specifically designed computer software and hardware attachments that accommodate video and audio transmissions, a student in Boston, USA, can receive instruction from a teacher in Sydney, Australia. Depending on the system design and configuration, a teacher can interact with one student or five hundred students at a time. The students can all be located in one site or in multiple locations. Because this technology is still being developed, there are limitations to the numbers and locations of students that can be reached by a single teacher at one time. Video conferencing also remains an expensive instructional option.

The obvious attraction of video conferencing is that the teacher and student no longer need to be in the same place for a student to receive instruction from a trusted teacher. Because the teacher and student have interactive visual and audio contact, many of the same instructional activities can take place, and a few enhancements are even possible. For example, a student can demonstrate a skill or show the teacher a video clip of a performance, and the teacher can analyze the performance with the student. The teacher can also show video clips or provide documents or presentation materials that are stored in computer files. Browsing the Web together is another option. A teacher can even administer a test over the Internet, or students can submit assignments in a variety of multimedia formats (e.g., text, video, audio, pictures, graphics). Although a video conference can't substitute for the personal contact between two or more people in the same place, it does provide a promising teaching tool.

Learning Centers

Have you ever considered allocating a small amount of space where students can come to learn more about a particular topic? Learning centers are self-contained learning spaces designed to promote individual or small group learning around a specific theme or task (Heinich et al. 1999) (figure 14.3). They can be as simple as a table and chair with a few

Figure 14.3 Learning centers are comfortable spaces where students can go to study more about the physical activity topics that most interest them.

resources such as books and magazines for independent exploration or as sophisticated as a multimedia site containing computers, video analysis, pictorial displays, and printed resources. Common items found in a learning center include books, articles, pictures, audiotapes, videotapes, and computers with software. The tasks students undertake in a learning center can vary but normally include one or more of the following: developing skills or increasing knowledge, exploring potential areas of interest, remedial activities, and enrichment challenges.

Learning centers are usually constructed to make them inviting to the learner, which places a premium on learner comfort and enjoyment. The location can be any secure, convenient place such as a classroom, hallway, office, or library. The advantage of a learning center is that it gives the students and teacher a degree of autonomy that allows the students to extend their learning without the presence of the teacher. Because of the relative ease of construction, self-service operation, and potential benefits to students, teachers should consider at least one learning center in their place of instruction.

Tools for Communication

In a recent study, teachers identified other teachers as one of their primary sources of knowledge (Fincher and Schempp 1994). Yet, on a daily basis, teachers work with students and athletes and often find themselves isolated from other teachers. The chance to communicate with their colleagues has traditionally been limited. Technology has changed this situation.

Electronic Mail

Electronic mail (e-mail) has become a common mode of communication. It permits communication between students and teachers, coaches and athletes, parents, colleagues, or others in a simple and cost-effective manner. E-mail requires a computer, a software program, and a connection to a server (usually from a modem in the computer). Using the software program, you can compose a message directly or import a message file from a word processing program.

Received messages can be printed and saved for later reference, and the reply function allows the receiver to quickly send a response if so desired. By using an address book, a single message can be communicated to as many individuals as you want. This technique is popular with coaches attempting to communicate with an entire team and teachers who need to communicate with an entire class.

Although e-mail isn't quite as fast as a phone call, it's significantly faster than the traditional postal service. It may take the post office several days to deliver a letter, but that same letter can be delivered in a matter of minutes (sometimes even much faster) using e-mail. And rather than hunting for stationery, stamps, and envelopes and then venturing out to find a mailbox, an e-mail message can be composed, corrected, and sent next door or around the world from the comfort of your computer chair. And a reply may be returned before you even leave your seat.

Coaches who find it difficult to locate athletes by phone or other means often find e-mail a valuable mode of communication. Famed Swedish golf coach Pia Nilsson is in regular contact with the golfers with whom she works. Pia may find herself in Sweden and yet wish to contact a player in Asia or the United States. Given their busy schedules, e-mail is a highly effective form of communication. Similarly, teachers who find it difficult to contact students by telephone find it a simple process to post assignments, information about an upcoming class, or answers to student questions by e-mail.

Listservs and Bulletin Boards

Active e-mail users often become members of listservs, sometimes referred to as an electronic discussion group (Elliot and Manross 1996a). A listserv, or electronic mailing list (EML; see chapter 13), is a form of e-mail in which multiple e-mail addresses are packaged together, and the people who respond or send messages to the listserv address are able to simultaneously communicate with all members of the group. A message sent to the listserv is automatically sent to all subscribers. This format is an excellent method of engaging in a professional dialogue on pertinent topics, soliciting information on a particular problem, or sharing ideas with people who hold similar concerns. Listservs have moderators who are responsible for, among other things, managing the operations of the service as well as regulating the messages sent to the group. Subscribing to a listserv is usually an easy process of contacting the moderator and informing him of your interest in joining the group. One of the more popular listservs for discussions on topics pertinent to sport and physical activity instruction is pe-talk (see www.lyris.sportime.com).

Bulletin boards are a specific type of listserv in which people post messages but responses are usually made in private. Many professional organizations host bulletin boards so that members can announce job openings, request information, announce upcoming conferences and related events, and keep members informed of policy changes and other news of the organization. Electronic bulletin boards are supplements to, and in some cases replacements for, the traditional newsletter printed by professional groups. Bulletin boards are faster and more cost-efficient than the traditionally printed and mailed newsletter.

Tools for Student Projects

Good teaching often requires that students make some effort outside the class to supplement instruction and promote their learning. Student projects are a good way for students to learn the subject in a medium other than a teacher-led class. Whether practicing a newly learned skill, training for an upcoming event, or monitoring a diet or exercise routine, students can learn and improve away from the teacher and the class. These projects and assignments are also valuable for evaluating student learning of the subject. Technology offers teachers and students effective, interesting ways to make such out-of-class activities pay large dividends.

Resource Location

One particularly popular activity with Internet surfers is locating information resources. The Internet offers what seems to be an unlimited supply of information on virtually any topic. Encouraging or even assigning "surfing projects" provides students with access to the extensive resources available on the Web. Providing some Web sites for them to visit is a good way to begin the "surfing safari." Searches can focus on the skills being learned, history, rules, related organizations, activities, events, and even personal Web sites from other sport or physical activity participants (Elliot and Manross 1996b).

Students don't need Internet access to locate resources, however. Learning is a lifetime activity, so having students assemble learning resources from a variety of areas will serve their learning for a long time to come as well as teach them how and where to look for resources pertaining to the topic at hand. Searching libraries for books, compiling a reading or video list, identifying relevant computer software, or locating other resources that might help them to learn more about the activity and increase their participation and enjoyment are all valuable activities.

Student-Designed Web Sites

Teachers might consider requiring students to design a personal Web site as part of their instructional program. Student-designed Web sites get the student online and connected to the vast information resources of the Internet. Students might place information on their Web sites about themselves and the course topics or subjects, or they may identify resources they've found useful in learning or participating in a sport or physical activity. There is a growing list of sport and physical activity participants who maintain Web sites on their sport or activity.

Student-designed Web sites are already becoming part of the teacher education requirements in some universities. Teachers graduate from these programs with a personal, professional Web site already up on the Web. At Central Washington University, for example, students construct Web pages and post unit plans for other physical education teachers (see www.pelinks4u.org/links/unitplans.htm).

Student Portfolios

Teaching places a premium on student improvement. What students do and learn is critical, and this learning is a developmental process. Technology allows students to document their learning by assembling a portfolio of progress. A portfolio might include a diary of thoughts and information using a word processor, a video archive of films made at various stages of the learning process, or a record of fitness scores, performance statistics, or practice times using a spreadsheet. A portfolio lets the teacher and student reflect on the progress made to date and plan the next stage in the learning process. A teacher might want to set standards and offer suggestions, but a portfolio documents the student's efforts, discoveries, improvements, thoughts, and accomplishments. Students should therefore be encouraged to construct the portfolio with documents, pictures, sound, and video that best represent their involvement in the learning process and their perspective on the activity being learned. Charting progress not only gives the teacher and student a tangible record of achievement but also details the steps along the way so that the progress can both be celebrated and continued.

A Teacher's Technological Toolkit

Tools for Finding Information	Tools for Analyzing Performance	Tools for Instruction
The Internet	Video recordings	Desktop publishing
The World Wide Web	Photographic images	Slide show software
Electronic literature search	Computer programs	Instructional videos
Courses and workshops	Virtual reality	Interactive multimedia
		Video conferencing
		Learning centers

Tools for Communicating	Tools for Student Projects
Electronic mail	Resource location
Listservs and bulletin boards	Web sites
	Portfolios

Summary

Technological improvements and innovations offer teachers and students new tools for teaching and learning. Future advances promise to change the way we teach and learn. Significant changes have already begun to take place in the way sport and physical activity is taught and learned because of technology, and this influence will continue to grow as new developments bring new opportunities. You must watch carefully for new ways to capitalize on the potential of technology for improving teaching and coaching.

Just because it is technology does not, however, automatically make it good or useful. Technology is a tool that will only be as serviceable as the user is skillful. The more technological tools a teacher can master, the greater the array of tools at his or her disposal in teaching. In this chapter, technological tools were presented that have proven successful for accessing information, analyzing performance, diagnosing performance problems, explaining concepts and skills, communicating away from class, and promoting supplemental learning. Teachers with a large collection of tools will be better equipped to meet the needs of their students and promote student development. Technology offers teachers an extensive and proven set of such tools.

Discussion Questions

1. Of the available forms of technology, which forms do you believe can potentially contribute to your effectiveness as a teacher or coach? How?

2. As a sport or physical activity participant, which forms of technology have you found to be the most valuable in helping you learn or improve your performance?

3. Discuss the advantages and any potential disadvantages of using videotape technology in your teaching.

4. In your position as a teacher or coach, what forms of technical equipment (e.g., computer, camera, printer, video) will you consider either necessary or desirable? Why?

Chapter 15

Improving Teaching

Knowing is not enough, we must apply. Willing is not enough, we must do.

— Johann von Goethe

DEVELOPMENT

Teaching requires both knowledge and skill. The degree to which you can improve your teaching skills and increase your knowledge is the degree to which you can improve your teaching. This chapter offers several techniques for refining teaching skills and escalating knowledge. To become better, it's important to incorporate regular assessments and reflections on the practices targeted for improvement. Therefore, the chapter opens with a discussion of strategies for reflective teaching and for monitoring instructional practices and perspectives. With an understanding of the areas to be improved, developing teaching skills comes next. In this process, current teaching practices need to be analyzed and areas for development need to be identified. Techniques for analyzing teaching will therefore be presented, followed by a review of practice strategies leading to improvement. Finally, the chapter ends with suggestions for increasing knowledge and continuing your education as a teacher. Used individually or collectively, these strategies and suggestions should help the conscientious and committed teacher find ways to improve teaching.

Reflective Teaching

Noted Dutch sport scholar Bart Crum wrote that "a conscientious practitioner should not stay on the safe high ground, but descend to the important problems" (1995, 5). To improve, you must honestly question the taken-for-granted and search for solutions to important and compelling problems. When teachers question their teaching, it's referred to as reflective teaching. The process of reflective teaching demands a continual searching and questioning. Hellison and Templin believe that reflective teaching "means to think about your teaching and especially to ask yourself two questions: What's worth doing? and Is what I'm doing working?" (1991, 3). The first question demands a focus on your values and beliefs as a teacher, whereas the second question leads to an analysis of instructional content, activities, and behavior.

Reflective Teaching Topics

There are many focus topics in reflective teaching, and all can lead to improvement. Just about any topic of importance to a teacher makes good subject matter for reflection. Reflection topics can range from the immediate concerns of the class to long-term implications for society. Organizing and managing the instructional environment, student learning, and the processes and practices of teaching are all common concerns scrutinized by reflective teachers. These are the day-to-day routines and practices that define your teaching and require periodic checks and adjustments.

Beyond the day-to-day practical concerns of teaching, reflecting on the limits of your current knowledge and seeking new information for a specific purpose provide avenues for instructional improvement through reflective teaching. Turning over old and recurring problems in your mind often leads to discovering new solutions. Understanding new techniques relative to a student's performance, training regimens, or even psychological theories of motivation may all be potentially fruitful topics for exploration. Reviewing what a teacher knows, and needs to know, about her students is a useful topic of reflection because the better a teacher knows and understands her students, the better equipped she is to provide instruction that motivates students and contributes to their overall well-being. The social dimension of a teacher's work is another reflection topic. Critical social reflection considers the role played by teachers in society as well as the

cultural values transferred and transformed through teaching. Issues of power, biases, and prejudices that may be formed or perpetuated in a teacher's class are checked. Included in the topics examined in critical social reflection are beliefs and practices based on race, social class, gender, sexuality, and religion.

Reflective Teaching Techniques

Taking a few minutes at the end of a lesson to think about the events just passed is perhaps the simplest way to reflect on your teaching. Expert teachers develop a routine of reflecting after each class. The successes from the lesson are stored for future use, while the problems are examined in hopes of finding better solutions should they arise again.

Reflective teachers develop characteristics and practices that allow them to maximize the findings of their deliberations (Cruickshank, Bainer, and Metcalf 1995). First, reflective teachers regularly, purposefully, and carefully judge their teaching. Their reflections lead to rational instructional decisions. Second, reflective teachers are open-minded. They question their own views and practices and openly explore options and other perspectives in the search for viable alternatives. Third, reflective teachers focus their deliberations on improving their practices and finding specific ways to help students maximize their potential. Fourth, reflective teachers take responsibility for their teaching and the results of their instructional practices. They see themselves as the sole proprietors of their teaching. No one else is going to make them a better teacher. Finally, reflective teachers are inquiry-oriented. They enjoy the process of exploring options and alternatives and are constantly questioning what they do and experimenting with new ideas and practices.

A technique that has proven useful in constructive reflection is maintaining a journal so that the products of reflection are recorded for future reference (figure 15.1). Famed basketball coach John Wooden (1985) kept a journal in which he would record not only his daily practice activities, but also his impressions, feelings, and judgments. He found his journal enormously useful for discovering those activities and practices that were most successful in shaping championship teams. A journal provides a place for recording important ideas that might otherwise be lost and helps ensure that a teacher can extract maximum benefits from moments of reflection.

Teaching Journal Entry
Nov. 3, 2002

Lots of questions today! A good sign! They seemed really into it. When the team handball unit started last week, there was a lot of grumbling and resistance. Now the enthusiasm seems to be growing. I think as they developed a bit of skill in passing and especially in shooting, their interest grew. The biggest spark, I think, comes from the small-sided games and scrimmages. Putting them into controlled and small competitive situations (e.g., 2 vs. 2 or 3 vs. 3) with people of like ability is lighting their fires. The idea of giving them a little information about the skill, brief practice, small game, followed by "debriefing" the skill (i.e., asking them how the skill worked in the game, and if it helped them perform at a higher level). This seems to make them see the value in learning the skill.

Also, the small-sided games are promoting more activity by more students. I've noticed some students sweating who would never break a sweat before. Isabel, Laura, and Euichang all seem to believe they have discovered a sport made uniquely for them. On the topic of students, Doug in fourth period continues to be a perpetual problem. His brother's arrest has thrown him into a belligerent funk. He hates the world and seems determined to make the world pay for it. I am having to isolate him from other students. It is a tough call. More than ever I think he needs to be with the rest of the kids, feeling some success and experiencing a little fun, but his behavior is making that all but impossible. I need to talk with other teachers about their strategies for engaging him, and if I end up not engaging him with others, maybe I can at least put him in situations that will decrease his destructive behavior and increase his happiness with himself. The challenges of teaching—they never grow old!

George Russell
Bassick High School

Figure 15.1 A technique that has proven useful in reflection is maintaining a journal.

Developing Teaching Skills

There is no substitute for experience when it comes to developing teaching skills. Through experience, teachers learn to express themselves clearly, identify effective forms of feedback, select stimulating learning activities, and develop organizational strategies that allow them to focus more on student learning and less on administrative tasks. But experience alone is not enough to bring about improvements in teaching. Unfortunately, many teachers continue to teach in the same way year after year with no detectable betterment in their instruction. Teaching becomes like handwriting: The same sloppy style is considered serviceable and never changed. It may even deteriorate over time. To improve and develop, you must thoughtfully analyze your teaching skills, understand the alternatives, and then practice the innovations. This section presents techniques for analyzing teaching skills and offers suggestions for establishing instructional routines, practicing teaching skills, and seeking instructional alternatives to persistent teaching problems.

Analyzing Teaching

Analyzing teaching is a three-step process. First, an observation must be made. To identify the quality of a teaching skill, the teacher must see it being performed. For teachers to analyze their own teaching, videotapes or cassette recordings are helpful. Direct observation is best to analyze the teaching of a colleague, a student teacher, or an assistant. After an observation, either live or recorded, the second step in the assessment takes place: analysis. Although sport instructors are often skilled at analyzing sport and physical activity skill performances, few are as skilled at judging a teaching performance. In the analysis phase, selected aspects of the teaching performance are either quantified or qualified.

The final step is forming judgments of the observed teaching skills. These judgments are based on the findings from the second step. For example, in applying criteria to the observation, it might be discovered that a teacher takes an average of eight minutes to explain and demonstrate skills at the beginning of class. Is this acceptable? Is a change necessary? Ultimately, it's the teacher who determines what needs to change and why. In determining the answers, the teacher identifies those aspects of his teaching he wants to improve as well as the magnitude of change.

Like any skill, current performance must first be analyzed before improvement can be targeted and strategies for refinement can be planned. In this section, four techniques will be suggested for analyzing teaching: directed observation, checklist/rating scales, systematic observation, and teaching journals. Within the descriptions of each technique, both the criteria and procedure for analyzing teaching are explained. By using a combination of these methods, teachers can best identify, analyze, and improve their instructional skills.

Directed Observation

A directed observation analysis is the simplest and most common of the analytic techniques. This technique requires no or few predetermined criteria when observing a teacher. As the observation unfolds, the observer makes notes as she sees fit. In some instances, a guide sheet is used to focus the observation into areas such as management and organization, quality of explanations and demonstrations, feedback, knowledge of the subject matter, and other areas of interest (see appendix J for an example).

The advantage of this technique is that, with no predetermined focus or criteria, it permits total observation of the environment, teacher, and students. Whatever captures the observer's interest becomes a potential item of analysis. The analysis can be responsive to the needs of the observer, teacher, administrator, or students.

The disadvantage of this technique is that it's unreliable and subject to bias. Two people watching the same teacher may come to two entirely different conclusions. The technique is also susceptible to the "good teacher/bad teacher" syndrome. That is, if the observer believes the teacher is "good," then the teacher's strengths are given greater weight in the report, while weaknesses are downplayed or ignored. If the observer believes the teacher is "bad," then the teacher's weaknesses are given center stage in the report, while any strengths are given average attention. This technique is therefore at the mercy of the observer's skill, knowledge, and sensitivity to the teacher and learning environment. The quality of the information and its ability to offer something meaningful to the teacher are strictly at the discretion of the observer.

Checklist/Rating Scale Analysis

Analyses using a checklist or rating scale have established criteria based on selected teaching activi-

ties. The observer watches the teaching and then completes either the checklist or the rating scale. If a checklist is used, the observer checks off those items that occurred. Rating scales require the observer to use a numerical sliding scale to rate the degree to which the activity occurred or failed to occur. Items contained in the checklist or rating scale are normally theoretically or empirically based on the characteristics of effective teaching and learning (see appendix K for an example).

Because of the predetermined criteria of the checklist or rating scale, this method of analysis is more reliable and objective than the directed observation technique. The rate of agreement between two or more observers will certainly be higher than what might be found in a directed observation. This technique will cover behavior and activities that might have been otherwise overlooked. Specific areas of interest can be determined, and the subsequent observation can be made to focus on these areas through the use of appropriate checklists and rating scales. In this regard, the information from the checklist or rating scale is more trustworthy for teachers planning improvements in their educational practice. Using multiple checklists and rating scales from a single observation leads to a more extensive and broader analysis of teaching skills.

Checklists and rating scales aren't without disadvantages. First, activities or behavior not included on the evaluation sheets cannot be analyzed. Therefore, a systematic bias occurs in that the behaviors analyzed are considered the most significant and critical aspects of teaching. Second, the events and behavior analyzed are often unrelated and out of context because the specific reference for the evaluation isn't included. The observer may check that feedback occurred in the lesson, but when, to whom, and under what conditions are not specified. Third, the later class events are often freshest in the memory of the observer and therefore receive greater weight in the analysis. Although the technique does hold several liabilities, it can still prove a valuable tool for teachers striving to be better.

Systematic Observation

The development of techniques to systematically observe teaching led to an explosion of research on teaching. These powerful tools allowed researchers to study specific aspects of teaching and coaching in a reliable and theoretically sound manner. These techniques, or at least scaled down versions, have also proven useful to coaches and teachers for improving teaching practices (Darst, Zakrajsek, and Mancini 1983).

Systematic observation requires two things. First, a specific set of criteria or categories to be observed, which focuses the observation. Examples of the types of categories used in systematic observation include feedback, student–teacher interaction, student time on task, content development, and coaching (Darst, Zakrajsek, and Mancini 1983). Second, a method of recording the observed behavior needs to be established. The recording procedure may be as simple as placing a tally mark next to the category listed on a recording sheet every time it occurs. For example, in a feedback system, the number of times positive feedback is observed is tallied in a positive feedback column. Other recording procedures include measuring the amount of time spent in each category, recording the most often occurring behavior in a given time frame, or sampling the group at specified intervals to monitor the predominant activity. Often the data can be entered directly into a preprogrammed computer and a statistical analysis produced almost immediately.

Systematic observation provides teachers with a clear and reliable picture of their teaching, so they can target the teaching practices they wish to improve. For example, if a teacher wishes to reduce student waiting and increase positive feedback, those behaviors can be identified and target goals set (e.g., have students wait no more than two minutes before moving; for every one criticism, give two comments of positive feedback).

The disadvantage of this analytic technique is that it is time-intensive. It takes time to adequately learn an observation system, and analyzing the data may take time as well. However, systematic observation has proven to be among the best ways to directly improve teaching and coaching practice. The time invested in gathering and analyzing the data pays the biggest dividends in improved teaching (see appendix L for an example).

Teaching Journals

Teachers often find keeping a journal a good way to catalogue and explore the decisions they make. The example of John Wooden made earlier is a case in point. A professional journal is a record of not only what the teacher or coach did but also why she made that decision and the outcome of that decision. Additionally, emotions, reactions, and insights are also recorded in a journal.

As Australian educator David Tripp (1993) noted from his work with teachers and their journals, teachers like to focus on the practical matters of their daily routines—classroom management, student relations, getting students' attention, and the like. In

a journal, a teacher can express himself as both a private individual and a trained professional.

> *On the one hand we each have an individual and unique set of experiences, interests, values, circumstances and such, that go to make us the kind of person we are; and on the other we subscribe in various ways and to certain degrees to a common set of professional norms that make us the kind of teacher we are. (1993, 142)*

According to Tripp, it's understanding the influence of the personal on the professional that leads teachers to develop the scope of and expertise in professional judgment. A journal is a good place to explore the personal in the professional.

Tripp suggests that teachers focus on recording detailed "critical incidents" in their journals (i.e., accounts of routine professional practice that are indicative of trends, motives, and structures of the class). These instructional events are easily recalled and remembered but often thought of as trivial because the significance is only recognized through reflective analysis. Teachers develop by reflecting on and critically interpreting the incidents recorded in their journals. Because the passages in a journal are "deeply contextualised in the culture of classrooms and the actions and values of teachers . . . interpretation of critical incidents offers a way to involve teachers as both clients and partners in research on the understanding and improvement of their practice" (1993, 152).

Improving Teaching Skills and Routines

To become a better teacher requires sustained, deliberate practice of specific and particular skills (Ericsson, Krampe, and Tesch-Romer 1993). As has been noted repeatedly in this chapter, deliberate practice begins by analyzing current teaching activities and then identifying those aspects of teaching that need to be developed. Next, a plan must be devised to practice those skills. Conscious, sustained practice of key teaching routines and skills is a proven path to becoming a better teacher. In this section, suggestions for developing routines, practicing teaching skills, and seeking alternatives are offered.

Developing Routines

Reflexive and repetitive behaviors are distinguishing characteristics of experts (Bloom 1986). To watch the lessons of experienced and expert teachers is to observe fluid, elegant, and seemingly effortless instructional practices. From years of experience and a familiarity with the environment, these teachers have rehearsed and repeated behavior patterns until they became subconscious, automatic routines. The advantage of instructional routines is that the lesson pattern becomes familiar to both the teacher and students. Familiarity with the more standard aspects of the lesson allows the instruction to proceed without the teacher making a constant series of decisions or the students being bombarded with a steady stream of directions.

Fewer decisions need to be made when routines are already established, so the teacher can focus more attention on more important issues like student learning. Because they need to think less about where they need to be, how to find equipment, or what they should be doing, students can devote more time to learning the lesson at hand. It's particularly useful to establish routines early in the instructional program (Siedentop and Eldar 1989).

Research has revealed several routine practices of effective teachers. Initiating the lesson with a statement of goals; asking many questions to gauge the students' understanding of the material being learned; offering immediate, positive feedback after selected student performances; and closing the lesson with a review of the main instructional points have all been identified as effective teaching routines (Baker, Schempp, and Hardin 1998; Rosenshine and Stevens 1986). The repetitive nature of these practices characterizes the teacher's instructional routine and cues the students as to what to expect in class.

If a teacher doesn't currently state a learning goal for the lesson or close with a summary of key concepts, deliberately practicing either or both of these activities for a sustained period will ingrain them in the teacher's instructional pattern. In time, these effective teaching practices will become a matter of routine. Management activities can also be routinized to make more time available for teaching. Consider routines for moving equipment, forming lines, taking attendance, making general announcements, and positioning students for explanations or demonstrations.

Practicing Teaching Skills

Routines allow the lesson to be carried off with greater ease, but actually improving teaching requires practicing specific teaching skills. In previous chapters in this book, many such skills have been identified and described. Chapters 5 through 12 all identify skills that help teachers help students to learn. However, simply reading about these skills won't make someone a better teacher any more than simply reading a basketball book will lead someone into the NBA. To improve teaching requires instructional skills to be put into practice and tried again and again.

There's little chance that any single teaching skill is going to bring increased success the first time it's tried. If a teaching skill isn't successful on the first or second attempt, the teacher should analyze the cause of failure, make corrections, and try it again. All too often when inexperienced or lower skilled teachers attempt something new, they find it doesn't work on the first attempt and quickly abandon it as a failure or inappropriate for their teaching. Few skills are mastered on the first attempt. Teaching skills are no different. Whether the skill is a new instructional strategy, an oral presentation technique, questioning students, or a planning scheme, it can only be mastered in the trial and error of sustained practice.

Although any time is a good time to develop a new teaching skill, for beginning teachers the best time to practice new skills is when a persistent problem occurs. For example, running short of good student practice activities during a lesson could signal a need to develop better planning skills. Continual in-class confusion may mean effective techniques for explaining material need to be developed. A lack of improvement by students might indicate insufficient time for practice or ineffective instructional feedback. For the more experienced teacher, feeling that the lessons have grown flat and monotonous would suggest that routines have overtaken the lesson and choked the life out of teaching and learning. To reinvigorate tired teaching practices, an experienced teacher might find new ways to build relationships with students, introduce technology to instruction, or incorporate a new learning strategy.

Seeking Alternatives

The very nature of teaching demands that instructors be creative. A continuous flow of decisions and challenges faces teachers with every lesson, and the instructional environment varies as new students, equipment, and subject matter are introduced. The teaching skills described in this book, although extensive, do not represent all the solutions to the many problems that teachers encounter. Rather, they represent what many teachers have found helpful. But all teachers are unique, as are the students they teach and the learning environments they share.

Because every teaching situation is different, there are yet undiscovered ways for a particular teacher, or student, or environment to achieve unlimited success. As long as teachers seek new solutions to old problems or alternative practices to meet changing challenges, there will be new innovations in the art and science of teaching. To a large degree, teachers are researchers, and their classrooms are laboratories. As they experiment, teachers continually discover new and better ways to help their students learn.

Strategies for Developing Teaching Skills

Here is a handy checklist of teaching skills to consider from this and previous chapters:

Analyze Teaching
- Directed observation
- Checklist/rating scales
- Systematic observation
- Teaching journals

Develop Instructional Routines
- Lesson openings
- Questions
- Positive feedback
- Lesson closings

Identify and Practice Teaching Skills
- Teaching styles
- Presentation techniques
- Planning
- Clear explanations

Seek Alternatives to Traditional Techniques
- New discoveries and innovations

Increasing Knowledge

Although knowledge can't guarantee that someone will be a good teacher, it's not possible to teach well without a substantial store of knowledge. For this reason, expert teachers are constantly in search of new knowledge (Schempp, Templeton, and Clark 1999), and those with less expertise do not strive with the same intensity. Teachers who flounder on the bottom gave up learning to teach long ago and generally blame circumstances or others for their inadequacies and shortcomings. Those who aspire to be the best never stop learning. In this section, strategies teachers use to increase their knowledge and become better teachers are discussed.

Listen and Learn

In two research studies, teachers identified both students and other teachers as important sources of knowledge for teaching (Fincher and Schempp 1994; Schempp, Templeton, and Clark 1999). Frequent problems and challenges are shared among teachers. Listening to one another gives teachers the chance to gain new perspectives on persistent problems, discover novel ways of meeting new challenges, or find support for ideas they incorporated into their lessons (figure 15.2). Teachers often make the best teachers of other teachers. Therefore, teachers who cultivate a network of peers develop a rich and continual source of new knowledge.

No one watches teachers ply their trade more than students, so few people are more qualified to comment on the practices of their teachers. A teacher's success is ultimately measured in the achievements and development of students. The best teachers are tuned to what their students say about their teaching both directly and indirectly. A teacher may ask a question directly to a student: "Did that work for you?" or "What did you think of that activity?" Indirectly, teachers observe the effects of their instruction on their students' learning and make adjustments as appropriate. When students are successful in a class, teachers know it. When students struggle, good teachers know that, too. In both cases, the students provide the teacher with important information about the teacher's instructional practices.

Figure 15.2 Teachers discuss physical education over lunch at a teachers workshop. There are many ways in which teachers can help each other to solve problems.

Trust Your Instincts and Develop Intuition

The suggestion to develop your instincts and rely on intuitive responses is not a call to abandon logic or reason on a grand scale. Rather, developing instincts and intuition promotes a greater sense and understanding of the instructional environment. Teachers who trust their intuitive senses in the instructional setting no longer need to deliberate about every action they take. Therefore, their instructional activity takes on a natural flow and timing.

Intuitive responses and heightened instructional instincts develop from recognizing similarities across teaching contexts and then making applications from one teaching situation to another. Teachers' intuition breeds from an intimate familiarity with and extensive knowledge of the learning environment. For example, if students encounter problems learning to serve a ball accurately, a physical education teacher may relate the problem to the same students having difficulties throwing accurately. With the connection made, the teacher can sense the potential problem, recall successful solutions, and make adaptations. The more often teachers reach across context to establish connections and see similarities, the better they become at anticipating problems and predicting workable solutions (Carter et al. 1988).

By increasing and applying knowledge across the instructional environment, that knowledge works from the conscious to the subconscious level. As decisions become more responsive and instinctive to variations in the teaching environment, intuition begins to develop (Tan 1997). Once a teacher begins relying on intuition, instruction becomes more dynamic because it's guided more by the teacher's "knowledge in action" than by preplanned lessons. However, a word of caution is in order. Only teachers with extensive experience and knowledge can afford to forgo lesson planning without a decrease in instructional effectiveness. Novices and teachers with limited knowledge of the subject being taught are better off preplanning lessons. This way, they'll have something to fall back on if their instincts and intuition fail to provide appropriate in-class actions and activities. Additional information on increasing intuitive activity in teaching will be offered in the next chapter on developing teaching expertise.

Professional Associations

A profession comprises an educated, experienced body of individuals who provide a recognized service to society for a fee. Because of their credentials and the services they provide, sport and physical activity instructors are recognized professionals. Members of a profession form organizations to promote their collective interests. The multiple benefits to both the individual and the profession make joining a professional association something every teacher should strongly consider.

Membership in a professional association normally results in five direct benefits (Kneer 1989). First, the opportunity to interact with other professionals at local, state, regional, or national association meetings is an important consideration. The chance to share ideas and meet people with common concerns is a vital link in the development of teachers. Friendships and connections made at meetings are often maintained over the years, and these important resources are only a phone call, letter, or e-mail away. Developing a network of colleagues and sharing ideas increase both knowledge and motivation.

Second, a collective group carries social power. As a group, the association can promote the interests of the members. This might take the form of a political action initiative with a legislative group, a promotional campaign to advertise the benefits of participating in the particular sport or physical activity, or some other collective action. Third, a professional association serves as a knowledge source. Most organizations publish journals and books that describe the latest innovations in the industry. Meetings are held in which prominent professionals share their knowledge and wisdom with those assembled. A professional organization may also sponsor research initiatives to solve major problems facing practicing professionals. Professional standards and certification programs are also within the scope of responsibility of these organizations.

Fourth, through elected offices and awards, organizations identify leaders who provide guidance and serve as role models for the profession. These individuals set the standards of the profession and lead the way in innovative practices. Finally, belonging to a professional organization is motivational. Most people come away from professional meetings feeling reinvigorated and supported in their efforts. From there, these teachers strive to improve the standards of their professional practice. Meeting other professionals, attending meetings, reading the latest developments, having your organization promote your profession, and meeting the leaders in your field are all ways of developing as a teacher and as a professional.

Continuing Education

In most areas of sport and physical activity instruction, some basic level of education is required before an individual is recognized as a professional and prepared to teach. The basic education may be as brief as a weekend workshop or as extensive as the college degree required to teach public school physical education. At best, these initial certification programs provide teachers with the basic knowledge, skills, and sometimes experiences to begin teaching. But as is true of any profession, continuing your education is a path to improving your practice. In this section, certification programs, in-service education, workshops, conferences and clinics, and advanced degrees will all be discussed as recognized methods for teachers to continue their education.

Certification Programs

Most sport and physical activity instructors receive an initial certification, either through a state agency for a public school teaching certificate or through a professional association for an initial teaching credential. Public school teachers commonly continue their education beyond the beginning certification and achieve a renewed or advanced certification. In some sport associations, advanced levels of training lead to master certifications. Both the United States Professional Tennis Registry and the Professional Golf Association, for example, have master professional certification programs. In all cases, additional or advanced certification programs offer teachers recognized ways to develop their knowledge base and increase their teaching skills.

Adding a certification in a second field may also be desirable. For example, a physical educator may want to also become a National Strength and Conditioning Certified Personal Trainer. Such a certification would not only provide additional information to be used in classes, but it would also provide additional employment opportunities when school is not in session. Professional associations offering teaching certification cover a wide variety of sports, including skiing (Professional Ski Instructors of America), rock climbing (American Mountain Guides Association), fitness (International Fitness Association), and martial arts (Independent Martial Arts Instructors Association). The American Master Teacher Program and the Coaching Effectiveness Program, both sponsored by Human Kinetics Publishers, are two popular programs offering a teacher or coach a series of workshops with follow-up activities. If the teacher or coach successfully passes the final evaluation, he receives a certification as a master

teacher or coach (see appendix I for Web sites of professional associations).

In-Service Education

In-service education represents the efforts and programs undertaken by teachers to develop and improve while "in the service" of teaching. The most useful in-service education for teachers is the informal education they receive on the job. Experience can be a wonderful teacher for teachers. Through experience, teachers learn which instructional styles and patterns lead to greater student learning, what management and motivational strategies keep lessons moving forward and students on-task, and how to meet the needs of a variety of learners. The opportunity to observe and talk with other teachers provides an important source of information for teacher improvement. Meeting with other teachers may also offer a chance to jointly design and evaluate teaching materials, share resources, offer support, find solutions to common problems, and discuss teaching practices.

Formal in-service programs are often designed around certification requirements or objectives of the teachers' employers. An important prerequisite for effective in-service programs is to view teachers not as passive, deficient recipients of information ready to make immediate and drastic changes but rather as professionals who require support in their efforts to grow and learn. Generally, using local experts and leaders is more effective than bringing in outside experts who are unfamiliar with the teachers' backgrounds and circumstances. Applied activities and examples, written materials, discussion periods, and follow-up activities with feedback are usually more helpful than one-time lectures by people unfamiliar with and unpracticed in the activities of teachers. Improvement through in-service education needs to be viewed as a long-term, ongoing process.

Workshops, Clinics, and Conferences

Few things are more valuable to a teacher than joining other teachers at a meeting to discuss a topic of professional interest. Workshops, clinics, and conferences are normally designed to assist teachers and coaches with the practical problems and challenges they face (figure 15.3). Topics may range from training and fitness to physical skills and drills to motivation and management. These sessions provide an efficient and enjoyable method of acquiring fresh insights and new ideas that teachers can directly and immediately implement into

Figure 15.3 Teachers present at conferences to educate and learn from their colleagues.

their programs. Workshops normally take place on-site and involve the teachers in a school or school district, with the format being lecture/discussion led by a local teacher or an outside consultant. Although the topics vary, they usually focus on the everyday problems and concerns faced by the teachers in attendance.

Workshops normally last a half-day or a full day. Clinics and conferences last from one to five days and are traditionally sponsored by professional associations. The sessions are normally led by outside consultants or experts on the topic under discussion. Again, the format tends to be lecture/discussion, but applied sessions with various demonstrations of equipment innovations or teaching techniques are also frequently offered. An added benefit of the clinic or conference is the opportunity to meet with other professionals for prolonged, informal discussions.

Coursework and Degree Programs

Universities and colleges offer a range of courses that teachers may find valuable in their work. Degree programs at the graduate or undergraduate level can prepare someone for a career in physical education, coaching, personal training, or other occupations rooted in teaching sport and physical activity. Many colleges permit teachers to enroll in particular courses as part-time or non-degree students. Junior colleges traditionally offer associate of arts or science degrees, while colleges and universities offer bachelor of arts or bachelor of science degrees.

Once a bachelor of science or bachelor of arts (the traditional four-year degree program) is completed, it's possible to enroll in post-bachelor or graduate degree programs at many colleges and universities. Post-bachelor programs allow students to take courses at a university or college without pursuing a degree. Students are free to choose any courses they wish to take. Many people with degrees outside of education take this program to complete a teaching certificate for public school teaching or acquire the knowledge necessary to effectively coach a sport. If a student chooses to pursue a graduate degree, several options are available, such as a master of arts (MA), a master of science (MS), or a master of education (MEd). Regardless of the type of master's degree, the required program is normally completed in two full years of study or several years of part-time study. The highest academic degree is the doctoral degree. The most common doctoral degrees in sport and physical activity are the philosophy doctorate (PhD) and education doctorate (EdD). These degrees traditionally take three to four years beyond the master's degree to complete.

Universities may also offer continuing education programs. Continuing education classes, generally held in the evenings or on weekends, are targeted at community members. Summer school courses are another way that teachers and coaches may gain useful new knowledge in areas such as foreign languages, organizational skills, fitness activities, or technological applications such as word processing for newsletters or designing Web sites. University and college courses provide an in-depth analysis of a variety of subjects that can help any skillful and clever teacher improve her teaching.

The Continuing Education of a Teacher

Ed Kenimer

After a 17-year business career, I became a first-year teacher for the second time. My first sojourn in education was a hectic two-job experience. I began as most new teachers, with all the answers and the ability to change the entire world. My coaching career soon became more important than my teaching, so I replaced workshops and my master's program with coaching clinics and scouting. Shortly after, teaching became a job, not a passion, and I left education after 5 years.

This time I entered education knowing I did not have all the answers and wanting to change the world one person at a time. I began my master's program the summer before my first day of teaching. What a surprise to discover that the pedagogy and teaching theories had changed! My professors and my classmates guided me into a new understanding of what a teacher can and should be in today's society. "Instructional Strategies in Physical Education" gave me new tools and methods that enabled me to be a better teacher. (Muska Mosston is great! See Mosston and Ashworth 2002.)

Beginning my third year, I had changed the sport-based curriculum with emphasis on team sports to a more lifetime-activity-based program with the emphasis on the individual. That year our school changed from a modified block schedule to a rotating seven period schedule with classes meeting four days. The following year the schedule modified to each class meeting every day. With class time per week cut by 30% in two years, my students were not progressing as before. I began to earnestly improve my own ability to teach children. I no longer had the perceived luxury of time.

That summer I began my final push to complete my master's degree. I enrolled in "Research Methods" and in the fall enrolled in "Evaluating Teaching in Physical Education." I was fortunate to have a knowledgeable professor and several highly experienced and accomplished teachers in my classes. The next six months were the most exciting and productive of my professional career to date. The research methods class gave me insight into previous and future research and readings. Now time spent reading professional publications, reviewing texts, and researching is truly beneficial to my students and me. My one regret is that I did not make this my first course of my studies.

The evaluation of teaching physical education class became my paradigm. Learning what it takes to be a master teacher, observing master teachers on film, and discussing teaching with classmates redefined my goals and self-expectations. Learning techniques and systems for evaluating classes and my own teaching has enabled me to improve the learning environment of my students. My ability to manage class time efficiently has increased my time on task for the students by an average of eight minutes per student. The students are advancing faster now with 30% less class time and are enjoying class more.

In closing, continuing education through workshops, classes, and reading is essential for improving as a new and experienced teacher. But the association with your colleagues and the interchange of experiences and solutions to educational challenges are the most important benefits of the process.

—*Ed Kenimer, Middle School Physical Education, Wesleyan School, Norcross, Georgia*

Strategies for Increasing Teaching Knowledge

Listen and learn.

Trust your instincts and develop your intuition.

Take advantage of professional associations.

Continue your education.

Certification programs

In-service education

Workshops, clinics, and conferences

Coursework and degree programs

Summary

Few teachers believe they can do it all well. Most experienced and expert teachers clearly recognize their limitations and strive hard to learn more about the matters that influence their teaching. Although initial certification programs may launch a teacher into the profession, to develop and grow in teaching takes a sustained desire to improve. In this chapter, strategies for improving teaching were offered. The first step is developing reflective teaching (i.e., to reflect on your professional practice and identify strengths and weakness in teaching). From here, you can seek strategies and resources that increase your skill and knowledge.

To develop teaching skills, you must thoroughly and critically analyze your teaching patterns and practices. Such analyses, whether using directed observation, checklist/rating scales, systematic observation, or a teaching journal, help teachers spot areas for development. Once identified, these areas can be improved if the teacher increases his or her knowledge and practices new skills. A teacher learns to teach better by deliberately practicing specific skills over time.

To increase knowledge, teachers have a variety of resources to draw from. A good start is listening to and learning from peers and students because these people are most familiar with your practices and work environment. Developing instincts and intuition is also necessary to elevate your level of expertise as a teacher. Teachers can find a wealth of new information on the latest research, equipment innovations, or teaching ideas by joining professional organizations or seeking ways to continue their education. Workshops, conferences, and clinics offer not only a chance to learn the latest teaching trends but also a chance to meet and exchange ideas and solutions for common problems. Finally, institutions of higher education offer both degree and non-degree programs that permit teachers to take advanced coursework on topics pertinent to their teaching concerns. The key to becoming a better teacher is to never stop learning to be a better teacher.

Discussion Questions

1. List the topics you believe would be of most value to you as a teacher or coach as you reflect on your practices in an effort to improve.

2. If you were to develop a systematic observation system to analyze your teaching or coaching, what would you like it to analyze? Specifically, what behaviors or instructional activities would you include in the system?

3. What routines would you like to establish in your lessons or team practices? How would you like to open and close each lesson? What routines would make it easier for your learners to move from one instructional station to the next or to retrieve equipment? Can you recall routines from your own experiences as a student or athlete that you might adopt as a teacher or coach?

4. How do you plan to stay fresh and up to date as a teacher or coach? What sources of knowledge will be most useful for providing solutions to recurring problems and offering new information to improve your teaching or coaching?

Chapter 16

Developing Teaching Expertise

Excellence is the gradual result of always striving to do better.

— Pat Riley

DEVELOPMENT

No one enters this world as an expert. Expertise is gained through years of practice and study. Differences in experience and knowledge separate the expert from the less expert in any given field or activity. Although certain natural abilities can account for someone learning faster or ultimately being able to perform at a higher level, a person cannot reach the highest levels of performance without learning and practice—no matter how much ability he or she may have. After an extensive review of research in expertise, Anders Ericsson (Ericsson and Charness 1994) concluded that it takes at least 10 years of deliberate practice to reach the level of expert. That offers good news for those who aspire to become great teachers because it means that investing in experience, intentional practice, and extended learning will pay dividends in developing instructional expertise.

Extensive knowledge and experience have led expert teachers to develop instructional practices that optimize student achievement, irrespective of the student or teaching conditions. Put another way, truly outstanding teachers find ways to be more successful with more types of students in almost any teaching environment. These teachers possess a combination of extraordinary teaching skills, a rich understanding of learners, and a vast knowledge of the subject matter and its instruction.

Expertise appears to grow in distinct and identifiable stages (Bell 1997). Examining these stages helps define what it takes to become an expert teacher or coach, thereby making it easier for others who wish to improve their instructional practice. This chapter offers suggestions for developing teaching expertise. First, the stages experts pass through are identified, followed by a description of the characteristics common to experts.

However, simply knowing the characteristics and qualities of an expert does not make you an expert. Remember that experts are individuals, and their thoughts and actions often take on an idiosyncratic, at times eccentric, quality. Therefore, when reading and considering the stages and the characteristics of each, understand that they represent commonalities among teachers rather than a prescription for being a teacher.

Based on research in the cognitive sciences, renowned educational psychologist David Berliner (1994) theorized that teaching expertise develops in discrete stages. In this chapter, four stages of teaching expertise based on Berliner's work will be explored: beginner, competent, proficient, and expert. These stages contain unique characteristics that represent the prevailing tendencies of teachers within them. Although these stages seem to imply a hierarchy, everyone must pass through them in developing expertise. No one starts in the middle. You can, however, choose where to stop in developing your expertise. The stages are presented here so that teachers may identify their current stages and recognize the skills, perspectives, and knowledge necessary to elevate to the next level and beyond (figure 16.1). A summary of the characteristics of each stage is presented in the box.

Figure 16.1 Student teachers can help themselves on the road to excellence by utilizing the experience of their mentor-teachers.

Stages of Teaching Expertise

Beginner

- Bound by rules (strictly follows rules and procedures)
- Lacks comfortable, efficient routines
- Does not take responsibility
- Learns best from experience

Competent

- Sees similarities across context (students, equipment, tasks)
- Develops strategic knowledge (knows when to follow and when to bend rules)
- Guided by goals and long-term planning (begins to "see the bigger picture")
- Uses contingency plans (if/then decision making); develops a sense of timing and maintains momentum
- Learns best from experience, but gains some knowledge from other sources (particularly other teachers and coaches)

Proficient

- Highly developed perceptual capacities
- Strong sense of personal responsibility
- Responds instinctively and begins to develop intuition
- Predicts likely outcomes of decisions and actions
- Learns most from others (e.g., coaches, players) and outside sources (e.g., reading, seminars)

Expert

- Extensive knowledge
- Intuition (result of extensive knowledge and experience)
- Automatic behavior
- Attends to the "atypical"
- Thinks "forward" to solve problems
- Self-monitors so learning and improving never stop

Everyone Begins As a Beginner

Those who become teachers seldom do so as pure novices. The years spent in classrooms as students, on playing fields as athletes, and in preparatory programs have familiarized new teachers with the skills, perspectives, and responsibilities of teaching. The instructional setting may have a ring of familiarity, but beginning teachers must still prove themselves as capable teachers.

Learning the Job Means Learning the Rules

To understand their new role as teachers and to prove themselves worthy, beginners learn the rules and norms governing life in their new workplace. Their perception of doing the job correctly includes following the rules and procedures, particularly those centered on establishing order and managing the learning environment. Beginners view neat, orderly classes with well-behaved and happy students as characteristic of competent teachers. This seems natural because through the naive eyes of a beginning teacher, it's relatively easy to notice students on-task, listening, following directions, and enjoying the experience. It's more difficult to discern students who are actually gaining knowledge, developing new skills, or improving performance. Only through experience will novice teachers begin to detect these subtle but significant changes in students.

Start to Develop Routines

During their initial teaching experiences, beginners try to detect the commonplace through objective facts and features of the situation but seldom sense the overall goal or see relationships between events. Novices sometimes get lost in tasks because of their lack of established routines and inability to see the interconnection of in-class events. For example, a beginning teacher may get caught up in taking attendance, securing equipment, or managing students (i.e., following standard procedures) while overlooking more important instructional tasks like lesson progressions, activity pacing, or student assessment (Carter et al. 1988; Leinhart and Greeno 1986). Through increased experience and conversations with other teachers, beginners start to develop effective routines that minimize the management functions of teaching and maximize the instructional focus of the teacher.

Cultivate a Sense of Control and Responsibility

Because beginners are so focused on enforcing rules and learning workplace regularities, they seldom feel any personal control over the conditions and events of the class. As a result, novice teachers may lack a sense of responsibility for their own actions. One manifestation of this is the common belief among beginning teachers that students are solely to blame for misbehavior and lack of achievement (Schempp, Tan, Manross, and Fincher 1998). Rookie teachers often deny responsibility for students' learning difficulties as well, blaming the learner's background or personal characteristics for deficiencies in learning or development (Schempp, Tan, Manross, and Fincher 1998). Believing that students bring their problems into the lesson and that the problems reflect current social ills and a lack of parental support, teachers with low levels of expertise often don't even attempt to support or assist struggling students because they believe such efforts would ultimately prove futile. This characteristic draws a dividing line in teaching, because those with the highest levels of teaching expertise never willingly give up on a student. Novice teachers and coaches with low expertise levels give up on students all too quickly. The drive to teach all students to their full potentials is one factor that propels great teachers to the heights they achieve. If you ever find yourself giving up on a student, realize that at the same time you're giving up on yourself as a teacher or coach. Refuse to give up on your students and you will be the better for it as a teacher—regardless of the students' ultimate success or failure.

Experience Is a Beginner's Best Teacher

Perhaps reflecting their limited practical experience, novices find their "real world" practice to be their most important source of information for increasing teaching expertise. Verbal or written information takes second place to trial and error in acquiring instructional skill and knowledge. Novices usually develop their instructional repertoires by combining observations of more experienced teachers, personal trial and error, and recollections of teachers from their days as students (Sikes, Measor, and Woods 1985). As has been stated before, there's no substitute for experience in becoming a better teacher. The more experiences and the greater diversity of those experiences (e.g., different students, facilities, teaching strategies), the more that beginning teachers will learn and the faster they will get to the next stage in expertise.

It would be reassuring to believe that you need only spend a certain amount of time teaching and the lessons learned through experience would elevate you to the next level of expertise. But, unfortunately, that is not a script that reads the same for all teachers. Teachers need to do more than simply spend time on the job to become better skilled. They need to learn from their experiences and gain more knowledge to reduce the number of mistakes they make and increase the number of successes they gain. Combining experience with the activities described in the previous chapter such as reflective teaching, journal writing, professional meetings, and conversations with other teachers will all help the beginner to get better. But a teacher must make purposeful and sustained efforts to improve. In the next section, the characteristics that signal the rise from beginner to competent professional will be identified and described.

Cultivating Competence

With experience and increased knowledge, teachers develop skills that allow them to minimize the time spent on noninstructional tasks such as management, which leaves more time and attention for instruction. Unfortunately, a common problem among physical education teachers, particularly secondary physical education teachers, is to simply be satisfied with having the managerial functions of teaching under control. These teachers don't aspire to develop instructional prowess or to help students learn sport and physical activity skills and concepts. If the students are "busy, happy and good" (Placek 1983), they have achieved sufficient success as teachers.

Fortunately, physical education teachers and coaches who aspire for more than simply mollifying students do exist. These teachers want to help students learn, develop, and grow. These are the teachers who want to make the most of their time with students and athletes, to have an impact on the students' lives, and to allow students to realize their potential as both activity participants and as people. These are the individuals who move from beginning teachers to the next level of expertise: competent teachers. In this section, the characteristics of competent teachers will be identified and suggestions for moving from a beginner to a competent teacher or coach will be offered.

Seeing and Connecting Similarities

As beginning teachers gain experience, recurring instructional events are remembered and recognized. As their knowledge of situations, students, and events expands, they detect similarities across contexts. Identifying commonalities across different teaching situations allows teachers to select from a variety of responses tested in prior experiences. Teaching competence begins to emerge when an instructor examines each new experience and searches for a solution or decision from previous experience rather than relying strictly on following established rules or a lesson plan.

Because they recognize similarities across situations, competent teachers make applications from one situation to another. For example, if a competent physical education teacher detects a student having problems learning an underhand serve in volleyball, she may relate the problem to the same or a similar student having difficulty with a badminton serve. With the connection made, the competent teacher can recall the successful solutions to the badminton problem and make an application to the volleyball dilemma.

Developing Strategic Knowledge

Competent teachers may still be somewhat rule-oriented but are now guided by circumstances and context when applying the rules. They develop a strategic knowledge that permits them to ignore or follow the rules as the situation dictates. For example, a teacher may choose to ignore students whispering and sacrifice the "No talking when the teacher is talking" rule in order to move ahead with a lesson. As a beginner, the same teacher would likely enforce a strict policy of no talking during instruction and thereby stop the learning of the students who were paying attention and on-task. The strategic knowledge of competent teachers lets them know when to ignore the rule when student talking contributes to, or least does not distract from, the learning.

Another example of the strategic knowledge of competent teachers may be illustrated in their feedback. Beginning teachers are schooled in giving positive feedback to bolster a child's self-esteem. Following this principle, novices are often heard sputtering "Good job," "Nice try," and other well-meaning but instructionally worthless responses to student efforts. Competent teachers have learned, however, that praise in certain instances may communicate low expectations and that, at times, constructive criticism serves as more effective feedback (Berliner 1994). Again, strategic knowledge lets them know what to say and when to say it.

Teachers develop strategic knowledge by combining their experience and understanding of the learning environment, the students, and the subject matter. It comes from trial and error and from being able to see similarities across different students, lessons, and subjects. Beginners looking to develop this form of knowledge need to do three things: gain experience, use reflective teaching to learn all they can from their experiences, and experiment with different decisions to see the results. For example, let students talk and see where it takes the class, or ask other students to provide feedback to a peer. It's only through teaching, learning about your teaching, and experimenting with your teaching that you'll become better at knowing what to do and when to do it—strategic knowledge.

Letting Goals and Long-Term Plans Guide You

While novices struggle to apply the rules, competent teachers work toward the larger goal of student learning. In other words, the practices of competent teachers are guided more by purpose, while policies and procedures are more likely to guide the practices of beginning teachers. To move from beginner to competent teacher, you must continually revisit the purposes behind the teaching practices being adopted and developed. If the purpose is simply to follow rules and maintain order, you are mired in a beginner's perspective. If the purpose of your instructional practice is to inspire student learning and development, a characteristic of competent teaching is evident. Competent teachers rely on long-term goals and plans to ensure that their practices work toward the "bigger picture" of student learning.

Developing Contingency Plans

With experience and increased knowledge comes another characteristic of competent teachers: contingency planning. Competent teachers develop the characteristic of "if/then planning." In other words, when they prepare a lesson, they plan for contingencies and changes by thinking "if/then." Let's use a teacher preparing to teach a class in running as an example. In planning the lesson, the teacher might think "If the students look tired in warm-ups, then I'll spend more time explaining the value of stretching. If the students look energetic, then I'll get them immediately into running activities." Again, experience allows the competent teacher to see similarities across context (e.g., the teacher realizes that students' energy levels affect their readiness to practice running skills) and provides the knowledge necessary to offer a variety of skills depending on the situation (i.e., strategic knowledge). With limited knowledge and experience, the beginning teacher doesn't have the skill to plan contingently. The ability to plan contingently also lets the competent teacher keep the lesson momentum flowing by timing one well-intentioned activity after the next—skills that were detailed in chapter 8.

Even with experience, competent teachers still lack the sensitivity and intuition to decipher potentially important cues in the lesson events. This inability to distinguish the important from the unimportant makes it difficult for teachers to accurately target their attention. For example, a teacher might get so caught up in monitoring one student who often goes off-task that he doesn't detect another student struggling to master the skill being practiced.

Learning From Experience and Others

Competent teachers are learning to teach as they follow established rules, recognize and classify contextual conditions, and label and categorize recurring events. Experience still remains their single largest source of knowledge, but they're beginning to rely on external sources like other teachers and books. They may still feel they don't completely and personally determine what happens in the lesson and therefore continue to lack a sense of responsibility for the events and actions of their lessons or activity area. The need or inclination to blame someone or something else for problems and failures still remains prevalent. Examples of this are teachers who perceive students' aggressiveness as caused by observing too much violence on television, attribute the lack of student motivation or work ethic to family background, or expect little learning to occur because the equipment is inadequate or the class is too large. What competent teachers often see as insurmountable obstacles, teachers with higher levels of expertise see as problems to be solved or challenges to be overcome.

Practicing Proficiency

If all teachers reached the point of competence, the level of instruction would be vastly improved in sport and physical activity. But gaining expertise takes a strong commitment, opportunities to learn, and perhaps some talent for the teaching field. Those with the desire to rise above competence and become great teachers and coaches seek opportunities to learn more about their chosen craft. These individuals are able to move from competent teacher to proficient. Proficient teachers occupy the top 20 to 25% of teachers and coaches. Proficiency is gained only after a significant number of years of teaching and prolonged and sustained efforts to increase knowledge of the subject, students, and instruction. Although proficient teachers hold many of the characteristics of competent teachers, this section will explore the characteristics that set proficient teachers apart from beginners and competent teachers.

Developed Perceptual Capacities

With considerable accumulated knowledge and experience, proficient teachers detect the subtleties in a learning environment that are significant to the events taking place. Thousands of hours of experience have honed their perceptual capacities, allowing them to recognize when something isn't working in a lesson. Possessing a keen sense of timing, they skillfully change the course of action in a direction that leads to greater instructional success.

Teaching physical education is a dynamic process in which many students are engaged in activities in a gymnasium or activity area. Although keeping the whole class interested and on-task is important, the challenge of focusing on individual performance is critical. Proficient teachers have the perceptual capacity to attend to individual student performances while monitoring the entire class. Beginners and competent teachers don't seem to have developed this skill (Housner and Griffey 1985). Because they can observe the students individually, proficient teachers try to meet the needs of every student and realize that students will be at differing skill levels. Some will be at the beginning stage, while others will be at the intermediate or advanced stage. Subsequently, expert teachers implement strategies tailored to meet the needs of students at each level of ability.

This developed perception also helps expert teachers sort the important from the unimportant. For example, a beginning teacher may notice a student's dress, choice of equipment, or friends, while a proficient teacher will overlook any extraneous factors that don't directly bear on students' learning. They thus devote more attention to student performance and lock tightly on the key components that most affect it. With this knowledge, teachers can provide the information and experiences that will most likely enhance that performance in the shortest possible time. A proficient teacher's perceptual capacities are not necessarily restricted only to performance characteristics. Proficient teachers quickly recognize that factors such as motivation and physical fatigue play a part in student learning, and they are therefore able to react accordingly. Again, with an inability to discern the important from the unimportant, beginners and competent teachers are less able to do this. The keen perceptual capacity of proficient teachers takes both extended knowledge and experience. However, beginning and competent teachers can speed along its development by first recognizing its importance to good teaching and then focusing on the environmental cues that are most pertinent to meeting the goals of the lesson or practice.

Strong Sense of Personal Responsibility

Proficient teachers are in command of the curricular and instructional activity in their domain. Because they're not as rule-focused as beginning or competent teachers, proficient teachers take more personal control of the learning environment. They feel a strong personal involvement in and responsibility for the successes and failures of their students. Proficient teachers hold themselves accountable for student learning problems and believe the solutions to these problems reside within both their abilities and responsibilities (Tan 1997). When learning problems arise, proficient teachers analyze the lesson, seeking alternative activities and resources that might help students learn more efficiently. It's at this level of expertise that teachers begin to believe they can teach anyone their sport or activity as long as the student wants to learn (Schempp, Tan, Manross, and Fincher 1998).

Responding Instinctively and Developing Intuition

As proficiency increases, instructional routines become so familiar to teachers that they respond instinctively to a situation rather than carefully and rationally analyzing it before coming to a decision. At this point, intuition is also developing and is beginning to gain prominence in their decision making. Teachers no longer have to consciously think about every action they make, and therefore their instructional behavior takes on a natural fluidity and timing.

At this level of expertise, teachers constantly analyze the flow of events in a lesson, attempting to select the activities or information that will make the biggest impact on the students' learning. Their experience and knowledge have become extensive at this stage, allowing them to respond less with rational thought and more with intuition. It's much like driving a car. After a significant number of hours behind the wheel of a car, you don't consciously have to consider which foot to use to depress the brake pedal or give thought to the brake pedal's location. The response is instinctive, and when certain environmental cues arise, such as a pedestrian who is likely to step into the path of the car, the braking process is intuitively begun. In a similar way, proficient teachers are able to anticipate likely events and respond to shifting changes in the learning environment as students progress in their learning.

Ability to Predict Outcomes

Because proficient teachers have become extraordinarily good at recognizing similarities across situations, they can predict potential outcomes of unfolding events with a high degree of accuracy and precision. This was demonstrated in a study in which teachers with advanced teaching skills were asked to comment on a series of slides of classroom events. The teachers provided rich commentaries about their observations and drew upon their own experiences to make judgments about what they viewed. The teachers "made many assumptions about what they saw, appeared to be looking for the meaning of events portrayed in slides in this task, [and] inferred relationships between actions and situations in the slides" (Carter et al. 1988, 28).

The ability to predict potential outcomes proves useful when selecting activities because it lets the teacher choose only those activities with the greatest chance of instructional success. Although it isn't an easy thing to gain, a "crystal ball" in teaching or coaching is extraordinarily useful. For a coach, with the final few seconds of an important game ticking down, being able to predict which play will have the greatest chance of success is an enormous advantage. For students, it's a major benefit to have a teacher who can predict which practice activities will help them learn in the most economical and efficient manner.

Proficient teachers can make these predictions because of years of experience. They have seen similar situations time and again and have become skilled at analyzing the outcomes of their decisions. To earn those powers of prediction, a proficient teacher must practice reflective teaching, experiment with new ideas, communicate with other teachers, and possess a strong desire to always find the solution that's in the best interest of the student.

Learning More From Outside Sources

Because of their extensive experience, proficient teachers look to sources outside their own teaching for new information. Other teachers and resources such as conferences and books are important sources of information for these teachers. Proficient teachers assume significant instructional responsibility, see similarities across different situations, use well-established instructional routines, have heightened perceptual capacities, and show a greater sophistication in problem solving by giving intuitive responses, but they still remain largely analytical and deliberative when making decisions. That is, they still demonstrate a logical progression in their instructional decision making. Most decisions are reached after a process of consciously analyzing the situation and deliberately selecting from a range of potential solutions. As we shall see, the expert begins to make decisions that, at times, appear to defy logic or explanation and yet still represent a superior solution to a given teaching problem.

Excelling to Expert

Experts are distinguished from those with less expertise by their consistently outstanding performance (Tan 1997). For expert teachers, this means that they are able to teach more students more subject matter in a greater variety of environments than less expert teachers. This does not mean that an expert can necessarily teach every student to master every skill in any learning environment. Rather, on an overall basis, students of expert teachers learn more than students of less expert teachers.

We'd like to think that anyone can become an expert, but that's not the case. It takes years of experience and extensive knowledge, but sometimes that isn't enough. Research has shown, however, that experts are made and not born (Ericsson and Charness 1994). This section analyzes the characteristics that experts share in an attempt to understand how they are made. Suggestions will also be offered on climbing to the highest level of professional practice in teaching and coaching. Although not everyone who aspires to become an expert will make it, there does seem to be plenty of room for those who want to try.

Extensive Knowledge

It perhaps seems obvious that an expert teacher has an extensive knowledge base, but the importance of this characteristic demands that it be examined thoroughly. There are many lessons for teachers and coaches in understanding what an expert knows. Experts make a significant investment in learning all they can about their fields (Tan 1997). Attend a workshop, clinic, or conference, and you will surely see an expert. Although the experts are the ones least likely to benefit from the information of the workshop, they got to be experts because they attended conferences and meetings to learn more long before they became experts. It is one reason that they are now considered such.

Experts enjoy talking almost endlessly about their subjects, gather others' views on pertinent topics, and have extensive libraries devoted to their fields (Ericsson and Charness 1994). Teachers use extensive resources to build a large store of knowledge. Experience and other teachers have been most often identified as key sources of teachers' knowledge, but books, workshops, certification programs, journals and magazines, athletic experiences, and even students have also been identified as important resources (Fincher and Schempp 1994; Schempp, Templeton, and Clark 1999). Walk into a teacher's or coach's office and look at his library. If there are no, or few, books to be found, it isn't likely that the person who works there is an expert. He may be good at what he does, but he's not at the top of his profession. Experts are vacuums when it comes to absorbing new knowledge. Less expert teachers are satisfied with what they know. If you stop learning, you stop getting better. Experts know that. Teachers wishing to elevate their expertise need to learn—read, talk with others, and attend workshops, clinics, and conferences.

Expert teachers possess a thorough knowledge of the subject matter they teach, classroom management, educational principles, and curriculum development (Rink et al. 1994; Ennis, Mueller, and Zhu 1991). Experts also synthesize their knowledge about a skill or activity into meaningful information for students to understand and apply (Siedentop and Eldar 1989). This extensive knowledge base gives them a palette of possibilities when selecting information that helps students understand and develop skills. If a student doesn't understand the teacher's explanation of an activity, an expert can try a different explanation or use a demonstration, audiovisual, or any number of other techniques. Teachers and coaches without a large knowledge base are generally restricted to only a few instructional options.

Expert teachers' superior knowledge permits them to use their teaching environment (i.e., equipment, facilities, and supplies) to greater effect than less expert teachers. They demonstrate greater flexibility in using equipment to facilitate student learning, and know different ways of using the same equipment for different purposes. For example, a hula hoop may be a target, boundary area, throwing object, or anything else the fertile mind of an expert teacher might concoct (Housner and Griffey 1985). Beginners see a hula hoop as a hula hoop.

When expert physical education teachers are faced with teaching subject matter they aren't quite familiar with, they make an effort to ensure they have a thorough understanding of what they are going to teach (Schempp, Manross, Tan, and Fincher 1998). In fact, they take great measures to do so by talking with people who are experts in the subject matter, reading all pertinent material on the topic, and even working on developing their own mastery of the skills. Experts know the importance of their own personal understanding of subject matter, so they go to great lengths to acquire all the information possible to increase their knowledge base.

Intuition

A major divide separating expert from less expert teachers appears to be a strong intuitive grasp of the developing learning environment. Experts use an intuition sharpened by years of experience and bolstered by an extensive knowledge base to make many of their instructional decisions (Tan 1997). They get a "gut feeling" and have the confidence to go with that feeling—even if it runs counter to accepted logic or convention (figure 16.2). This would be a dangerous practice for beginning or perhaps even competent teachers, but it is the *modus operandi* for the expert. It takes years of reflective teaching, experimentation, trying, failing, and succeeding to gain an expert's intuitive ability. What separates the expert from the less expert is not intuition itself but rather the superior performances and solutions that the process yields for the expert.

Figure 16.2 Teachers gain confidence and control of their classes as they gain experience.

Because of the reliance on intuitive decision making in their teaching, expert teachers often forgo formal written plans. With a wealth of knowledge, a depth of experience, and the role of intuition in their teaching, they can afford to do so. In fact, because they are such masters of the learning environment, they can teach more effectively without constraints placed on them by prior decision making. For expert teachers, planning is best done responsively during the lesson and without the use of formal lesson plans. Siedentop and Eldar (1989) refer to this as "plan independent," where expert teachers plan on past experiences and class events. Indeed, when teaching familiar subject matter, experts often show little concern for advanced formal planning (Manross and Templeton 1997). They are so familiar with the lessons, student abilities, and equipment that they often spend very little time outlining a detailed lesson plan. Teachers with less experience and knowledge would not be nearly as effective without carefully written plans and would be hard-pressed to craft a meaningful lesson without careful forethought. A beginning teacher who believes he can teach well without a lesson plan is much like a person with a new driver's license believing he can successfully drive in the Indianapolis 500 or Monaco Grand Prix.

Automatic Behavior

Because experts are intuitive and don't often use linear, step-by-step approaches to decision making,

their responses and performances appear fast, fluid, and natural. Characteristic of the expert performance is a high degree of automaticity, which Bloom (1986) described as "knowing-in-action." Extensive hours of practice are an important prerequisite for developing the automatic aspect of expert performance. Automaticity in experts' teaching practices is found in their daily routines. These routines are the repetitive activities that seemingly occur with little practice or forethought. Siedentop and Eldar (1989) attribute an expert's automaticity to an ability to discriminate information early and respond quickly.

Automaticity begins to be noticeable in proficient teachers, but it's even more pronounced among experts. Lesson openings, closings, demonstrations, explanations, and even interactions with students are performed with seemingly little effort but result in remarkable outcomes. In a study I completed with expert golf instructors (Schempp 1999), Jane Frost (LPGA Teacher of the Year) would declare a pop quiz at strategic points in the lesson and then ask her student questions about what was just learned in an effort to check the student's level of comprehension. Checking student comprehension by questioning is one of the characteristics of an effective teacher, so I wasn't surprised to see this in Jane's instructional repertoire. Several years later, Jane and I were conducting a teaching seminar together when she used the exact same phrase with the seminar participants. When I asked Jane if she was aware of her pop-quiz routine, she said she was not. When I produced the tape made several years earlier and showed her that even her intonation was the same, she was embarrassed to discover the automaticity in her behavior and the unconscious use of this routine. I attempted to assure her that it was a characteristic of an expert teacher, and it only further reinforced my belief that she was indeed at the top of her profession. This automatic behavioral routine allowed Jane to focus completely on the purpose—the student's comprehension—because she had to give no thought to the method of extracting the information. Experience had already effectively ingrained an "autopilot" technique into her teaching.

In the previously mentioned study of golf instructors in which Jane was a participant, the expert teachers had routines for opening the lesson, giving instructions, positioning themselves during a lesson, pacing the content, and closing the lesson (Baker et al. 1998). When teaching, experts use certain routines for starting and stopping class and for disciplining and monitoring student behavior. Because of these automatic routines, students understand what is expected of them at all times. Teachers or coaches looking to raise their level of expertise should review the routines they currently use or consider developing routines that will allow them more time to teach and to teach more effectively. The routines used for opening and closing a lesson or practice seem particularly key to instructional effectiveness, so that's a good place to begin.

Attending to the Atypical

When discriminating information (i.e., sorting the important from the unimportant in the learning environment), experts attend to the atypical in a situation. Carter and colleagues (1988) found that experts assessed teaching events as either typical or atypical, and this assessment affected how they processed information. If a situation was assessed as typical, the need to process the observable events was minimal. The teachers would simply let the lesson unfold. If a situation appeared to be unusual, or atypical, experts attempted to make sense of the irregularities. While observing a swim class, for example, a teacher may notice an arm swing rising from the water in an unusual pattern. Once the atypical action is spotted, the expert teacher then seeks to discover its cause and take appropriate action.

When tending to the atypical, experts draw on their extensive and highly organized knowledge to efficiently sift the information and determine their next set of actions (Tan 1997). When things are working in a normal pattern, however, they tend not to reflect on what is occurring but rather simply monitor the process until something seems out of line. Detecting the atypical signals the expert's attention. Their reliance on intuition in decision making, large quantity of knowledge, and different analytical framework for monitoring ongoing events all contribute to the distinct and effective instructional activity of the expert teacher and coach.

Thinking Forward to Solve Problems

Experts invest time identifying, defining, and analyzing a problem before searching for a solution. They realize if they don't get the problem right, they have no hope of finding the right solution. Even though experts are sometimes slower than novices in the early stages of problem solving (i.e., absolute time spent on initial problem representation is longer for experts), it seems time well spent because experts still solve problems faster than novices.

In the beginning of the problem-solving process, experts try to better understand the problem by analyzing it qualitatively. During this analysis, experts rely on their extensive knowledge base to construct a mental representation of the problem that helps define the situation, identify constraints, isolate factors causing the problem, and evaluate and justify possible solutions (Voss and Post 1988). In analyzing and representing problems, experts rely more on underlying principles and metaphors rather than literal and practical categorizations (Chi, Feltovich, and Glaser 1981).

Experts spend time gathering all the facts before making decisions. For example, expert coaches spend significant time reviewing tapes of game performances to analyze all facets of the game in an effort to link specific occurrences to the outcome. Beginners spend less time and are more easily satisfied that they have found the right answer. For example, a beginning basketball coach remembers that with two seconds left in the last game, his player missed a free throw that would have tied the game. He therefore has his players practice free throws for 15 minutes every practice the following week. An expert coach viewing the same game may realize that even though the player missed a key free throw, the team made 70% of the free throws in the match (acceptable to the coach's standard). After further analysis and study, the expert coach discovers her team had 16 turnovers that directly resulted in the opponent scoring 32 points. The expert coach then devotes significant practice time to dribbling and passing.

When solving routine problems (e.g., physics, medical diagnoses), expert problem solvers tend to work forward from known facts to the unknown. Forward reasoning is usually contrasted with backward reasoning, in which the problem solver works from a hypothesis about the unknown back to the given facts (Patel and Groen 1991). In teaching, an example might be seen in a physical education teacher observing that a class isn't paying attention to his soccer instruction. A beginner would see the problem as students not paying attention, which might have two solutions: punish those not paying attention or make the instruction more interesting (e.g., more enthusiasm, shorter explanations, rewards for paying attention). An expert teacher would take the time to find out why the students were not paying attention before attempting a solution. Perhaps talking with the students would be the first step (see John Hichwa's story in chapter 7; John provides a superb example of an expert teacher thinking forward to solve a problem). An expert would not attempt a solution until he has developed a firm grip on the exact nature of the problem. Perhaps the students had previously poor experiences with soccer, were already sufficiently skilled in soccer, or believed that they would never have the opportunity to play soccer. With the real reason at hand, the expert teacher is prepared to solve the problem.

Self-Monitoring

More than one expert teacher has told me "Just because I know more than most people about teaching doesn't mean I know everything." An interesting phenomenon occurs in teaching. Beginners appear to have a great deal more confidence in their knowledge and practices than do experienced teachers. In reality, expert teachers are very good at understanding the limits of their knowledge and skills, tend to be more critical of their work, and love what they do to such a degree that they strive to be even better than they are now—regardless of any success or awards they may have received (Schempp, Tan, et al. 1998).

Beginning teachers may simply be unaware of how little they know. Expert teachers are keenly aware of errors they make and can predict which teaching problems will prove most challenging for them. They also insightfully understand why they fail to comprehend certain elements of a problem

if something doesn't work as intended. Further, they are acutely aware of the appropriateness or adequacy of the solutions they attempt and practices they employ in their teaching and coaching. By objectively and honestly assessing their shortcomings and knowledge deficiencies, they are better able to analyze the cause of their failure and take corrective action. This self-monitoring process is one reason they are experts. For example, while a beginning teacher may give up on a struggling student learning a martial arts kick as a hopeless cause, and a competent teacher may be satisfied that she tried her best and made at least some progress, regardless of any initial success—or failure—an expert teacher will reflect on the lesson until he discovers ways he might have taught the skill better and then make a mental note of the discovery for the next time a similar situation arises.

The characteristic of self-monitoring might have been best recognized and celebrated in the poetry of Henry Wadsworth Longfellow:

> The heights by which great men reached and kept
>
> Were not attained by sudden flight.
>
> But they, while their companions slept
>
> Were toiling upward in the night.

Summary

This chapter identified the characteristics of the four stages in teaching expertise: beginner, competent, proficient, and expert. Suggestions for becoming more expert at teaching and coaching were also offered. Not everyone has the ability, desire, or opportunity to reach the highest levels of professional practice. But by identifying, formulating, and developing the elements of expertise in your own professional practice, you are well on your way to becoming more expert. Our society would certainly benefit from more expert teachers and coaches in sport and physical activity.

Discussion Questions

1. As a beginning teacher or coach, what do you believe will be your biggest challenges? How will you meet these challenges? What will help you move to the level of competent teacher or coach?

2. Planning is an important skill for any teacher. How do the planning strategies change as you move through the stages of expertise?

3. Instinct and intuition seem to be two characteristics of more expert teachers. Do you believe these characteristics can be developed? If so, how?

4. Do you know any expert teachers or coaches? Do they seem to possess the qualities described in this chapter?

The Final Story

Most of the chapters in this book have included a story to illustrate a significant point made in the chapter. This being the final chapter, this is the place for the final story. But I can't write the final story because the final story is you. As I wrote in the beginning, this book is intended to serve you in your quest to be a better teacher and coach. Will this book help you become a better teacher? Only you can decide that. So I leave the final story to you. What kind of a teacher or coach do you wish to become? How good do you want to be and why? Years from now, when your students and players recall their time with you, what is it you want them to remember?

Let me know how your story goes (you can reach me at pschempp@arches.uga.edu). I'd like to know how this book ends.

Appendix A

Sample Lesson Plan

Course: Beginning Golf

Instructor: Schempp

Lesson: Pitching

Objectives:

1. The student will learn the proper address, swing, and follow-through for hitting the pitch shot.
2. The student will learn when to hit a pitch and when to chip.

Key Points:

1. <u>Pitch Shot</u>
   a. Address: open stance, ball in middle of stance, hands ahead of the clubhead, weight on left side of the body
   b. Backswing: length depends on distance
   c. Impact: left wrist firm, focus on striking the back of the ball and then ground, hands remain ahead of the clubhead
   d. Follow-through: focus on where the ball was (don't look up too soon), weight completely on left side, finish with elbows high

2. <u>Chip or Pitch?</u>
   a. Chip: poor lie, downhill lie, green is hard, wind, stress
   b. Pitch: good lie, uphill lie, green is soft, obstacle is in the way

Activities:

1. Place bag about 10 yd away and land balls on bag.
2. Hit over a bunker. Can you land and stick on the green?
3. Place balls at 10 yd, 20 yd, 30 yd, and hit to a different target each time.

Enrichment and Back-Up Activities:

1. Pitch and hole out. Can you get down in two from 15 yd?
2. Practice with the clubhead open at various degrees. Can you change trajectory?
3. Play "catch" with a partner using a pitch shot (pitch to your partner's feet).
4. Play pitch and putt with a partner. Alternate shots.
5. Play pitch and putt with an opponent.

Appendix B

Sample Unit Plan

Baseball

Activity:	Baseball	**Dates:**	March 16 to April 16
Facilities:	Baseball field, classroom	**Equipment:**	1 dozen balls, 6 bats, gloves, helmets, 3 batting tees
Class Size:	24 high school freshmen		

Purpose: On completion of this unit, students will have acquired the fundamental skills of baseball, be able to apply those skills in a game situation, and have a sufficient knowledge of the game's rules so they may enjoy the game as both participants and spectators.

WEEK 3/16

Monday	Tuesday	Wednesday	Thursday	Friday
Introduction of unit Rules: field	Warm-up Rules: equipment Skills: overhand throw	Warm-up Review: throw Skills: catch (fly and grounder)	Warm-up Rules: outs Skills: outfield positions and play	Warm-up Rules: batting Review: throw and catch Skills: cut-offs and relays

WEEK 3/23

Monday	Tuesday	Wednesday	Thursday	Friday
Warm-up Skills: infield positions and play	Warm-up Rules: running Skills: first base play	Warm-up Review: positions Skills: cut-offs and relays	Warm-up Skills: backing up Test: throw and catch skills	Warm-up Review: infield play

WEEK 3/30

Monday	Tuesday	Wednesday	Thursday	Friday
Warm-up Skills: pitching (wind-up, stretch)	Warm-up Skills: pitching (fastball, curve)	Warm-up Skills: pitching (position play)	Warm-up Skills: baserunning Game: modified using batting tee	Warm-up Review: pitching

(continued)

Sample Unit Plan *(continued)*

Baseball (cont.)

WEEK 4/6

Monday	Tuesday	Wednesday	Thursday	Friday
Warm-up Skills: batting (stance, grip)	Warm-up Skills: batting (swing fundamentals)	Warm-up Skills: batting (bunting)	Warm-up Review: stance, grip, swing Skills: batting (hit to location, power)	Warm-up Review: batting Game: batting game

WEEK 4/13

Monday	Tuesday	Wednesday	Thursday	Friday
Warm-up Game: regulation (three innings) Review: game situations	Warm-up Test: batting and pitching	Warm-up Game: regulation (three innings) Review: game situations	Warm-up Test: rule knowledge Game: modified	Warm-up Game: regulation (three innings)

Summary: key skills and knowledge

Appendix C

Sample Long-Range Plan

Beginning Racquetball

Week	Topic
1	Equipment, court dimensions
2	Preparation for play (fitness, stretching, skill, warm-up)
3	Grip, ready position, footwork
4	Forehand stroke; review ready position
5	Backhand stroke; review footwork
6	Rules
7	Volley shots; review grip
8	Overhead shots; review forehand stroke
9	Serve: power, lob; review backhand stroke
10	Serve: cross-court, Z, overhead
11	Passing shot: straight, two-wall
12	Kill shot; review overhead shots
13	Ceiling shot, lob shot, three-wall shot
14	Strategy: serve, playing out-of-shape opponents; review rules
15	Strategy: opponent hits hard or soft shots; review rules
16	Strategy: using the backwall; review kill shot
17	Tournament play: ladders, round-robin, double elimination
18	Challenge play

Appendix D

Sample Take-Home Practice Diary Sheet

Basketball Skills
Practice Schedule

Name: _____

Record the practice date and number of baskets made as indicated for each practice activity.

Date: _____ _____ _____ _____ _____					
Short shots: shoot within 3 feet of the basket; emphasize using wrist and fingers to make the shot *# of shots out of 10 that do not touch the rim*					
Jump shots: from outside paint, middle left *# made out of 30*					
Jump shots: from outside paint, middle right *# made out of 30*					
Free throws: from foul line *# made out of 30*					
3-point shot: from right side *# made out of 10*					
3-point shot: from left side *# made out of 10*					

Appendix E

Kurt Street Elementary School
Physical Education
Fundamental Motor Skills Unit

Task Card: Striking

Skill Description:

The striking pattern is used in many sport activities. Most of the activities involve hitting an object with some part of the body or an implement that is controlled by the hand. The object to be struck may be stationary or moving. The striking pattern is much the same as that involved in any throwing motion.

No matter what plane the striking implement follows, the speed of the struck object is governed by the same principles as those involved in throwing. The amount of momentum developed depends on the length of the backswing, the number of muscles brought into play, and their orderly sequence of action. The object to be struck should be contacted at the instant the maximum speed of the swing has been reached. The implement must follow through in the direction of the target. The implement should be held out and away from the body and swung in a plane that is a right angle to the object to be hit. A stance that provides a solid base is important if fast-moving objects are to be struck and propelled any distance.

Equipment Needed:

Playground balls, volleyballs, foam balls, fleece or yarn balls, tennis balls, Wiffle balls, paddles, bats, Wiffle ball bats, rackets, cones, drum with beater, hula hoops, volleyball standards with hanging targets, milk crates, garbage cans, cardboard boxes

Activities: (use a variety of striking implements)

1. Strike an object with an emphasis on base of support and body position.
    a. Strike an object with one hand or an implement held by one hand while standing with the feet in a stride position and either close together or far apart.
    b. Repeat previous step using two hands or an implement held with two hands.
    c. Use the underhand, sidearm, or overhead patterns with one or both hands to strike an object.
    d. Use the previous striking patterns while standing, kneeling, sitting, and lying.
    e. Lean the trunk forward, backward, and to both sides while using the different striking patterns.
    f. Strike an object on the left side of the body and on the right side of the body.

2. Strike an object with an emphasis on speed, rhythm, force, and flow.
    a. Strike a stationary, resting, rolling, and airborne object lightly, firmly, slowly, and quickly.
    b. Strike an object and emphasize the follow-through beyond the point of contact.
    c. Strike an object so that a verbal cue or drum beat accentuates the point of contact and the transfer of weight.

3. Strike an object with an emphasis on range, level, and direction.
    a. Strike an object rolling on the floor or airborne at different levels with one hand, two hands, or with an implement.
    b. Strike an object from above and below, from the right and left, and from other angles.

4. Strike an object with an emphasis on combination, environment, and creative expression.
   a. Strike a rolling object with the hand as you walk or run alongside (hula hoops are ideal for this).
   b. Using an implement, strike a vertical or horizontal pole with different targets.
   c. Strike an object into the air and catch it.
   d. Strike an object as if you were angry, strong, a giant, an elf, happy, weak, and so on.
   e. With one object (ball), an implement or two, and a partner, invent a new game.
   f. Move about the room keeping an object above your head using striking actions.
   g. Volley a ball against a wall using striking patterns (how many times can you hit it?).
   h. Strike an object over a piece of equipment and onto or into a target.

Appendix F

Mac George High School
Physical Education Department
Archery Contract

I, _____, am signing a contract to receive a grade of "A" for the physical education course in archery. I understand that I must complete all of the following requirements in order to earn this grade:

Activity Completed	Teacher's Signature	Date
1. Grade of 85-100 on the final written exam	_____	_____
2. Complete four written assignments	_____	_____
3. Complete six independent skill assignments	_____	_____
4. Complete 12 archery course rounds in class	_____	_____
5. Visit a local archery range/meet range officer	_____	_____

Should I not complete the above requirements, I shall receive the grade for which I meet all of the requirements. I further understand that I can sign a contract for another grade at any time during the course. I will, however, give my best effort to fulfill all the terms of this contract as I now understand them.

_____   _____

Student's Signature   Date

Appendix G

Mac George High School
Physical Education Department
Archery Course Evaluation

Welcome to the world of archery. This course is designed to maximize your enjoyment and appreciation of one of civilization's oldest sports. In ancient times, skill with a bow and arrow was necessary for survival; today, it is a very popular recreational activity. It is the instructor's hope that you leave this course with a basic understanding of archery and a desire to include it among your free time activities.

The content of this course is presented in a manner that allows you to work at your own pace and interact with your peers yet permits the instructor to assist you on an individual basis. If at any time you have a question or concern, please feel free to talk with the teacher.

Student Evaluation

Your final grade in this course is based on a contract you will sign with the teacher. After reading the terms of the contract and selecting the grade you wish to earn, please notify the teacher as to which level of contract you choose to enter. The instructor will ask you to sign the appropriate contract, and you can then begin the appropriate activities. You will receive the grade for which you meet the requirements. You must meet all requirements for that grade. At first, there may appear to be a considerable amount of work, but our time is short and the assignments represent the essential knowledge necessary for the enjoyment of archery. The terms of the contracts are as follows:

1. For the grade of "A" you must complete or achieve the following:
   a. Grade of 85-100 on the final written exam
   b. Complete four written assignments
   c. Complete six independent skill assignments
   d. Complete 12 archery course rounds in class
   e. Visit a local archery range and meet the range officer
2. For the grade of "B" you must complete or achieve the following:
   a. Grade of 75-84 on the final written exam
   b. Complete two written assignments
   c. Complete five independent skill assignments
   d. Complete 10 archery course rounds in class
   e. Visit a local archery range and meet the range officer
3. For the grade of "C" you must complete or achieve the following:
   a. Grade of 65-74 on the final written exam
   b. Complete one written assignment
   c. Complete three independent skill assignments
   d. Complete 6 archery course rounds in class

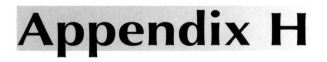

Appendix H

Mac George High School
Physical Education Department
Archery

Independent Skill Assignment #1

Skills: Selecting, Stringing, Unstringing a Bow

Student's Name:_____ Partner:_____

Skill Assignment Purpose

The purpose of this assignment is to enable a student to select the proper bow weight so that the student may shoot with ease and accuracy. The student will also learn to properly string and unstring a bow.

Bow Selection Information

An inexperienced archer should use a lighter weight bow than an experienced archer. As skill increases, a heavier bow can be used. A bow weight of 15 to 25 pounds is recommended for a beginner. A heavier bow can project the arrow farther, but a lighter bow permits the beginner to be more accurate—and accuracy is more important than distance in archery as it is easier to adjust the distance one shoots by selecting the distance to the target. The bow weight is normally printed on the side of the bow near the handle, but at times it may be located somewhere else or not found on the bow at all. As you gain skill in archery, your height, weight, strength, and shooting purpose will all factor into selecting the appropriate bow weight. If purchasing or renting a bow, ask for assistance from the sales representative, who should be skilled in helping someone select the proper bow weight.

Instructional Cues

1. In selecting a properly weighted bow, you should have to strain slightly when drawing the bow.
2. Push-pull method of bracing (stringing) the bow:
   a. The left hand grips the handle with the string side facing downward.
   b. Wedge the lower end against the arch of the left foot.
   c. Pull on the handle and push the upper limb down and slide the string up simultaneously.
3. Step-in method of bracing (stringing) the bow. Recommended for heavier bows.
   a. Place the right leg between the string and bow belly.
   b. Place the lower end of the bow above the instep of the left foot. The bow handle will rest against the back of the thigh.
   c. Press against the top of the bow with the right hand and slide the string with the left hand.

Skill Practice

Individual Activities

	Repetitions	Date Completed
1. String and unstring a bow using the push-pull method.	5	
2. String and unstring a bow using the step-in method.	5	

Partner Activities

1. What bow weight would you recommend for your partner and why?

	Repetition	Partner Evaluation
2. String and unstring a bow using the push-pull method.	1	_____
	2	_____
	3	_____
	4	_____
	5	_____

3. String and unstring a bow using the step-in method.	1	_____
	2	_____
	3	_____
	4	_____
	5	_____

Appendix I

Recommended Web Sites

Physical Education Organizations

www.aahperd.org American Alliance for Health, Physical Education, Recreation and Dance. AAHPERD is the largest organization supporting and assisting those involved in physical education, leisure, fitness, dance, health promotion, education, and all specialties related to achieving a healthy lifestyle.

www.aahperd.org/naspe National Association for Sport and Physical Education. NASPE seeks to enhance knowledge and professional practice in sport and physical activity through scientific study and the distribution of research-based and experiential knowledge to members and the public. An organization within AAHPERD.

www.napehe.org The National Association for Physical Education in Higher Education. NAPEHE provides a forum for interdisciplinary ideas and concepts relative to physical education programs and scholarship.

Sport and Fitness

www.aausports.org Amateur Athletic Union. A large nonprofit volunteer sports organization dedicated to the development and promotion of amateur sport and physical fitness programs.

www.AFPAfitness.com American Fitness Professionals and Associates. AFPA's goal is to provide excellence in health and physical fitness education that is both practical and scientifically up to date for health and fitness professionals and enthusiasts.

www.fifa.com Fédération Internationale de Football Association (FIFA). The largest organization dedicated to the game of soccer. The Web site provides news and competition descriptions.

www.ifpa-fitness.com International Fitness Professionals Association. Information on certification, P.T. support, and a store.

www.lpga.com Ladies Professional Golf Association. Certification and education programs for golf teaching professionals. Despite the name, certifies both women and men as teaching professionals.

www.ncaa.org National Collegiate Athletic Association. Web site news and information related to athletic events and activities of the NCAA.

www.olympic.org International Olympic Committee. Features information on all aspects of the Olympics and provides links to governing sport federations.

www.pga.com Professional Golf Association. Certification and education programs for golf teaching professionals.

www.softball.org Amateur Softball Association. The governing body of softball in the United States. Information available on competitions, umpiring, youth and adult softball, plus a hall of fame.

www.uspta.com United States Professional Tennis Association. An organization that promotes the tennis profession and awareness of the game. Information on education, programs, and membership.

www.usptr.com United States Professional Tennis Registry. Certification and education programs for tennis teaching professionals.

www.usta.com United States Tennis Assocation. The governing body for tennis in the United States. The Web site offers information on lessons, equipment, travel, competition and tennis news.

www.womenssportfoundation.org Information and resources on competitive, professional, and recreational sports as well as health and fitness for girls and women.

Coaching Associations

www.abca.org American Baseball Coaches Association. News, committees, programs, and links.

www.afca.com American Football Coaches Association. News, conferences, clinics, library, and links.

www.ahcahockey.com The American Hockey Coaches Association. Information on the organization, hockey news, drills, and special features.

www.avca.org American Volleyball Coaches Association. Online information source for volleyball coaches.

www.baseballcoaches.org National High School Baseball Coaches Association. Provides services and recognition for baseball coaches. Member information, publications, and convention announcements are posted on the Web site.

www.coachingforthefuture Coaching for the Future is an international company dedicated to comprehensive and integrated coaching education.

www.dsr.nsw.gov.au New South Wales Sport and Recreation site. Information on organizing and conducting effective coaching sessions.

www.HumanKinetics.com This Web site provides a listing of books from the leading publisher of books, journals, and videotapes in sport and physical activity. Gives information on the American Master Teacher Program and the Coaching Effectiveness Program.

www.nabc.com National Association of Basketball Coaches. Coaches corner, press releases, conventions and clinics, resources, recruiting news, and links.

www.nagce.org National Association of Golf Coaches and Educators. Serves as a resource for golf coaches, physical education teachers, and youth leaders.

www.nhsca.com National High School Coaches Association. Provides leadership and support for high school coaches. Web site has information for coaches in general as well as by specific sport.

www.nscaa.com National Soccer Coaches Association of America. Information on coach education, job openings, and coaching tips.

www.nsca-lift.org The National Strength and Conditioning Association. Offers information on careers, certification, publications, special interest groups, and resources.

www.swimmingcoach.org American Swimming Coaches Association. Information on education, certification, news events, and membership.

Practice Activities

www.activeteamsports.com A wealth of ideas for many popular sports and physical activities. Includes practice ideas, coaching tips, and health and fitness suggestions.

www.gamecentralstation.com/gcshome.asp A wealth of games related to sport and physical activity. Most games are categorized based on skills and age appropriateness.

www.goldmedalperformance.co.nz Personalized coaching systems designed over the Internet.

www.homestead.com/rugbycoach Tips, fitness ideas, positions, and strategies for rugby teachers and coaches.

www.eteamz.com A wealth of ideas for many popular sports and physical activities. Includes practice ideas, coaching tips, and health and fitness suggestions.

www.pelinks4u.org/links/unitplans.htm A listing of instructional unit plan Web sites designed by physical education students from Central Washington State University.

www.sportsId.com Features videoclips of athletes performing skills in many different sports. Also offers information on learning, preparing for, and participating in a large selection of sports and physical activities.

www.teacher2teacher.com Online resources for teachers. Includes interactive projects and resources. Specializes in technology training for teachers.

www.tennisteacher.com Offers tennis instruction over the Internet.

www.yahooligans.com/Sports_and_Recreation Links to a large variety of sports and recreation sites that feature tips, instructional ideas, and activities.

Sample Physical Education Program Sites

http://schools.eastnet.ecu.edu/pitt/ayden/physed.htm Web site for Ayden Elementary School's physical education program, Ayden, NC. Contains program descriptions, photographs, and links to hundreds of related Web sites.

www.fargo.k12.nd.us/schools/Jefferson/PE/index.htm Provides the philosophy, program highlights, special events, and other information for Jefferson Elementary School, Fargo, ND.

www.fmhs.cnyric.org/physed/index.html Fayetteville-Manilus High School Physical Education. Offers fitness tips, program descriptions, philosophy, and a monthly calendar.

Creating Web Sites and Electronic Mailing Lists

http://werbach.com/web/wwwhelp.html Provides assistance and resources for creating Web pages.

www.everythingemail.net Information on all aspects of using e-mail and e-mail lists.

www.lsoft.com Software that allows you to manage and control e-mail lists on a private network or on the Internet.

Sample Sport Instructor and School Web Sites

www.pelzgolf.com Information and descriptions offered by leading golf instructor Dave Pelz. Includes information on schools, clinics, and corporate programs.

www.snowvalleybasketball.com Web site for the Snow Valley Basketball School. Information on upcoming events, frequently asked questions, and school contacts.

Teaching

www.antion.com Presentation skills, public speaking, professional speaking. Online articles and information for public speakers.

www.coe.uga.edu/sportlab Sport Instruction Research Laboratory. Research on sport instruction.

www.ericsp.org Educational Resource and Information Clearinghouse on Teaching and Teacher Education. Research on all aspects of teaching.

www.pecentral.org Physical Education Central. A national clearinghouse of information on all aspects of physical education. This Web site provides teachers with education news and research updates plus links to career training, distance education, schools, classroom management, and industry contacts. Ideas for lesson plans as well as information on professional conferences are also available.

Public Speaking

www.selfgrowth.com/public.html Self-improvement online. Recommended and reviewed public speaking Web sites.

Lesson and Unit Planning

www.new-teacher.com Veteran educators give newcomers tips on substitute teaching, job hunting, classroom management, and professionalism. Absorb the wisdom, or submit your own articles.

www.pelinks4u.org A compilation of Web site listings that provide a wealth of information in all categories of knowledge for sport and physical activity instructors.

www.pelinks4u.org/units.htm Some very well done unit plans by physical education students and teachers.

www.teacher2teacher.com Online resources for teachers, primarily public school teachers. Includes interactive projects and resources.

Appendix J

Directed Observation
Guide Sheet

Name:_____ Date:_____

Lesson:_____ Students:_____

Observer:_____ Location:_____

1. Pre-Lesson Preparation (equipment, facilities, lesson content)

2. Lesson

    a. Lesson opening

    b. Explanations and demonstrations

    c. Student activities

    d. Feedback

    e. Lesson closing

3. Post-Lesson Activity (student evaluations, lesson critique)

From *Teaching Sport and Physical Activity: Insights on the Road to Excellence* by Paul Schempp, 2003, Champaign, IL: Human Kinetics.

Appendix K

Teaching Skills Rating Scale

Name:_____ Date:_____

Lesson:_____ Students:_____

Observer:_____ Location:_____

Rate these teaching skills (1 needs most improvement, 10 needs no improvement).

1. Instructional Pacing

   a. Student practice time

      1   2   3   4   5   6   7   8   9   10

   b. Activities briskly paced

      1   2   3   4   5   6   7   8   9   10

   c. High rates of student success in practice activities

      1   2   3   4   5   6   7   8   9   10

   d. Expectations for student mastery made clear

      1   2   3   4   5   6   7   8   9   10

2. Instructional Form

   a. Begins lesson with goals and overview

      1   2   3   4   5   6   7   8   9   10

   b. Stresses main concepts throughout lesson

      1   2   3   4   5   6   7   8   9   10

   c. Transitions between activities clear and quick

      1   2   3   4   5   6   7   8   9   10

   d. Information presented in clear, concise manner

      1   2   3   4   5   6   7   8   9   10

   e. Teaches with enthusiasm

      1   2   3   4   5   6   7   8   9   10

   f. Closes lesson with review and summary

      1   2   3   4   5   6   7   8   9   10

From *Teaching Sport and Physical Activity: Insights on the Road to Excellence* by Paul Schempp, 2003, Champaign, IL: Human Kinetics.

Appendix L

Systematic Observation
Feedback Analysis System

Name:_____ Date:_____

Lesson:_____ Students:_____

Observer:_____ Location:_____

After each feedback statement, place a tally mark in all applicable columns.

Students

Individual	
Group	

Target

Correct movement	
Incorrect movement	
Neutral	

Specificity

Specific to movement	
General	

Character

Positive	
Negative	
Neutral	

Intention

Evaluative	
Prescriptive	
Descriptive	
Affective	

From *Teaching Sport and Physical Activity: Insights on the Road to Excellence* by Paul Schempp, 2003, Champaign, IL: Human Kinetics.

References

Ayres, A., ed. 1990. *The wit and wisdom of Mark Twain.* New York: New American Library.

Baker, K. 2001. Promoting your physical education program. *Journal of Physical Education, Recreation and Dance* 72(2):37-40.

Baker, K., P. Schempp, and B. Hardin. 1998. *Science and golf III: Proceedings of the World Scientific Congress of Golf.* Champaign, IL: Human Kinetics.

Baumgartner, T., and A. Jackson. 1999. *Measurement for evaluation in physical education and exercise science.* Boston: MCB/McGraw-Hill.

Bell, M. 1997. The development of expertise. *Journal of Physical Education, Recreation, and Dance* 68(2):34-8.

Berliner, D.C. 1994. Expertise: The wonder of exemplary performances. In *Creating powerful thinking in teachers and students: Diverse perspectives*, ed. J. Mangieri and C. Block, 161-86. Fort Worth, TX: Harcourt Brace College.

Bloom, B. 1986. Automaticity. *Educational Leadership* 43(5):70-7.

Broekhoff, J. 1985. The effect of physical activity on physical growth and development. In *The academy papers*, 75-87. Champaign, IL: Human Kinetics.

Brophy, J., and T.L. Good. 1986. Teacher behavior and student achievement. In *Handbook of research on teaching*, ed. M.C. Wittrock, 328-75. New York: Macmillan.

Byra, M., and M. Sherman. 1993. Preactive and interactive decision making tendencies of less and more experienced preservice teachers. *Research Quarterly for Exercise and Sport* 64:46-55.

Calderhead, J. 1996. Teachers: Beliefs and knowledge. In *Handbook of Educational Psychology*, ed. D.C. Berliner and R.C. Calfee, 709-25. New York: Macmillan.

Carnegie, D. 1990. *The quick and easy way to effective speaking.* New York: Pocket Books.

Carter, K., K. Cushing, D. Sabers, P. Stein, and D. Berliner. 1988. Expert-novice differences in perceiving and processing visual classroom stimuli. *Journal of Teacher Education* 39(3):25-31.

Cazden, C. 1986. Classroom discourse. In *Handbook of research on teaching*, ed. M.C. Wittrock, 432-63. New York: Macmillan.

Chapman, V. 1999. *Style versus substance in public debate: Smoke or mirrors?* ERIC document number ED4455362.

Cheffers, J. and V. Mancini. 1978. Teacher-student interaction. In *What's going on in gym: Descriptive studies of physical education classes*, eds. W.G. Anderson and G.T. Barrette, 25-38. Newtown, CT: Motor Skills: Theory into Practice. Monograph 1.

Chi, M.T.H., P.J. Feltovich, and R. Glaser. 1981. Categorization and representation of physics problems by experts and novices. *Cognitive Science* 11(2):121-52.

Covey, S. 1989. *The 7 habits of highly effective people.* New York: Simon & Schuster.

Cruickshank, D.R., D. Bainer, and K. Metcalf. 1995. *The act of teaching.* New York: McGraw-Hill.

Crum, B. 1995. The urgent need for reflective teaching in physical education. In *Better teaching in physical education? Think about it!* ed C. Pare, 1-19. Trois-Rivieres, Canada: University of Quebec.

Cutlip, S., A. Center, and G. Broom. 2000. *Effective public relations.* 8th ed. London: Prentice Hall International.

Darst, P., D. Zakrajsek, and V. Mancini. 1983. *Analyzing physical education and sport instruction.* Champaign, IL: Human Kinetics.

DeMarco, G. 1997. *Profiles in expertise.* Unpublished doctoral dissertation. Athens, GA: University of Georgia.

Dewey, J. 1938/1963. *Experience and education.* New York: Macmillan.

Doyle, W. 1986. Classroom organization and management. In *Handbook of research on teaching.* 3rd ed., ed. M.C. Wittrock, 392-431. New York: Macmillan.

Driskell, J., R. Willis, and C. Copper. 1992. Effect of overlearning on retention. *Journal of Applied Psychology* 77:615-22.

Elliot, E., and M. Manross. 1996a. Physical educators and the Internet. Part one: Using e-mail. *Teaching Elementary Physical Education* (September):6-9.

———. 1996b. Physical educators and the Internet. Part two: The World Wide Web. *Teaching Elementary Physical Education* (October):6-9.

Ennis, C., L. Mueller, and W. Zhu. 1991. Description of knowledge structures within a concept-based curriculum framework. *Research Quarterly for Exercise and Sport* 62:33-40.

Ericsson, K.A., and N. Charness. 1994. Expert performance: Its structure and acquisition. *American Psychologist* 49(3):725-47.

Ericsson, K.A., R. Krampe, and C. Tesch-Romer. 1993. The role of deliberate practice in the acquisition of expert performance. *Psychological Review* 100(3):363-406.

Evans, J., ed. 1988. *Teachers, teaching and control in physical education*. Lewes, England: Falmer Press.

Evertson, C., and A. Harris. 1992. What we know about managing classrooms. *Educational Leadership* 49(7):74-78.

Feiman-Nemser, S., and R. Floden. 1986. The cultures of teaching. In *Handbook of research on teaching*, ed. M. Wittrock, 505-26. New York: Macmillan.

Feiman-Nemser, S., and M.B. Parker. 1990. Making subject matter part of the conversation in learning to teach. *Journal of Teacher Education* 41(3):32-43.

Feingold, R.S. 1994. Making connections: An agenda for the future. *Quest* 46:356-67.

Fincher, M., and P. Schempp. 1994. Teaching physical education: What do we need to know and how do we find it? *GAHPERD Journal* 28(3):7-10.

Fink, J., and D. Siedentop. 1989. The development of routines, rules, and expectations at the start of the school year. *Journal of Teaching in Physical Education* 8:198-212.

Fitts, P. and M. Posner. 1967. *Human performance*. Belmont, CA: Brooks/Cole.

Freire, P. 1970. *Pedagogy of the oppressed*. New York: Basic Books.

Gall, M. 1970. The use of questioning in teaching. *Review of Educational Research* 40:707-20.

Ginsburg, M. 1987. Reproduction, contradictions and conceptions in professionalism: The case of pre-service teachers. In *Critical Studies in Teacher Education*, ed. T. Popkewitz, 86-129. London: Falmer Press.

Gowan, G.R. 1992. Canada's National Coaching Certification Program (NCCP): Past, present, and future. *Journal of Physical Education, Recreation and Dance* 63(7):50-54.

Graber, K.C. 1991. Studentship in preservice teacher education: A qualitative study of undergraduates in physical education. *Research Quarterly for Exercise and Sport* 62:41-51.

Griffey, D., and L. Housner. 1991. Differences between experienced and inexperienced teachers' planning decisions, interactions, student engagement, and instructional climate. *Research Quarterly for Exercise and Sport* 62:196-204.

Griffin, L., S. Mitchell, and J. Oslin. 1997. *Teaching sport concepts and skills: A tactical games approach*. Champaign, IL: Human Kinetics.

Griffin, P. 1984. Girls' participation patterns in a middle school team sports unit. *Journal of Teaching in Physical Education* 4:30-8.

———. 1985. Boys' participation styles in a middle school team sports unit. *Journal of Teaching in Physical Education* 4:100-10.

———. 1998. *Strong women, deep closets*. Champaign, IL: Human Kinetics.

Grossman, P. 1990. *The making of a teacher: Teacher knowledge and teacher education*. New York: Teachers College Press.

Gruber, J. 1985. Physical activity and self-esteem development in children: A meta-analysis. In *The academy papers*, 30-48. Champaign, IL: Human Kinetics.

Hackbarth, S. 1996. *The educational technology handbook: A comprehensive guide*. Englewood Cliffs, NJ: Educational Technology Publications.

Harrison, L. 2001. Understanding the influence of stereotypes: Implications for the African American in sport and physical activity. *Quest* 53:97-114.

Harrison, L., and T. Worthy. 2001. Just like all the rest: Developing awareness of stereotypical thinking in physical education. *Journal of Physical Education, Recreation and Dance* 72(9):20-4.

Hastad, D.N., and A.C. Lacy. 1998. *Measurement and evaluation in physical education and exercise science*. 3rd ed. San Francisco: Benjamin Cummings.

Hastie, P., and N. Vlaisavljevic. 1999. The relationship between subject matter expertise and accountability in instructional tasks. *Journal of Teaching in Physical Education* 19:22-33.

Hebert, E., and D. Landin. 1994. Effects of a learning model and augmented feedback on tennis skill. *Research Quarterly for Exercise and Sport* 65:250-7.

Heinich, R., M. Molenda, J. Russell, and S. Smaldino. 1999. *Instructional media and technologies for learning*. 6th ed. Upper Saddle River, NJ: Merrill.

Hellison, D. 1993. The coaching club: Teaching responsibility to inner city students. *Journal of Physical Education, Recreation and Dance* 64:66-70.

———. 1995. *Teaching responsibility through physical activity*. Champaign, IL: Human Kinetics.

Hellison, D., and T. Templin. 1991. *A reflective approach to teaching physical education*. Champaign, IL: Human Kinetics.

Hichwa, J. 1998. *Right fielders are people too*. Champaign, IL: Human Kinetics.

Hisley, J., and T. Kempler. 2000. What's everybody so excited about?: The effects of teacher enthusiasm on student intrinsic motivation and vitality. *Journal of Experimental Education* 68:217-36.

Housner, L.D., and D. Griffey. 1985. Teacher cognition: Differences in planning and interactive decision making between experienced and inexperienced teachers. *Research Quarterly for Exercise and Sport* 56:44-53.

———. 1994. Pedagogical content knowledge in motor skill instruction: Wax on, wax off. *Journal of Physical Education, Recreation and Dance* 65(2):63-8.

Huberman, M. 1989. The professional life cycle of teachers. *Teachers College Record* 91:31-57.

Hutchinson, G.E. 1993. Prospective teachers' perceptions on teaching physical education: An interview study on the recruitment phase of teacher socialization. *Journal of Teaching Physical Education* 12(4):344-54.

Jewett, A., L. Bain, and C. Ennis. 1995. *The curriculum process in physical education.* 2nd ed. Madison, WI: Brown & Benchmark.

Jones, D., D. Housner, and A. Kornspan. 1997. Interactive decision-making and behavior of experienced and inexperienced basketball coaches during practice. *Journal of Teaching in Physical Education* 16:454-68.

Kneer, M. 1989. The influence of professional organizations on teacher development. In *Socialization into physical education: Learning to teach,* ed. T. Templin and P. Schempp, 123-44. Indianapolis: Benchmark Press.

Kluka, D. 1999. *Motor behavior: From learning to performance.* Englewood, CO: Morton.

Kolb, D.A. 1984. *Experiential learning: Experiences as the source of learning and development.* Englewood Cliffs, NJ: Prentice Hall.

Kounin, J. 1970. *Discipline and group management in classrooms.* New York: Holt, Reinhart, & Winston.

Lacey, C. 1989. Foreword. In *Socialization into physical education: Learning to teach,* ed. T. Templin and P. Schempp, xv. Indianapolis: Benchmark Press.

Land, M. and L. Smith. 1979. Effect of a teacher clarity variable on student achievement. *Journal of Educational Research* 72(4):196-97.

Landau, G. 1996. Critical theory in German sport pedagogy. In *Scientific development of sport pedagogy,* ed. P. Schempp, 223-36. Munster: Waxmann.

Lavay, B., R. French, and H. Henderson. 1997. *Positive behavior management strategies for physical education.* Champaign, IL: Human Kinetics.

Lawson, H.A. 1983. Toward a model of teacher socialization in physical education: The subjective warrant, recruitment, and teacher education (Part I). *Journal of Teaching in Physical Education* 2:3-16.

———. 1989. From rookie to veteran: Workplace conditions in physical education and induction into the profession. In *Socialization into physical education: Learning to teach,* ed. T. Templin and P. Schempp, 145-64. Indianapolis: Benchmark Press.

Leadbetter, D., D. Smith, N. Price, and J. Huggan. 1996. *Faults and fixes: How to correct the 80 most common problems in golf.* New York: Harper.

Leinhardt, G., and J.G. Greeno. 1986. The cognitive skill of teaching. *Journal of Educational Psychology* 78:75-95.

Leshin, C., J. Pollock, and C. Reigeluth. 1992. *Instructional design strategies and tactics.* Englewood Cliffs, NJ: Educational Technology Publications.

Lirgg, C. 1993. Effects of same-sex versus coeducational physical education on the self-perceptions of middle and high school students. *Research Quarterly for Exercise and Sport* 64:324-34.

Locke, L.F., and S.E. Woods. 1982. Teacher enthusiasm! *Journal of Teaching in Physical Education* 1(3):3-14.

Lortie, D.C. 1975. *Schoolteacher.* Chicago: University of Chicago Press.

Magill, R. 1990. Motor learning is meaningful for physical educators. *Quest* 42:126-33.

———. 2001. *Motor learning: Concepts and applications.* 6th ed. Boston: McGraw-Hill.

Mancini, V., D. Wuest, J. Cheffers, and S. Rich. 1983. Promoting student involvement in physical education by sharing decisions. *International Journal of Physical Education* 20(3):16-23.

Manross, D., and C. Templeton. 1997. Expertise in teaching physical education. *Journal of Physical Education, Recreation and Dance* 68(3):29-35.

Martin, K., S. Moritz, and C. Hall. 1999. Imagery use in sport: A literature review. *The Sport Psychologist* 13:245-68.

Martinek, T. 1997. Serving underserved youth through physical activity. *Quest* 49:3-7.

———. 1996. Psycho-social aspects of student differences in physical education. In *Scientific development of sport pedagogy,* ed. P. Schempp, 82-102. Munster, Germany: Waxmann.

Martinek, T., and D. Hellison. 1997. Fostering resiliency in underserved youth through physical activity. *Quest* 49:34-49.

McCullagh, P. 1993. Modeling: Learning, developmental, and social psychological considerations. In *Handbook of research on sport psychology,* ed. R. Singer, M. Murphy, and L. Tennant, 106-26. New York: Macmillan.

McCullick, B.A. 2001. Practitioners' perspectives on values, knowledge, and skills needed by PETE participants. *Journal of Teaching in Physical Education* 21:35-56.

McCullick, B., P. Schempp, and R. Cumings. 1999. The professional orientations of expert golf instructors. *International Journal of Physical Education* 36:15-24.

Melograno, V. 1996. *Designing the physical education curriculum.* Champaign, IL: Human Kinetics.

Metzler, M.W. 2000. *Instructional models for physical education.* Boston: Allyn & Bacon.

Meyer, C. 1992. What's the difference between authentic assessment and performance assessment? *Educational Leadership* 49(8):39.

Milo, F. 1997. Getting the word out: Why public relations should be on your board's agenda. *American School Board Journal* 184(10):46-7.

Mohnsen, B. 1998. *Using technology in physical education.* Cerritos, CA: Bonnie's Fitware.

Mosston, M., and S. Ashworth. 2002. *Teaching physical education.* 5th ed. San Francisco: Benjamin Cummings.

Nichols, M. 1995. *The lost art of listening.* New York: Guilford Press.

Oliver, K., and R. Lalik. 2000. *Bodily knowledge: Learning about equity and social justice with adolescent girls.* New York: Peter Lang.

Parker, J. 1995. Secondary teachers' views of effective teaching in physical education. *Journal of Teaching Physical Education* 14:127-39.

Partlow, K. 1992. American Coaching Effectiveness Program. *Journal of Physical Education, Recreation and Dance* 63(7):36-9.

Patel, V., and G. Groen. 1991. The general and specific nature of medical expertise: A critical look. In *Toward a general theory of expertise,* ed. K.A. Ericsson and J. Smith, 93-125. Cambridge: Cambridge University Press.

Patrick, B., J. Hisley, and T. Kempler. 2000. What's everybody so excited about?: The effects of teacher enthusiasm on student intrinsic motivation and vitality. *Journal of Experimental Education* 68:217-36.

Penick, H., and B. Shrake. 1992. *The little red book.* New York: Simon & Schuster.

Placek, J. 1983. Conceptions of success in teaching: Busy, happy and good? In *Teaching in physical education,* ed. T. Templin and J. Olson, 46-56. Champaign, IL: Human Kinetics.

Rink, J., K. French, A. Lee, M. Solmon and S. Lynn. 1994. A comparison of pedagogical knowledge structures of preservice students and teacher educators in two institutions. *Journal of Teaching in Physical Education* 13(2):140-62.

Roberts, G., ed. 1992. *Motivation in sport and exercise.* Champaign, IL: Human Kinetics.

Rosenshine, B., and N. Furst. 1971. Research on teacher performance criteria. In *Research in teacher education,* ed. B. Smith, 37-72. Englewood Cliffs, NJ: Prentice Hall.

Rosenshine, B., and R. Stevens. 1986. Teaching functions. In *Handbook of research on teaching.* 3rd ed., ed. M.C. Wittrock, 376-91. New York: Macmillan.

Rovegno, I. 1992. Learning to teach in a field-based methods course: The development of pedagogical content knowledge. *Teaching and Teacher Education* 8(1):69-82.

Safrit, M. 1998. *Introduction to measurement in physical education and exercise science.* New York: McGraw-Hill.

Safrit, M., and T. Wood. 1989. *Measurement concepts in physical education and exercise science.* Champaign, IL: Human Kinetics.

Sage, G.H. 1989a. Becoming a high school coach: From playing sports to coaching. *Research Quarterly for Exercise and Sport* 60(1):81-92.

———. 1989b. The social world of high school coaches: Multiple role demands and their consequences. In *Socialization into physical education: Learning to teach,* ed. T. Templin and P. Schempp, 251-68. Indianapolis: Benchmark Press.

Sardo-Brown, D. 1990. Experienced teachers' planning practices: A US survey. *Journal of Education for Teaching* 16 (1):57-72.

Schempp, P.G. 1993. Constructing professional knowledge: A case study of a high school teacher. *Journal of Teaching in Physical Education* 13(1):2-23.

———. 1999. *The role of knowledge and experience in expert sport instruction.* Paper presented at the AIESEP International Congress, Besancon, France.

Schempp, P. and K. Graber. 1992. Teacher socialization from a dialectic perspective. *Journal of Teaching in Physical Education* 11:329-48.

Schempp, P., D. Manross, S. Tan, and M. Fincher. 1998. Subject expertise and teachers' knowledge. *Journal of Teaching in Physical Education* 17(3):342-56.

Schempp, P., A. Sparkes, and T. Templin. 1993. The micropolitics of teacher induction. *American Educational Research Journal* 30:447-72.

Schempp, P., and P. St. Pierre. 2000a. The magic of metaphors. *Golf Science International* 9:6-7.

———. 2000b. The use of video technology in teaching. *Golf Science International* 8:2-5.

Schempp, P.G., S. Tan, D. Manross, and M. Fincher. 1998. Differences in novice and competent teachers' knowledge. *Teachers and Teaching: Theory and Practice* 4(1):9-20.

Schempp, P., C. Templeton, and E. Clark. 1999. The knowledge acquisition of expert golf instructors. In *Science and golf III,* ed. M.R. Farrally and A.J. Cochran, 295-301. Champaign, IL: Human Kinetics.

Schmidt, R.A. 1987. *Motor control and learning: A behavioral emphasis.* 2nd ed. Champaign, IL: Human Kinetics.

Schmidt, R. A., C.A. Wrisberg, and C.N. Wrisberg. 2000. *Motor learning and performance.* 2nd ed. Champaign, IL: Human Kinetics.

Schon, D.A. 1983. *The reflective practitioner: How professionals think in action.* New York: Basic Books.

Scribner, J.D., and D.H. Layton. 1995. *The study of educational politics.* Washington, DC: Falmer Press.

Seefeldt, V., and M. Milligan. 1992. Program for Athletic Coaches' Education (PACE): Educating America's public and private school coaches. *Journal of Physical Education, Recreation and Dance* 63(7):46-9.

Shor, I. 1987. *Freire for the classroom: A sourcebook for liberatory teaching.* Portsmouth, NH: Heinemann.

Shulman, L.S. 1986. Those who understand: Knowledge growth in teaching. *Educational Researcher* 15(2):4-14.

———. 1987. Knowledge and teaching: Foundations of the new reform. *Harvard Educational Review* 57(1):1-22.

Siedentop, D., ed. 1994. *Sport education: Quality PE through positive sport experiences.* Champaign, IL: Human Kinetics.

Siedentop, D., and E. Eldar. 1989. Expertise, experience, and effectiveness. *Journal of Teaching in Physical Education* 8(3):254-60.

Siedentop, D., and D. Tannehill. 2000. *Developing teaching skills in physical education.* 4th ed. Mountain View, CA: Mayfield.

Sikes, P., L. Measor, and P. Woods. 1985. *Teacher careers: Crises and continuities.* London: Falmer Press.

Sisley, B., and D. Weise. 1987. Current status: Requirements for interscholastic coaches: Results of NAGWS/NASPE coaching certification survey. *Journal of Physical Education, Recreation and Dance* 58(7):73-85.

Smith, L. and K. Sanders, K. 1981. The effects on student achievement and student perception of varying structure in social studies content. *Journal of Educational Research* 74:333-36.

Sparkes, A.C. 1989. Culture and ideology in physical education. In *Socialization into physical education: Learning to teach,* ed. T. Templin and P. Schempp, 315-38. Indianapolis: Benchmark Press.

Sparkes, A., T. Templin, and P. Schempp. 1990. The problematic nature of a career in a marginal subject: Some implications for teacher education programs. *Journal of Education for Teaching* 16:3-28.

Stillwell, J., and C. Willgoose. 1997. *The physical education curriculum.* 5th ed. Boston: Allyn & Bacon.

St. Pierre, P. 1998. Distance learning in physical education teacher education. *Quest* 50:344-56.

Swanson, H., J. O'Connor, and J. Cooney. 1990. An information processing analysis of expert and novice teachers' problem solving. *American Educational Research Journal* 27:533-56.

Tan, S. 1997. The elements of expertise. *Journal of Physical Education, Recreation and Dance* 68(2):30-3.

Templin, T., and P. Schempp. 1989. *Socialization into physical education: Learning to teach.* Indianapolis, IN: Benchmark.

Templin, T., R. Woodford, and C. Mulling. 1982. On becoming a physical educator: Occupational choice and the anticipatory socialization process. *Quest* 34(2):119-33.

Teven, J. and J. McCroskey. 1997. The relationship of perceived teacher caring with student learning and teacher evaluation. *Communication Education* 46 (1):1-9.

Tharp, R., and R. Gallimore. 1976. What a coach can teach a teacher. *Psychology Today* (January):75-8.

Thomas, J., and K. French. 1985. Gender differences across age in motor performance: A meta-analysis. *Psychological Bulletin* 98:260-82.

Treanor, L., K. Graber, L. Housner, and R. Wiegand. 1998. Middle school students' perceptions of coeducational and same-sex physical education classes. *Journal of Teaching in Physical Education* 18:43-56.

Tripp, D. 1993. *Critical incidents in teaching: Developing professional judgement.* London: Routledge.

Veeneman, S. 1984. Perceived problems of beginning teachers. *Review of Educational Research* 54(2): 143-78.

Voss, J.F., and A. Post. 1988. On the solving of ill-structured problems. In *The nature of expertise,* eds. M.T.H. Chi, R. Glaser, and M.J. Farr, 261-85. Hillsdale, NJ: Erlbaum.

Waller, W. 1932. *The sociology of teaching.* New York: Russell & Russell.

Weber, M. 1964. *The theory of social and economic organization.* Translated A. Henderson and T. Parsons. New York: Free Press.

Weinberg, R., and Gould, D. 1995. *Foundations of sport and exercise psychology.* Champaign, IL: Human Kinetics.

Whitehead, A.N. 1929. *The aims of education.* New York: Mentor Books.

Wiese-Bjornstal, D., and M. Weiss. 1992. Modeling effects on children's form kinematics, performance outcome, and cognitive recognition of a sport skill. *Research Quarterly for Exercise and Sport* 63:67-75.

Wild, T. 1992. Effects of perceived extrinsic versus intrinsic teacher motivation on student reactions to skill acquisition. *Personality and Social Psychology Bulletin* 18:245-51.

Wooden, J.R. 1985. *They call me coach.* Waco, TX: Word.

Yinger, R., and M. Hendricks-Lee. 1995. Teaching planning. In *International encyclopedia of teaching and teacher education,* 2nd ed., ed. L. W. Anderson, 188-92. Oxford, England: Elsevier Science, Ltd.

Zeichner, K., B. Tabachnick, and K. Densmore. 1987. Individual, institutional and cultural influences on the development of teachers' craft knowledge. In *Exploring teachers' thinking,* ed. J. Calderhead, 21-59. London: Cassell Educational.

Index

Note: The italicized *f* following a page number denotes a figure on that page. The italicized *ff* following a page number denotes multiple figures on that page.

About the Author

Paul Schempp, EdD, is a teacher first and foremost. He loves teaching and continually strives to find ways to improve—a quest that has led to his extensive research on instructional expertise in physical education and a variety of sports. Known worldwide for his research in the pedagogy of sport and physical education, he has served on the faculty of five different universities in three different countries and has presented the results of his research in 18 countries.

Schempp currently heads the department of physical education and sport studies at the University of Georgia and directs the university's Sport Instruction Research Laboratory. He also has served as a senior Fulbright research scholar in Germany, as a member of the National Education Advisory Board for the Ladies Professional Golf Association (LPGA), and as a technical consultant to the Swedish National Golf Team. As the scientific consultant on instruction to *Golf Magazine,* he also assists in the annual selection of America's top 100 golf instructors.

Schempp holds an EdD in human movement studies from Boston University. A resident of Athens, Georgia, he enjoys spending his free time playing golf, fly fishing, and scuba diving.

You'll find
other outstanding
teaching sport resources at

www.HumanKinetics.com

In the U.S. call

800-747-4457

Australia 08 8277 1555
Canada 800-465-7301
Europe .... +44 (0) 113 255 5665
New Zealand 09-523-3462

HUMAN KINETICS
The Information Leader in Physical Activity
P.O. Box 5076 • Champaign, IL 61825-5076 USA